BILLIE: THE NEVILL LETTERS

BILLIE

THE NEVILL LETTERS

1914-1916

Ruth Elwin Harris

This edition is published by
The Naval & Military Press Ltd
2003

First published in Great Britain 1991 by Julia MacRae
an imprint of the Random Century Group Ltd

This edition published by
The Naval & Military Press Ltd
Unit 10 Ridgewood Industrial Park,
Uckfield, East Sussex,
TN22 5QE England
Tel: +44 (0) 1825 749494
Fax: +44 (0) 1825 765701
www.naval–military-press.com

THIS BOOK WAS WRITTEN FOR MY SONS,

JONATHAN AND RICHARD.

IT IS DEDICATED TO THE MEMORY OF BILLIE AND AMY NEVILL

AND ALL WHO SERVED WITH THEM.

CONTENTS

ILLUSTRATIONS & MAPS

Maps

The letter writers of all ages give us a far finer and more vivid picture and estimate of the times in which they lived than their historians. It is the human document that has the power to make history really live for us. In all probability some of the letters that are now passing to and from the trenches will make the poignant history of these – our own times – live for descendants far more thrillingly and truly than all the memoirs of the Joffres and the Hindenburgs and the Grand Dukes that will come out after the titanic struggle is ended.

The Sphere, 20th November 1915

Here are – perhaps – two million men in arms, of whom not five per cent had stood to attention a year ago, practically all of whom were plying a trade or at least earning a civilian wage last August – officered to a very large extent by erstwhile professional men and youths from the Universities and Schools.

AN OFFICER, *The New Army in the Making*, 1915

Most of us were too young to have any standards of comparison. This was our life. We had been pitchforked headlong into khaki from school or college. The war was just another experience as first our preparatory school, and then our public school had been. We were not philosophers in uniform. The majority of us were hardly mature enough to philosophise at all.

SIDNEY ROGERSON, *Twelve Days*, 1933

ACKNOWLEDGEMENTS

It would be impossible to write a book of this sort without the co-operation of the family concerned. I am deeply indebted to Elizabeth Anderson, daughter of Howard Nevill, and to Anthony Bond, son of Dorothy, for allowing me to use the letters and papers of their relatives as the basis of this book. In addition, Mrs Anderson lent me family papers, answered questions and entertained my husband and me. I am more grateful than I can say, and hope that both she and Mr. Bond are happy with the portrayal of the Nevill family which appears in the following pages. I am only sorry that Howard's widow, Mrs. Poppy Nevill, did not live to read the manuscript.

I am also greatly indebted to the Imperial War Museum – to the Department of Photographs and the Department of Art for help with illustrations, to the Department of Printed Books, for their advice and the speed with which they dealt with my queries, and to the Department of Sound Records for their interview with Lt.-Col. Irwin. My biggest debt must be to the Department of Documents where I first met the Nevills while researching the background for a novel with a V.A.D. heroine. Especial thanks are due to Mr. Roderick Suddaby, Keeper of the Department, for his invaluable help and encouragement, both of which eased the difficulties in writing a book far from its manuscript sources. I particularly appreciated the patience with which he answered questions that too often revealed my ignorance of the military world.

My thanks are also due to Mrs. A.P. Dennis, Mrs. A. Hemming, Mr. I.P. Kirkpatrick and Maj. C. Thorne for allowing me to quote from their relatives' papers deposited in the Imperial War Museum.

I am very grateful to Lt.-Col. L.M.B. Wilson of the Queen's Royal Surrey Regimental Association, who must have wondered if he was ever going to see his regimental histories again; to the staff of the Regimental Museum of the Queen's Royal Surrey Regiment, Clandon Park, and of Queen Alexandra's Royal Army Nursing Corps Museum at Aldershot, for their interest and help; to Mr. Annetts of Dover College, Mr. George Capel of Harrogate Reference Library and the staff of various branches of the City of Westminster Reference Library.

Extracts from John Jolliffe's *Raymond Asquith: Life and Letters* are reproduced by permission of HarperCollins Ltd. and those from Martin Middlebrook's *The First Day on the Somme* by permission of Penguin Books Ltd. The extracts from Volume II of Siegfried Sassoon's *Diaries* and from his *Memoirs of an Infantry Officer* appear by permission of Faber and Faber Ltd. The lyrics of 'Neville' from *Bric-à-Brac* by Wimperis and Monckton, are reproduced by permission of International Music Publications; Touchstone's verses by permission of the *Daily Mail*. I thank them all.

Unfortunately not all my efforts to contact copyright holders have been successful. I apologise to those whose copyright I have infringed and would be pleased to hear from them through my publisher.

For the illustrations, I must thank Mrs. Anderson for allowing me to use photographs 1, 5 and 6. Nos. 2, 12, 13, 15, 18, 21, 23, 25 and 26 are reproduced by permission of the The Trustees of the Imperial War Museum; nos. 4, 10, 11, 16, 17, 19, 20, 27, 28 and 30 by permission of the Regimental Museum of the Queen's Royal Surrey Regiment, Clandon Park; no. 14 by permission of the Queen Alexandra's Royal Army Nursing Corps Museum, Aldershot, and no. 22 by permission of *The Illustrated London News* Picture Library. I would like to thank Mr. Peter Holloway and Major Cornelius Thorne for supplying nos. 9 and 24 respectively, and Barbara Johnson for no. 29. The poster of Kitchener's appeal and the portrait of Major-General Maxse by Francis Dodd are reproduced by permission of the Trustees of the Imperial War Museum.

Finally, I am very grateful to my brother, Roger Elwin Harris, for help with photography, and to my husband, Christopher, who acted as driver, translator and even, on one occasion and much to his surprise, as secretary.

The Nevill Family

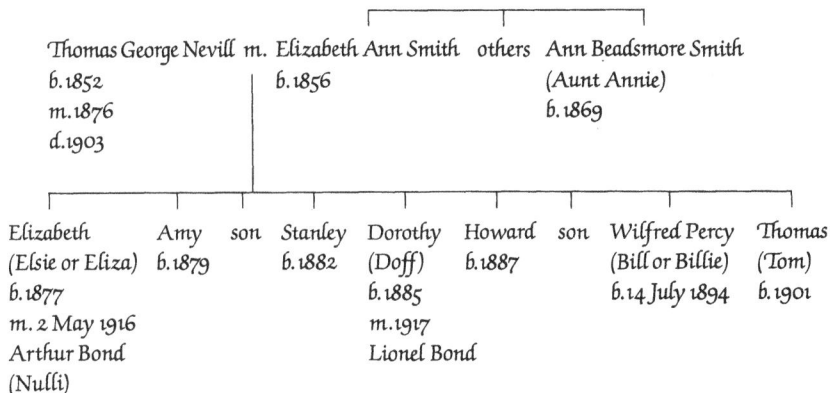

Thomas George Nevill m. Elizabeth Ann Smith others Ann Beadsmore Smith
b. 1852   b. 1856   (Aunt Annie)
m. 1876   b. 1869
d. 1903

Elizabeth	Amy	son	Stanley	Dorothy	Howard	son	Wilfred Percy	Thomas
(Elsie or Eliza)	b. 1879		b. 1882	(Doff)	b. 1887		(Bill or Billie)	(Tom)
b. 1877				b. 1885			b. 14 July 1894	b. 1901
m. 2 May 1916				m. 1917				
Arthur Bond				Lionel Bond				
(Nulli)								

The Schooling Children

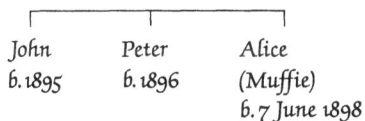

John   Peter   Alice
b. 1895   b. 1896   (Muffie)
                     b. 7 June 1898

INTRODUCTION

The Nevill letters came to light during the making of a television docu-
mentary on the Battle of the Somme, shown on July 1st 1976, the sixtieth
anniversary of the battle. When Malcolm Brown, writer and producer of the
programme, visited the Reverend T.S. Nevill to find out more about an incident in which Tom Nevill's brother, Wilfred, had taken part, he was
shown a hat box full of letters, the majority of them from Wilfred himself.

Those letters, now in the Imperial War Museum, are the basis of this
book.

Wilfred Percy Nevill – more usually called Bill or Billie by his family – was
twenty when he answered Kitchener's call to arms in 1914; just twenty-one
when he sailed to France with the 18th Division, and fourteen days short of
his twenty-second birthday when he fell on the first day of the Battle of the
Somme, one of nineteen thousand who were killed on that day. In less than
two years, almost the entire lifetime of Kitchener's army, he underwent instruction at the Staff College, Camberley, trained in England with the 8th
Battalion of the East Surrey Regiment and spent eleven months in and out of
the trenches in Picardy, before achieving fame on July 1st 1916 by providing
footballs for his company to kick across No Man's Land towards the German
trenches. His letters from that time describe his life as a member of Kitchener's army during its build-up towards the big battle, his dealings with the
French in the billeting towns behind the front line and his experiences in the
trenches, this last usually accompanied by assurances of his own safety at
the front and of the absence of any danger. Over two hundred letters to his
mother and sisters still survive.

Also in the collection of letters at the Imperial War Museum are those of
Billie's elder sister, Amy, who nursed with the Voluntary Aid Detachment
from 1915 to 1919, first in France and then in Italy. Amy's letters could scarcely be more different from those of her brother. To someone who was
Victorian in upbringing and almost middle-aged by the standards of the
time (she was twenty-one when Queen Victoria died, thirty-six the summer
she went to France) the situation in a base hospital in France must surely

have seemed extraordinary, yet Amy rarely mentions her work and accepts her circumstances with little comment. While Billie welcomed and took advantage of every new experience offered – '[It] is rather new to me, so I like it,' he said, when deputising for the adjutant [119] – Amy seems to have had little curiosity about her surroundings. Billie learnt to ride, rapidly became fluent in French[1], was interested in anything and everything that went on around him, and he matured in command. Amy never managed to cut the umbilical cord, her thoughts and interest remaining all the time with her family on the other side of the Channel. 'What a ripping time you seem to have had,' was Billie's usual reaction to accounts of family outings; 'if only I could have been with you,' was Amy's. The most interesting aspect of Amy's letters, in fact, is the relationship they gradually reveal between Amy and Mrs. Nevill's youngest sister, Ann Beadsmore Smith, the formidable Aunt Annie.

Nine children were born between 1877 and 1901 to the Nevills. Seven survived childhood. Despite the wide age range they were a close, affectionate family. 'There are not many families that are such real friends together as we are,' Howard told his mother in 1916. Stanley worried about Billie's rheumatism; Billie about Tom's education. Elsie and Billie were both prepared to act as marriage brokers for brothers and sisters, if need be.[2] Dorothy copied out Billie's letters to send to those members of the family who were abroad to help keep them in touch. Both Billie and later Howard made great efforts, not all of them successful, to visit Amy in France and later in Italy, and when Elsie, the oldest of the family, married in the spring of 1916, Amy, Billie and Howard all managed to return home on leave from their particular theatre of war – a not inconsiderable feat at such a time. Both Mr. and Mrs. Nevill came from large families so aunts, uncles and cousins are frequently mentioned in the letters.

The family lived in north London until the death of Mr. Nevill in 1903, when Billie was just nine and Tom, the youngest, not yet two, after which they moved to Tennyson's House[3], 15 Montpelier Road (now Row), in Twickenham.

The family was staunchly Christian. Billie's favourite text, singularly appropriate to the situation in which he found himself, was 'Be strong and of good courage; be not afraid, neither be thou dismayed; for the Lord thy God is with thee whithersoever thou goest.' Both he and Amy were concerned about the difficulties of worship in France, while Howard, writing home after his first Sunday in the Navy told his mother that 'we had no service on board at all. I did suggest it to the Captain, pretty strongly as a matter of fact, but he would not do it. It was nervousness chiefly, I think.' The family supported a settlement[4] at Hoxton; both Billie and Amy sent back money for it during their time in France.

Mr. Nevill had owned a coal business and had also been managing direc-
tor of Kelly's Directories. The family was comfortably off, owning a house in
Canonbury and one in Westgate-on-Sea, where Billie had been at preparatory school. Later Mrs. Nevill was to buy a cottage at Holmbury St. Mary
near Dorking in Surrey, a village Billie remembered with affection when in
France. Mrs. Nevill took the waters at Harrogate, Christmases were spent in
Torquay; holidays taken abroad, Italy having been a favourite choice with
Mr. Nevill. Billie, at least, had enjoyed winter sports; Elsie, an artist, spent
holidays sketching in France, sometimes with Aunt Annie. While Stanley
and Howard, the eldest boys, had been educated at the Merchant Taylors'
School, down the hill from their home in Highbury, Billie went away to
Dover College.

During school holidays Billie not only had his next-door neighbours, Jack
and Peter Schooling, for company but also their little sister. Muff – chris-
tened Alice but known as Muff or Muffie all her life – was four years
younger than Billie. She climbed trees with the boys, punted on the river
with them, played with them in Marble Hill Park beside Montpelier Road,
and read the books of Kipling that Billie gave her. 'You know how desperately shy I am,' Billie was to write later of his dealings with the opposite sex,
but he does not seem to have had any difficulty where Muff was concerned.
He even used two Player 50 cigarette tins and waxed string to rig up a telephone line between their houses so that he and she could have secret con-
versations. Just when he began to regard Muff more romantically is not
recorded, but by early 1915 the prospect of seeing her the following day
could give him a sleepless night. Unfortunately for Billie, Mr. Schooling did
not regard him as a possible suitor for his daughter. Meetings with Muff became difficult after the Schoolings' move to Hastings, and needed Mrs.
Nevill's help and diplomacy to arrange.

The letters conjure up delightful vignettes of the family, particularly of
Mrs. Nevill and Elsie, the eldest child. Both were somewhat eccentric, Elsie
the more so. 'My pump handle flies up and down like Mother and Elsie
going to catch the 'bus, & forgetting an umbrella, or a purse, or the tickets
etc. etc. !!!!' [28] Mrs. Nevill was vague, she muddled addresses ('Why do
you persist in putting D Coy, when I'm B Coy now,' Billie asked [195]); she
had difficulty deciphering the coded messages in Billie's letters, and when
Tom went to Dover College she even misspelt the name of his headmaster.
'By the way, Mother, it's Mr. LEE not LEA at Dover, W.S. Lee, O.D.,' [94]
Billie corrected her; and corrected her again later, 'Cecil is probably at
LARKHILL not Park Hill.'

One is filled with admiration for Mrs. Nevill. She was not young, even if she seemed so. 'Are you sure it is not [your] 50th you mean!' Howard said, of her sixtieth birthday in 1916, 'because really it seems almost impossible.' She was 'jolly' when seeing her sons off overseas. She organised the sending of what must have amounted to dozens of parcels to children and relatives – even to Billie's orderly. She entertained her children's friends when asked to do so – 'could you ring him up and ask him over some time?' Howard would write. With Elsie she visited those friends when they were lying wounded in hospital. 'I hope you will see Donald fairly often,' Billie said, of his badly wounded friend from Dover College, Donald Campbell, 'as he has never had the advantage of a home (it's a bit late to start reforming him now) & it would do him a lot of good.' But she was always appreciated. 'I gather that he likes you all very much,' Billie reported to the family of Donald [88]. Later he wrote on his own account, to thank her for the parcels she sent him. 'May I take this opportunity of saying how splendid you are in sending out exactly what I ask for & not something you thought would perhaps do.'

Billie appreciated Elsie, too. 'You seem to have been doing an awful lot at the 'Back' so to speak, not quite so flashy as wearing uniform & spending Govt. money in France, but every bit as necessary I know. Don't crock up, please.[5]' [34]

Billie was undoubtedly closest to Elsie of his three sisters. He was seventeen years Elsie's junior; she may well have had more to do with his upbringing than had Mrs. Nevill. Although Billie was happy for anyone to read his letters, and indeed expected them to be handed round, his most revealing remarks were always made to Elsie. She encouraged him in his writing – 'Elsie has a journalese and Daily Mailian idea' – and when he wrote an article on the anniversary of the 8th East Surreys' formation it was Elsie who tried to place it for him, though without recorded success. He sent her £5 to go towards her headache cure – an astonishing sum when one considers that another £5 sent by him was expected to provide dinner in the West End and theatre tickets for 3 or 4 people. The cure was apparently a success, for later he wrote that 'The news about your heads is splendid, those congestions would account for lots of things about you which have up to the present been a mystery to me. Trains for instance. I hope they've tapped the 'hurrierup' bump!' [94]

Sadly there is no one left of that generation to elaborate on certain incidents that one would dearly like explained. 'You couldn't picture Elsie being married quietly and calmly. She's sure to be late, or forget the day, or marry the wrong man,' [180] is one example; 'The post has just come in, bringing an enormous letter from your eldest daughter. I hope she'll not get in to any great trouble about the picture. I'll be prisoner's friend if she's court-martialled. But oh! how typical,' [56] another.

None of Billie's letters to his brothers survive. Howard, seven years his senior, is the most frequently mentioned. After leaving school he had worked for a stockbroker for two years before joining the Bank of England. Here he became friendly with the two brothers, Arthur (Nulli) and Lionel Bond, who would later marry Elsie and Doff respectively. An assistant pay-master in the Royal Naval Reserve, Howard had joined his ship the day war was declared.[6] His attitude to life seems to have been very like Billie's, the account of his experience in the sinking of the *Louvain* on January 23rd, 1918, being as casual as any of Billie's descriptions: 'After about 5 minutes [in the water] I found I was still smoking my pipe! I thought I had better save my breath so I put it in my pocket, worse luck it floated out after so I lost it in the end.'

Stanley and Doff, the third and fourth children, are more shadowy figures, the former no doubt because he was already married and a father. A mechanical engineer with his own engineering business, he served in the Royal Flying Corps in Egypt and Salonika and was, one imagines from Bil-lie's advice, a forthright character. 'Tell him not to call anyone above a Briga-dier 'a fool' to his face! It's not done!' [67] Anxiety about suitable accommo-dation for 'Ethel and Baby' appears frequently in Amy's letters, one reason being family doubts about Ethel's capabilities as a mother. 'I tremble to think of Joan after being away so long from our home influence,' Amy wrote in 1918, when Ethel and her daughter had moved away from the Nevills. [73]

Dorothy, known as Doff, was a teacher, the cleverest of the three girls and, according to Amy, not above making out her sisters to be fools, 'at least to her many admirers, but she herself doesn't really think it of us.' [68]

The youngest, Tom, was twelve when war broke out. Following in Billie's footsteps, he started at Dover College in 1915 shortly after Billie crossed to France. Billie sent him letters of advice, about deportment before he started, and later about games. 'In the sports in the 2nd half of next term go in for everything & see how you get on. Don't be shy of entering for things & don't overtrain to start with.' [119] Tom collected butterflies – Billie sent him specimens from France – and stamps. He was obviously a typical schoolboy, with a dislike of letter-writing – 'for the 100th time did he receive a knife from me besides the one in the food bag.' [30]

Billie himself had had an exceptional career at Dover College. For four out of his five years there he represented the College in cricket and hockey, finishing as captain of both, as well as head boy. From his second year on he headed the bowling averages and was in the top half of the batting. He played fives, gained a marksman certificate and his running colours and was in the College Officers' Training Corps. While there is no record of his academic prowess, the anonymous account in the school magazine of the activities of the 1913 O.T.C. summer camp has a distinct flavour of Nevillian prose. Dover College's O.T.C. seems to have been a flourishing training ground for the military – ten boys from the school were at Sandhurst in the autumn of 1913, one of them Billie's closest friend, Donald Campbell – which may explain why Billie was fortunate enough to have a period of instruction at the Staff College, Camberley, in 1914 before joining his regiment.

In the autumn of 1913 Billie went up to Jesus College, Cambridge, to read Classics. He played hockey for the College – 'He can deal the ball a shrewd blow,' was the college magazine's comment in the 1914 Lenten Term issue – but the outbreak of war at the end of his first year gave him no opportunity to make any greater mark. His original intention to become a schoolmaster did not last long in the army. Army life suited both his character and his abilities. Promotion was rapid as a result. Gazetted a second lieutenant on November 27th, 1914, he was a temporary captain by the following spring. After six weeks' service in France he applied for a commission in the Regular Army.

A photograph of Billie comes as a surprise, even a disappointment. 'I'm not a fool though I may look it,' was his own verdict [155]. There seems little connection between the face in photographs and the lively, engaging personality that is evoked by his letters and the comments of his companions, both before and after his death.

'One of the most popular characters in the battalion,' P.G. Heath, a fellow officer, wrote in his memoirs years later. 'He had an uproarious sense of humour all his own, and he was for ever thinking up new ideas.' 'Our mess is a very happy little family, led by the brilliant and priceless Nevillus,' another officer, A.E.A. Jacobs, told his parents, 'who recently told us his story: the Nevills are relatives of the old Warwicks and how any of his ancestors escaped Tyburn beats him and me. I believe one of the whole warren managed to push the hangman's face and hence the Nevilides.'[7] ('I'm not romancing,' Billie insisted, describing some episode of trench warfare, 'it's true.')

'It is seldom, even in the Army, that a man gains the love of his fellow men, but our feelings towards Capt. Nevill were deeper than mere admiration, & there wasn't a man in the Battn. who would not have followed him anywhere,' Humphrey Cunnington, a sergeant for seven months in Billie's company, wrote to Mrs. Nevill after Billie's death. Such sentiments have become a cliché in the myths of the Great War, but in Billie's case they appear to have been true. 'Quite a little retinue' applied to accompany him when he was transferred from C company to D in order to help bring the latter up to standard, though only his servant, Marker, was allowed to do so.

Condolence letters from commanding officers and fellow officers in World War I followed a standard pattern, the same phrases recurring. The rarer, less articulate letters of other ranks are the more telling in comparison. Another sergeant, Sergeant Cutting, wrote to Mrs. Nevill:

> I do trust you will not think this a liberty, but – though I was only a Sergeant and your son a Captain – I can safely say he was my friend.
> Therefore I feel that, as one who knew him well, one who sat with him for many hours in the trenches, one with whom he so often talked, I must write just a few lines & tell you how we all loved him.
> I was never good at saying to others those things which affect me very nearly so perhaps you will read between these few stammering lines thus perceiving what a MAN he was, how we all loved him & respected him.
> . . . Your son was a brave man he was a good man. He made us better men for having known him.

'Nevill was my ideal hero,' Jacobs told Mrs. Nevill, 'a perfect pattern of the British officer and the British Gentleman and I feel his loss personally more than any other.'[8]

Billie was well aware of the change in himself brought about by the war.

> You know sometimes I sit down & laugh to myself when I think what I was before this bally War. Now I've got 200 odd men solely under me, to feed, pay, clothe, house, advise on every conceivable subject, lecture to, teach, & order about in emergencies, organise, act as judge to, in fact every blooming thing, & the funniest part of it all is that it doesn't worry me a bit or awe me, though the thought of it in England used to frighten me a bit. [171]

He had changed in other ways. In August 1915 war was 'the greatest fun imaginable.' [22] 'What a ghastly thing war is nowadays,' he was writing less than a year later.' [202] With that knowledge came the inevitable hardening. Whereas the death of a fellow officer in September 1915 depressed him greatly, the death of a cousin six months later merely brought forth the remark 'Bad luck.' When Muffie's brother, Peter, was killed a month later at the age of 19, Billie was almost casual. 'I'm so sorry for poor old Muff, & the others, mais c'est la guerre, as everyone says & it's very true.' [171]
Unlike some, notably Robert Graves, Billie got on well with the French

during his time in France. He admired the way in which they as a nation were facing up to the Germans, and considered that England was not making half their effort. '[The French] take the war quite differently to us,' he noted, within a couple of days of landing in their country. 'No one left except the very very old people and the absolute kids. Not a single young man about. It's a grand example to anyone.' [25] While making the occasional protest about the behaviour of the French – 'after all we're over here defending their blooming country, & they've got to lump us' [43] – he was generally sympathetic. 'I'm glad your poor are flourishing,' he wrote home. 'I don't think the French are, but I don't think they ever are, so far as I can see,' and later in the same letter said, 'I do feel sorry for some of these old people, who perpetually have Tommies and officers and mud, let alone horses, etc. billeted on them.' [42] The East Surreys seem to have been more fortunate than Robert Graves, who complained bitterly about the quality of French hospitality encountered in billets. D company's billets in Ville-sur-Ancre for much of the winter of 1915/1916, where the officers were mothered by the nineteen-year-old Alcinie and her mother, Madame de la Porte, were exceptionally happy – on both sides, it would seem, for after the company was moved to 'not so nice' billets a mile down the road, Billie received two touching letters in French from Alcinie:

> *Ville-sur-Ancre*   29th February 1916
> My dear Captain,
>   . . . We often talk about you and unfortunately we shall never have
> any more officers like you, so friendly so kind and above all very
> polite, we are very sorry that you will never be able to come back to
> Ville . . .
>   Last week we had a visit from Mr Pegg, Mr Hetherington, and Mr
> Wigtman [Wightman], and on Sunday yesterday a visit from Captain
> John Bowen and Mr Pegg again . . .
>   Yes we are hoping to see you soon and often, your visit will give us
> a lot of pleasure, your cup of coffee is waiting for you and your glass
> of wine, hurry up and come back.
>   Now at the house we have Sergeant Majors, just 2 to sleep, they are
> very nice, but it is not the same as you.
>   So, cher Monsieur, I finish in the hope of seeing you soon.
>   Mother asks me to remember her to you.
>   In sincerest friendship
>   *Alcinie*

Germany, like France, came in for Billie's admiration for its war effort in comparison with that of England. 'If we settled down to it as a nation like the huns have, we'd be home in 6 months,' was his opinion. [143] His opinion on the Germans themselves – variously referred to as huns, Bosches (with a variety of spellings, often in the same letter), Jummuns and the Brethren – though occasionally belligerent was more often muted. As he pointed out, 'the Huns are 'for it' just as much as you.' [40]

In view of his opinion of England's war effort – 'half steam ahead' – it seems surprising that Billie should disapprove of conscription. Commenting on a draft of men from England – 'jolly fine fellows they looked too' – he said that 'as long as we can feel there are batches like this just waiting till we send for them, we shan't ever need to worry. In fact it's the old, old cry, ensure more men & more & more again.' [34] But not, apparently, conscripts. 'You see I've seen what you are glibly contemplating sending thousands more to, I'm not thinking of the slackers but the thousands of good chaps who will become conscripts and be branded slackers. How are you going to pay them? Who do you think will mix with them? Who will officer them? There seem to be enormous difficulties.' [43]

He never doubted England's eventual victory.

The only danger to my mind is that some near sighted and fat headed people will say 'oh anything to stop the War' and when Germany proposes terms of peace, jump at them & make peace, on the pretext that we've lost so much already & so many valuable lives . . . That's just what Germany will want . . . a decent 5 years breathing space to refit, and then she'll start again. [93]

Only occasionally did he look to the future. 'I shall bring my wife and fam (?) to visit these places, when I've grown up!' [40] he wrote, soon after his arrival in France, and after a period in the unpleasant Tambour section of the trenches, 'Perhaps some day I'll take you all over this ground & we'll follow it all from letters & look up everything again.' [110] The only doubt he ever expressed came soon after his arrival in France: after describing a house with one side blown away and the furniture 'just waiting for peace, when it will carry on as if there never had been a war,' he added, 'I wonder if we shall.' [35]

The letters should be read in the context of the time in which they were written. The emotional patriotism expressed by Rupert Brooke in his war sonnets may be disparaged now, but in 1915 he spoke for his generation, as any reader of letters and diaries of the period will know. Disillusionment, as expressed by war poets such as Siegfried Sassoon, had yet to surface. Billie had been dead six months before Wilfred Owen landed in France. Right up until July 1st the majority of Kitchener's men, like Billie, regarded the fight against Germany much as a crusade. ('England is of course the one hope against 'Hunnism' now, and I hope she'll realise it,' Billie wrote in the autumn of 1915 [56]). Part of the value of Billie's letters is the picture they give of the training and attitudes of those who rushed to enlist in the early days of the war.

There is much 'cheeryho' jauntiness in the letters. 'Ripping' is a favourite and, at times, over-used adjective (Howard's was 'topping'). Most of the humour is of the schoolboy variety. 'Can you tell how it's a howitzer? Sorry.' 'Bill in Stillets' he headed one letter (the previous one had been 'Still in Billets') adding, 'Please laugh.' It was not so long, after all, since he had been a schoolboy, and children remained children for longer in the early decades of the century than they do now. Besides, the humour was deliberately done. 'I'm not certain whether I shall try to make this comic or not. It's so dreadful to try & write a funny letter & feel at the end that you won't be really amused at all, but merely think I've got shellshock.' [88] His wish not to alarm – it must be remembered that he was writing to three women, one of them his mother – often vied with his desire to record accurately his life at the front.[9] 'I will put in a few 'incidents' of the real scrapping each time, if any occur, but you know how scared I am of frightening you, or of appearing to seek pity & sympathy, when there are such crowds of poor people about who really are in a bad way and do want sympathy.' [80] Writing to Elsie during his first tour in the trenches, he told her that his letters 'were the result of much careful thought, and it requires a somewhat deceitful turn of mind to produce them.' [37] Any strain from the life he was leading was only unwittingly revealed. 'I expect you'll find me a wee bit quick worded,' he warned before returning home on leave, 'but don't mind that; also don't make unnecessary noises or bangs.' [106]

He wrote with enjoyment nonetheless. 'Do say if all this bores you but I do love to chat.' [35] he said on one occasion, and on another promised that 'if my letters are too wordy & boring I'll trim them up, but I love to ramble on as you know.' [29] He wrote either in pencil with the 'indellibles' supplied by Tom or, very occasionally, in ink. 'I'm writing this with my trusty Onoto [fountain pen], to show you how desperately civilised we are still,' he wrote during his first tour in the trenches. 'At times when I scrawl off hurried notes, I always feel I ought to put "Please excuse our country manners," or something like that.' [30] Conditions were not easy for letter-writers. Mosquitoes swooped down on the unwary behind the lines, while dug-outs in the trenches were cramped, badly lit and often crowded, with the unexpected likely to happen at any moment. 'Our dug-out is haunted by

Artillery F.O.O.s and mining R.E. officers, and the tunneling coy., so with ourselves we are a crowd sometimes, it's nice and sociable of course, but worries me to death, if I want to write or sleep.' [69]

After his leave in December 1915, his letters changed. 'I know I'm not writing those long rambling letters Doff mentions, like I used to,' he wrote in January, 'but somehow I just can't.' At the time he was deputising for the battalion adjutant while the latter was on leave, which gave him little opportunity to write, but there were other reasons. He had been able to talk of his experiences while on leave. What was new on his return was 'mostly censurable & of purely military interest.' He assumed too that he had been able to allay their fears about his safety. 'There doesn't seem to be the need to keep you disalarmed about me now.' [138]

The letters became shorter still and sparser after his leave the following May. Training for the coming battle allowed little free time, but there may have been another reason of which Billie himself was unaware. To many in the army, life in England became increasingly remote from their military experience. Awareness of the divide between home and the front seems often to have occurred during that second leave. This may well have been the reason for the unexplained rift between Billie and Muff.

It must be remembered that the letters of both Billie and Amy were written in haste. The use of apostrophes was erratic or non-existent, and these have been tidied up, as have some of the most glaring errors – the omission of the letter 's' in obvious plurals, for instance. Otherwise the letters are as they were written, spelling mistakes and lack of paragraphs included. This may be unkind, particularly where Billie is concerned for he excused himself for both, as well as commenting on the occasional badly constructed sentence. 'I'm writing this by two candles' light hence any bad spelling,' he said on August 23, and on October 24th, 'I hope the omission of paragraphs is not too confusing' (paper was after all in short supply). Editorial additions are always in square brackets.

Lastly, either the date or the number of each letter is given in brackets in the text, for those who wish to refer to the original.

NOTES

1. 'We broke a chair here yesterday, and our old landlady is still howling, poor soul, only one of us can speak well enough to try to comfort her, namely Twigg(ie), but he only roars with laughter, the heartless blighter,' Billie wrote on September 4th, adding, 'No, I didn't bust the chair.' Exactly four months later on January 4th, 1916, he was able to say that he could 'talk French much more freely now & only rarely get into difficulties.'

2. 'I'm on the shelf now as far as I can

see & likely to remain there,' Howard wrote to Elsie on July 18th, 1918. 'Your desperate efforts last leave seemed doomed to failure but I shall expect you to have dug someone up for me by the time I come back next . . . You know my style more or less. Don't, when I come back, say you could only think of Daisy Ardon or I shall half slay you.' He did not marry until 1922 – and then not to Daisy Ardon.

3. Tennyson had lived in the house during the eighteen fifties. He found Twickenham 'too bustling', however, and within three years moved away to the more peaceful Isle of Wight.

4. The settlement movement began in 1894, with the setting up of Toynbee Hall in the east end of London and an invitation to university students to help 'settle' a deprived area. Most settlements provided cultural, educational and recreational activities for the working class of the area. There were several in Hoxton, including one run by Quakers, but it is not known which the Nevills supported nor whether they did more than contribute financially.

5. It is not known what Elsie was doing at this time. Later in the war she worked for the War Graves Commission.

6. Billie and Howard were staying at the Brambletye Hotel in Forest Row, Sussex, at the beginning of August 1914. Howard later wrote that, 'August 2nd at 12.30 was when I

heard that the R.N.R. had been called out. It took just six minutes for Wilfred and me to pack up and start off to Twickenham in the Morgan. It was a splendid start and the car went beautifully, in 1 hour 10 minutes we were home and found every one in a great state of excitement. I wired off to the Admiralty to say I had received their order and then said goodbye to Mother and went off to Waterloo. Elsie, Wilfred and Nullie came with me and Stanley met us at the Station. I got down to Portsmouth about eight o'clock in the evening.' He had to wait until the 4th, however, before his ship came in – 'and at first I was staggered. The S.S. Ramillies . . . is [a] 2,000 ton Black Sea Collier and she looked it. Dirty, small, slow and full of vibration . . .'

7. 2nd Lieut. A.E.R. Jacobs, 16.12.16. In the Nevill collection.

8. All letters of condolence quoted are in the Nevill collection.

9. 'Life out here is rather a strain on one,' wrote one of Billie's subalterns, 2nd Lieut. C.W. Alcock, a married man of 34, 'but I think it is much worse for the people at home – writing & suspense are so trying.' (27th July, 1916, to Miss Nevill, probably Doff.) The efforts of those serving in France to protect their families meant that there was widespread ignorance in England of conditions on the Western Front.

1 KITCHENER'S MAN

'Over by Christmas' was the general expectation when war was declared on August 4th, 1914. Lord Kitchener, appointed Secretary of State for War the following day, was one of few in the country who foresaw a long struggle. Realising that such a conflict would require a vast number of men to augment the existing small, but professional, British Army, he estimated that it would take three years to raise the necessary seventy divisions (about a million and a half men). Unlike the continental countries, however, Britain did not have conscription. Kitchener's famous appeal for volunteers, the 'First Hundred Thousand', made at the beginning of August, received an immediate and overwhelming response. On August 25th he was able to tell the House of Lords that the first hundred thousand recruits 'have been already practically secured'. By the end of the month these recruits had been allotted to battalions in one of the six divisions that collectively became known as K1, or the First New Army.

Kitchener's appeal on August 28th for the second hundred thousand received an even bigger response, 174,901 men enlisting in one week alone. Among the battalions formed from these volunteers was the 8th battalion of the East Surrey Regiment.

Not surprisingly, the Army was overwhelmed by the sudden influx of such numbers. Feeding, accommodating and training so many men was an administrative nightmare. Even eating was difficult, with the shortage of utensils and mess tins. Tents provided shelter, but only while the weather remained fine and anything more substantial took time to design and erect. Despite the waterlogged condition of the East Surreys' site in Essex – 'the swamps of Purfleet' one officer later described it – it was December before the battalion was able to move into huts. There were no facilities, and few Regular officers available to train the new recruits. 'We had to keep them fed if we could and quiet if we could and amused,' A.P.B. Irwin, the East Surreys' adjutant, said of his men at this time. It was not the most effective way of building up a fighting force, but Sir John French, Commander-in-Chief of the battered British Expeditionary Force in France, was understandably reluctant to release experienced men for training purposes in England, however great the need.

The problem was addressed as far as the East Surreys were concerned by bringing two officers out of retirement to take command of the battalion. It was not a satisfactory solution, however, and could only be temporary. The men concerned were elderly ('a dear old thing' was Billie's description of his C.O.), they were out of touch, and they relied too heavily on the battalion's adjutant, a 26-year-old Regular Army lieutenant from the 2nd East Surrey Regiment, who had no administrative experience whatever. In every other aspect the battalion was fortunate in its adjutant. On home leave from India when war broke out, Irwin was one of a number of officers on leave from different regiments abroad who were recalled by the War Office to help organise and train the newly formed service battalions. To him must go much of the credit for the transformation of one thousand citizens into a fighting force.

The first days of the 8th East Surreys, as recorded by Irwin, were no doubt typical of many battalions in Kitchener's army.

I stood in the station yard at Purfleet and waited for the men to arrive. All I had for battalion headquarters was in my haversack. Three trains arrived during the day, bringing 1,000 men who had been wished upon us before any attempt had been made to provide accommodation.

We only had two elderly retired officers and a quartermaster, and a very good sergeant major was the only n.c.o. We were given a dozen old Reservists, who we promptly made lance-corporals, much to their horror and indignation. Then the whole battalion was paraded and an appeal was made for anybody who had ever been in charge of anyone else, or who wanted to be. About forty men stepped forward; we tied white tape around their arms and made them lance-corporals too. A rough and ready system, but it worked out well and nearly all of them made good.[1] [Later tradition had it that it was the men in bowler hats who were selected.]

Despite its regional name, the 8th East Surreys contained men from all over the United Kingdom – Welsh miners, Sussex farmers, 300 Norfolk men and men from Suffolk ('splendid chaps,' said Irwin of these last). In order to give the battalion some cohesion, Irwin placed men from the same area together. Londoners were in A company, Welsh miners in D. Most of C company came from Suffolk. B company contained the rest. The men themselves were equally varied – one captain was a London University professor, while the N.C.Os included a middle-aged barrister and a steam crane driver from the London docks. There were city clerks and grave-diggers, an exwarder of Dartmoor Prison, and several who had apparently known him in his former capacity and tended to avoid him as a result. Those with previous army experience were not necessarily an asset: one ancient reservist, winner of the Victoria Cross in an earlier war, turned out to be incompetent and re-tired after a few months to become a Beefeater at the Tower of London.

Billie was late in coming to the East Surreys because of an illness from which it took some weeks to recover. 'I hope that old Bill is much better now & that Westgate will do him lots of good,' Howard wrote home on October 2nd, 'the water on the knee seems a funny combination with rheumatic fever.'

Billie's commission as 2nd lieutenant finally came through on November 27th, the day that he had been told to report to the Staff College at Camber-ley. The College had been closed down on August 5th and its staff dis-persed, but on November 27th it reopened its doors to accommodate 180 newly appointed officers for a month-long course at the Royal Military Col-lege next door. Billie was fortunate to be one of the few Kitchener's men to get a modicum of professional instruction.

Not many of Billie's letters survive from this period and those that do are less descriptive than those he was later to write from France. There was no need yet to reassure the family of his continuing existence, and weekend leave, from Saturday lunchtime to Sunday evening, gave him time to return home and report in person on his new life. Consequently letters from Cam-berley tend to be practical rather than informative. 'Please address my letters with My Name very clear & distinct as I have to hunt through a large pile each day.' 'If you think of it send me some very small safety pins and some old dustery things for cleaning leather & brass.'

He lists one day's programme:

6.55 – 8	Physical Training
8.30	Breakfast
9 – 10.30	Wire entanglements
10.35 – 1.30	Rifle firing on the R.M.C. Range.
	Lunch
2.30 – 3.30	Musketry
3.30 – 4.15	(Revolver range
	(Voluntary
6 – 7	Lecture on Sanitation
8	Mess

and describes another day:

We had bayonet fighting and pip-tock (p.T.) (physical Training) before breakfast, then I had charge of the people for orderly room. Then a parade for instruction in musketry. This after brekker then a lecture on Military Topography, and again one on Tactics, chiefly dealing with outposts, and all adapted to the conditions of the front. This afternoon we've had an hour's right, left & about turning, under a staff Sergeant so our feet are warm.

We have a pause today from 3-6 & that is now. At 5.55 I have to see everyone is in our lecture hall & call the roll, and report absentees. The lecture is on 'Organisation'. All these lectures are the first of a course, of course, (sorry).

The account of his return from weekend leave suggests that the recently opened College was still not entirely prepared for its new role.

I arrived last night about 11.30, the train being hideously late. I found my old bed occupied, my draws empty & my belongings far & wide. After a diligent search I collected my things & found a note, bidding me to oblige someone by going to no. 4 room instead of No. 2. Well my old room was No. 6.

I eventually reached No. 4 & found a bed & two other people evidently training for a snoring match. Creeping gingerly, like Agag[2], I put my belongings in an empty chest of ds. & crawled up the dark landing to see why I should have had to go to no. 4 instead of No. 2. With the aid of a match I found out, & also that I was Divisional orderly officer for the next day, i.e. to-day. Help help. I pulled myself together, & was just saying Sneeze Kid, your brain's dusty, when the match sortit & burnt mes doigts. I spent about 3 halfpence worth of matches learning up my various duties, & shivering with cold and fear of the morrow, I slipped in to bed about 12.30, hardly daring to go to sleep at all, for fear I should again oversleep, as I was jolly tired by then and my first duty was to see that all my division (30) were on parade by 6.55.

He must have had some difficulty getting both himself and his division onto the parade ground in time that morning as it was 6.40 before he woke, 'with a bad head, however, I've had too busy a day to notice it, & its gone.'

'The course included instruction in squad drill, company drill, physical training, entrenching and topography, practical and theoretical,' an officer who had been on the course with Billie wrote after the war. 'Most of us picked up a great deal of knowledge at Camberley and I shudder to think what we should have been without the course.'[3] It was the route marches, important in building up stamina, that worried Billie after his recent illness, unnecessarily as it turned out. 'To-day I have marched about 10 miles,' he said, at the end of his first week, '& my knees seem perfectly fit.' [2]

When not working or copying up his notes, Billie tried, with some diffi-culty, to get himself properly equipped. 'I went into Aldershot this after-noon to get some boots,' he wrote on December 3rd, '& found all the shops & cafés shut. So I rushed in for a cup of tea, with another chap to the Station Hotel & was rooked 1/3. We bussed & walked in & took the train back [it was the day of the ten-mile march], it was awful, all K's Army.' It wasn't until December 14th that he was able to report: 'I got a priceless pair of 'K' boots to-day. 23/6 and very good & cheap I think for what they are. Very comfort-able, so I've got that off my chest. That is my chief news . . . I can't think of anything else, it's just the boots I'm so bucked about.'

Arms were another problem. 'We have been advised to get auto-pistols rather than the G.S. (Government Service) pattern revolver, as the latter fires dum dum bullets and the Germans kill you if they catch you.'

The course ended on December 23rd, enabling Billie to spend Christmas with his family before joining the battalion at Purfleet. First impressions of his new surroundings were not altogether favourable, although the pros-pect of seeing Muff must have eased the transition from home.

[Postmarked 31 December 1914]   *Purfleet*
                                                           Essex

Dear Mother,
. . . This is the most miserable place on earth. No cabs or anything, I lugged the suit-case from the station, only about ½ a mile, and stole a bed & some blankets and lay shivering. I got up about 5 to 8 for 7.45 brekker & nipped in at 8.2, fully dressed but, would you believe it, unwashed. The Colonel is a dear old thing, but my Coy. Commander is rather grim. My servant seems to be a fairly decent lad. He sweated in with my valise and I have hopes of a decentish night, if I can get to sleep, because I'm a bit excited, as I hope to see Muffie tomorrow. All leave off work is stopped, but on the excuse of getting my camp kit, bed, washandstand, table etc. I managed to get leave from lunch tomorrow. I hope to spend from 5.30 till 9 tomorrow at Hastings. Some turn, but absolutely the last chance, of seeing her, I can get leave from 4.30 till parade next morning, most evenings but not too often, so I shall hope to slip up & meet you all sometime quite soon. This is a topping Regiment on the whole. I'll write again soon,
   with very best love to you & all
   from
      Billie
   I mean
      Wilfred

The most notable characteristic of Kitchener's men was their keenness. However unpleasant the conditions under which they lived and trained – and in Purfleet during the winter of 1915 they were dreadful, with the camp waterlogged and the training ground six miles distant – nothing seemed to dampen their enthusiasm. Regular Army officers who remarked on it included the commander of the 18th Division, of which the East Surreys were a part. In a paper circulated to Kitchener himself, Maj.-Gen. Ivor Maxse wrote of

the excellent physical and moral qualities of the subaltern officers. They have tackled the job of commanding war strength platoons with a zest and a fearlessness which augurs well. They spend eight hours a day with their platoons and identify themselves with the men's interests both on and off parade. Their keenness to learn the work of training men to fight makes some think that after six months' service they will be as good platoon commanders as the average subaltern of the old Army. This also is the opinion of several Commanding Officers.[4]

The 18th Division was fortunate in its commanding officer. Ivor Maxse was to prove outstanding, both as a leader and for the thorough, professional training he gave those he led. Known as the 'black man' throughout his division, he looked rather like a bad-tempered bulldog, and suffered neither fools nor the inefficient gladly. He had a warm heart, however, and particularly liked those who were prepared to stand up to him. His training methods, like his language, were all his own, but they achieved results.

'Attending his fortnightly conference was like a university course on how to make a fine fighting division out of 20,000 semi-trained, albeit enthusiastic soldiers,' one of his officers remarked[5], while another marvelled at 'the feat he used to perform when he would pass the Battalion, Brigade and later the Division in review on the line of march, and greet by name every subaltern that passed.'[6] His summoning of Billie for an interview when the latter was recommended for a captaincy is an example of the interest Maxse took in even his most junior officers.

Command of the 8th East Surreys itself had improved radically when the two officers brought out of retirement were found, tactfully no doubt, to be medically unfit for service overseas and were replaced. The battalion's new C.O. was a Major Powell of the North Lancashire Regiment, recently recovered from a wound received at Givenchy in France, in an action for which he was to be awarded the D.S.O. Comparatively young, efficient, and battle-experienced, he was a very different commander from Billie's 'dear old thing'.

Billie was later to describe this period in the battalion's life:

I don't need, I think, to describe our slow and weary-some growth . . .
how the officers' uniforms started to come down in the most exciting
parcels; how the regiment, like a caterpillar, crawled out of its civilian
skin into blue serge and came to be recognized as one of K's crowd:
how this again slowly turned into khaki, and how, to keep up the
metaphor, we got our sting in the shape of rifles that really fired!

Lack of equipment continued to be a serious problem in the Division until
it left for France. According to Maxse, each battalion of approximately 1,100
men had only 100 service rifles between them, no long bayonets, no entrenching tools, no haversacks and no water bottles. Very little khaki uniform had arrived to replace the gaudy blue serge, and only a few greatcoats.
The majority of recruits were still having to wear the civilian coats in which
they had enlisted the previous autumn. There were no machine-guns nor
service field guns in the whole Division and only twenty per cent of the required number of horses. In view of the gun shortage perhaps the lack of
telephones for the artillery was irrelevant.

The East Surreys' time at Purfleet was taken up with drilling, physical training, rifle training and field exercises. A rugby team was set up, which beat
the 7th West Kents 37 – 3 in its first match, its success hardly surprising
when one considered the quality of the players – five Welsh internationals
from D company, a rugger blue from Cambridge, two who had played for
Dublin University and several, Billie included, who had played for their
school. Even with such diversions, everyone was heartily sick of Purfleet
and the training ground by the time the battalion moved up to Colchester,
headquarters of the 18th Division, for battalion and brigade training. There
were unexpected difficulties. An outbreak of meningitis meant that Ipswich
was out of bounds and route marches consequently longer. Epidemics were
something the New Armies had had to contend with from their formation:
three of Billie's men developed measles during their time in East Anglia.

Billie's journey was not entirely trouble-free. On a picture postcard of Bar-
rack Lane, Ufford, he wrote,

Dear M. We are here to-night, after a jolly hard day. My men lost all
their kit, so I got a farm waggon & fetched it. Also I borrowed a
civilian bike and generally had a pretty busy evening. Very fit. We
move to Hollesley to-morrow evening.   WPN

In his account of the battalion's beginnings Irwin describes recruits arriving with suitcases of clothes as if expecting to live in some comfort. Billie must have been one of them.

> *8th East Surrey's*
> *Colchester*
> 27th

Dear Mother,
 I have sent home a sack with all the things I don't want. I hope it will arrive safely. We go on trek tomorrow, marching fighting & billeting each day for a week. Letters sent here will be brought on by car to wherever we are.
 I am leaving a lot of stuff here as we are coming back here on the 5th. Then we have 4 days leave & go on the 9th to Royston near Cambridge. This is our probable course.
 Also some photos of my own fair face will arrive with a bill for 17/6 which I'd love you to pay, as they are for you & the family & I shall want my money for odd things for my men on the trek. I've been recommended for promotion to lieut. now for some time & hope to get it dated back a month or two . . .
 I hope to be second in command of A company before we go out. The C.O. is I know very bucked with me.
  with my v.b. to you & all
   from *Wilfred*

The trek referred to was the culmination of the Colchester training, a week-long exercise designed to test units in a variety of battle situations. The Divisional Cyclist Company took the part of the enemy, and umpires, visible and invisible, were appointed to note 'points of march discipline, fitness of troops, handling and management of transport, etc.' Specific problems were allotted to each day, starting out with a comparatively easy march to the area of the exercise – 'We marched in a boiling sun, on a hard road from Col. to Ipswich only 18 miles, but very tiring' – and finishing with one of sixty-two miles over the last forty-eight hours, officers and men alike carrying full marching order. One day, spent attacking a wood, was designed 'to bring out the value of a retired position, and the difficulty of issuing from a wood if the enemy's infantry and artillery are well placed'; another, 'to bring out the difficulties of assembling a force scattered in billets at night, a night approach deployment and the assault of a "jumping off" position under cover of darkness.'[7]
It was very different from the training given to many sections of the New

Armies, where infantry tactics were those used in the Boer War and subalterns frequently had no idea what they were supposed to be doing or why. Indeed, during the Battle of the Somme fifteen months later, a Regular officer in the division was to attribute the 18th Division's successes in that battle to their time at Colchester. 'The outstanding lesson in my mind is that given sufficient time to get troops into action and explain what is required at least to c.o.s these new army battalions are capable of doing all they are asked.' Lt.-Col. Shoubridge wrote in July 1916. 'I think the value of the old Colchester & Codford training still exists among the survivors [of July 1st] & I personally think it was the remains of that training that helped us to get TRONES Wood and hold it.'[8]

The Colchester exercise was carried out under full service conditions. 'Preserved Meat and Biscuit' were included in the rations instead of fresh meat and bread, for instance, and the accommodation provided was supposed to be as close as possible to that expected in France or Belgium. This meant comfort for Billie, as well as for J.R. Ackerley and P.G. Heath, two subalterns with whom Billie had become friendly, for all three were billeted on 'an awfully nice doctor, one Ward, hot baths, dinner & sheets!!' Other ranks were not so fortunate. 'Their billets have really been very bad on the whole,' Billie complained. Divisional instructions stated that straw would be provided where there were earth or stone floors, which was no doubt the reason why, when asked their identity by a passer-by, one of Billie's men on the march shouted out, 'The East Surreys, the men with the Iron feet who live in pig-styes.' [8]

The greatest excitement during the week, as far as Billie was concerned, was the battalion's first contact with the enemy – the real enemy, that is, rather than the Divisional Cyclist Company. The first Zeppelin air raid of the war had been on King's Lynn three months previously; there would be nineteen more such raids over England during the summer of 1915 before improved air defences meant airships became too vulnerable and the Germans used aircraft instead. A full moon on the night of April 30th allowed the airship LZ38 to follow the main road from Ipswich to Bury St. Edmunds, where it dropped four explosive bombs and more than forty incendiaries. There is no reason to believe, however, that the attack was as personal as Billie imagined.

8th East Surreys
Colchester
1.5.15
My Dear Mother,
. . . It's rather a rag as the "Boches" are trying to bomb us but they

don't get the dates quite right, only once. Listen. On the morning of
the 29th we left Ipswich & they bombed our old billets that evening.
We went to Woodbridge & Melton & Ufford on the night of the 29th
and that night they passed over us on the way to Ipswich and just
dropped one for luck at Melton. It didn't go off, but fell bang in the
middle of the village, & is now on exhibition at the local Police
Station.

We left Ufford etc for Hollesley on the morning of the 30th and
found that they had dropped some eggs here as well, on the 29th.
Also lights have been seen near our billets here. And a man is
undoubtedly giving us away but we can't catch the beggar. Joe
Ackerley & I slept out last night on a hill just above our billets with
loaded revolvers & thick sticks but we had no luck, although we
heard either Zeps or aeros go right over very high up about 11.30 last
night. You see, the beggars have got our trek mapped out exactly as
other brigades have done the same trek, but they've got the dates
wrong at present. However, we are here till Monday morning. To-
night we are out fighting all night, back about 7 to-morrow morning.
This is of course a war or prohibited area and only the most dithering
old farm people are left and no lights allowed. Yesterday a German
Aviatik aero went smack over the Brigade on the march near here. We
reported, i.e. our Brigadier-General reported at once to Divisional
H.Q.s & the War Office . . . It will be an awful sell if they bomb us
while we are all out to-night.

The above was all written before I saw the morning paper. Now I
read that 1 Zep. did go over here to Ipswich & go there about 12.15. It
was going very slow (judging by the length of time I heard it) & that
would mean it went over here about 11.30 as I said earlier. It's the one
that bombed Bury St. E.

We are fully expecting to be bombed to-night, but we shall miss it
as we shall be out. It was very quaint to think while one lay out &
looked up at the stars listening to the faint buzz of the propellers, of
the scene going on up there. I pictured to myself the close-cropped
Boches officers leaning over with glasses discussing where they were,
& I was quite dissappointed not to see the little blue streak and hear
the whizz of a bomb. Although it was clear & starry you could see
nothing at all. This all sounds rather sensational but it's quite true and
is a bit interesting.

'We are as brown as berries & as fit as fiddles,' Billie wrote, after a week that
had tested physical fitness to the limit, '& I do hope we shall get our 4 days'

leave alright if only to show you how well I am. My hat it did hurt shaving this morning, I fairly scraped one half peeled layer of skin off.' [8]

After leave, the 18th Division reassembled for further training on Salisbury Plain. Billie's journeys seem to have been unusually eventful and the one to Codford in Wiltshire was no exception.

Monday night   *8th East Surreys*
17.5.15   *Codford*
Dear People All,
    We got down to Aldershot & had tea, then on to Winchester where we had dinner. It was nearly 10 pm. when we had finished and it was raining hard, the road was cruel & I couldn't get more than about 30 out of the bike so we left it at Winchester and went on through about 2 miles of half drunk Saturday night crowds in Morse's car, when the road overcame one of the back tyres and we put on the Stepney, I holding matches in the rain and Morse doing the dirty work. Then we got hopelessly lost and finally got to Salisbury about 11.45, only 25 miles. We took the wrong turning out of Salisbury 3 times, and had to stop every mile or two, get out & read the sign posts by matches. It was cold & miserable, but Morse was an excellent companion & how I blest him & his car. We got to camp about 1.30 am. where the car stuck in the mud. [9]

    Considering Billie's map-reading ability, it was probably as well that the weather continued to be bad. 'I was to have lead the battalion by compass across an utterly desolate part of the Plain to-night, but it was too wet.' One hopes that his catering abilities were better than his map-reading for he was now in charge of A Company's messing. 'It's rather a job feeding 192 hungry men at the rate of 4d per man a day to buy butter, cake, jam, flour, cheese, vegetables, sausages, eggs, kippers & all breakfast dishes!!! The Govt. supply bread, meat, tea, sugar (a little) only. Some job.'[9]
    He had been promoted to lieutenant some time previously but it was not until May 21st that the promotion was listed in the London Gazette, when it was backdated to April 11th. Five days before its appearance he wrote, 'feeling fearfully bucked,' to his family:

The Great news is that I've been recommended by the C.O. for a captaincy (3 stars & 2 rings) . . . I was as you [know] very junior, owing to my illness, so this is a great step up. The General saw how junior I was, & when he got the recommendation he sent for me to

have a look at me. He seemed satisfied & promised to send in my
papers at once. As a Captain I shall get 15/6 a day, instead of 10/- &
that will probably date from to-day <u>when</u> it appears. I should be
careful how you mention it to anyone as it may take a month or more
from now. Of course it will mean leaving my beloved No. 2 platoon,
acknowledged to be the crack platoon in the battalion. [9]

Thanks awfully for your letter & congrats [he wrote to Elsie on May
22nd]. Perhaps you saw in the Gazette yesterday that I was a 1st lieut.
to date from April 11th, that is 40 days ago, so you see how long these
promotions take to go through. Of course I get the additional 1/- a day
pay for that 40 days in a lump (£2) & now I get 8/6 a day & 2/6 field
allowance.[10] My Captaincy has been in about a week now so if that is
to take 40 days as well, I shan't see it for some time to come . . . I'm
2nd in command of C Company now or 2nd Captain as it's called,
under an Oxford man called Pearce, rather a quaint man, but
tolerable. My job is now the accounts; pay & all interior economy of C
Coy. and of course I command the coy. whenever Pearce is away, ill,
or a casualty (200 men). Of course I'm now over all the platoon
commanders, so I'm in rather an awkward position (as they were
mostly senior to me) or rather I <u>should be</u> if everyone was not so
awfully decent & apparently genuinely pleased about it. No. 2 say
they are awfully sorry I've left them, but are very pleased I'm an s.i.c.
[10]

Five weeks later he was telling Elsie to 'Watch the gazette carefully & add
on 4/6 a day for the days between the date given & the date on the paper. I
shall get that in a lump of back pay.' Nothing had appeared in print by the
time he left England at the end of July. When giving his mother his future
address he took care to underline the correct rank – '<u>Lt</u>. W.P.N.' – as if Mrs
Nevill were already addressing him as captain. He had had to reprove his
family for military ignorance before – 'Coy. is the correct abbreviation for
company not co. (you civilians!!).' [11] It was not only his mother in whom
he lacked confidence; he told Elsie that Stanley, 'who offered to get anything
for me that I might want, is getting some envelopes printed with my address
for you to use in writing to me, so as to ensure my getting the letters.' [15] A
supply of the envelopes was also to be sent to Muffie down in Hastings.

The tale of his promotion was a sorry one. There was a mix-up in the
paperwork and on August 12th, nearly three months after the first news, he
wrote from France to say that

The C.O. can't understand about Paull & me & is furious about it, we

were both up but my name was up about 2 months before Paull's
that's the extraordinary part. [28]

He returned to the subject two days later.

About Paull getting his captaincy & not me, you see, my name went
up & then Paull's, & they've dated Paull's back to mine really, so
when mine comes I may not get nearly so much back pay, you see
he's got nearly £30, which should have been mine. Our Colonel is
furious about it, & I've seen his letter on the subject leave our Orderly
Room, so in time something may happen, but I fear I've done in. [29]

And again, the next day,

The C.O. came up to see us again today, and said how sorry and angry he
was about Paull getting my captaincy, of course he has written complaining
and is trying to get mine dated back to its proper time, as well as Paull's.
Paull's of course can't be altered now to a later date. [30]

Eventually, but not until September 9th, he found on his plate at breakfast
a note from Cecil Clare, the battalion adjutant: 'Dear Nevill, I enclose cutting
from the London Gazette, from which you will see that the War Office have
made the amend honorable by Gazetting you from April 11th.' [48] In the
end Billie did rather well. Backdating to April 11th meant that he had been a
lieutenant for less than a day.

Once the division reached Salisbury Plain, Maxse took care to see that junior
officers felt that they were the keystone of the division, while Irwin 'tried to
make it a rule to let the men understand what we were trying to teach them
all the time. We'd have discussions on what we'd seen that was new to them
and that sort of thing and before any day's work if I could find out what we
were supposed to be doing that day I would get hold of the officers and just
ask them to pass on to the men what we were going to do, try to get them interested.' There was much greater variety in the training than there had
been at Purfleet.

I've been riding all morning & feel jolly sore now [Billie wrote on May
30th], otherwise I'm very fit. I sleep out on the haystack with Ackerley
(Joe in future) & Heath, I've been out each night last week, all
weathers ['The frost is ghastly here,' he had said earlier in the same
letter]. It makes you sleep, is very comfy & all the windows are open!

. . . We start another musketry course soon now. All our horses are to be at the firing pt. to get used to rows. We are all going to see our artillery fire soon. We are to stand & watch just between the guns & the target. Rather a rag, eh? [11]

Equipment was still short. Irwin talks of dummy guns. 'I'm now on a 'spring gun' course but the gun has not turned up yet,' Billie wrote on July 21st, less than a week before the battalion's departure for France. 'Nor have some patent catapults.' [15] The trench catapult eventually arrived on the day the battalion left England.

Life on Salisbury Plain was not all work. There was an opportunity for families to visit. 'You must come,' Billie wrote.

I shall probably be about looking out for you. Don't mind going fearlessly through the huts, it's a good short cut & saves a lot. You go through the Royal West Kents camp, Camp 15. Don't get taken for spies . . . I'll give you lunch in my hut & we'll go to the Divisional Horse Show in the afternoon, then you can either go home about 6.30 or 8.30 pm or stay the night in Salisbury, 15 miles off by rail. I'm sure you'd get beds in Sal. somewhere, you certainly won't here. I'll have to slip down to Codford with this to express it & I hope it'll get home in time. Do come, I'd love you to see it all, far more than Purfleet of course. [12]

A more august visitor was George V, who inspected the Division near Stonehenge towards the end of June, which meant that embarkation could be expected at any time. Rumour was rife.

One bit of news is that I am almost for certain going to the Dardanelles[11] [Billie had told his mother at the end of May]. We seem to have bitten off a shade more than we can chew down there, but France is alright now I think & the passage to Russia (via Archangel) is open now. So we can give her shells, but her corn is all down south. I'd far rather have a whack at the Huns proper, than the wretched Turks, but doubtless we'll find some down there. [11]

'We may fly any moment, almost for certain to the Dardanelles, I'm afraid. There's no doubt about [it] now,' [12] he confirmed two weeks later. To Elsie he admitted, 'We're fed up with this & dying to get the first 5 minutes over & be wounded bad enough to keep [us] home for a bit, after that is of course, we've bagged a fair quota of the Bosches.' [13]

By mid-July the destination had changed. 'Rumours fly like bees still,' he told Elsie on July 21st. 'But as a Division we are for France, though I hear some regiments may be drafted out to the Dardanelles.' [15]

The formalities of courtship in the first part of this century made a farewell visit from Muff difficult to arrange. The Nevills and the Schoolings had been neighbours for years, the children growing up together, but it was still necessary to invite Muffie's younger brother to come with Muff as chaperone. 'I'm afraid Peter simply must come up, they'd never let Muff without him,' Billie told Elsie, adding hopefully, 'Muff swears he's alright now & absolutely converted.' It was Elsie who offered help, in spite, or perhaps because, of an incident in the past when Billie had unwittingly acted in Peter's current role.

Postmarked 20 June 1915   *8th E. Surreys*
                                                          Codford
                                                          Wilts

Dear Else,

Thanks no end for your letter & very sound advice. Both Muff and myself are working our hardest to arrange either to lose Peter (which wd. at once bring about the very debâcle which you foreshadow) or else, better still, to find someone for him to cart round & so we should hold him in the hollow of the hand & he wd. have no evidence. I think we shall be alright, anyhow he'll have to lie pretty prodigously to get anything against us that would annoy papa Schooling. Papa S. bagged one of my letters the other day, read it through and handed it back saying "He writes a very good letter."[12] Rather amusing . . . I think Muff & I might not have been very much missed if we'd punted all alone all Sunday, as per programme. Not with a brother on board, as you had to suffer that Windsor trip! You know I never realised about that till the end. You were both too sporting to suggest I should not come, and really you took it most awfully well, so that I never realised I was so terribly 'de trop' till I thought it over afterwards. That's a back number though now. [13]

To circumvent the censor once he was overseas, Billie arranged to put dots under the appropriate letters, either in pencil or a pinpoint, to spell out the message. 'It will always be at the beginning,' he told Elsie. 'I won't put "see page 3" or they might smell a rat. On this you will find a few names or smaller towns which might be our route one day for instance.' [15] Still in England he tried the system out with his mother, apparently with little success for a week later he was telling her, 'I simply dare not put the dots any plainer, you can do em with [a] magnifying glass. You see if the censors catch a letter, they stop all the letters of that battalion!!' [17]

As the day of departure approached he did his best to reassure Mrs. Nevill. 'We shan't scrap or rather be near any fighting for ages.'

Please, please don't worry about me. It's as safe as the East Coast where we are going. The only thing I'm worrying about is the crossing & after that perhaps the rheumatism. The Dardanelles would have done my knees a world of good, so of course they put me in a swamp. Still a safe swamp is better than a risky sun. [14]

He wrote again before leaving Salisbury Plain.

Everyone is now ready and it's like hanging about at the end of your last term at School . . . Don't worry about me please, Mother, I feel as happy as I ever have in my life. Muffie is simply topping, the family goes without saying, I've no bills of any standing or size, why worry. I shall be alright, really there's no danger. [18]

The 18th Division crossed to France between July 25th and 27th, 1915. It was a period of intense activity as far as the Channel ports were concerned. As Billie wrote later, 'They put through 8000 infantry alone, a night, for nearly 3 weeks on end, without a single hitch. Does the Navy do anything? Think of the horses & guns for all that infantry & it's simply incredible how the Navy does it at all, let alone control the Sea as well.' [56]

The transport and machine-gun section under Captain Irwin, the first part of the East Surreys to leave, crossed from Southampton to Le Havre on July 26th. In England Irwin had fallen foul of Colonel Powell, who threatened to get rid of him and appoint another adjutant. 'He didn't really like me or my methods very much,' Irwin remembered. 'Very efficient chap himself and he didn't want anyone else doing anything, I think.' Irwin was in charge of billeting arrangements in France before the arrival of the full battalion and was fortunate enough to find such a magnificent billet for Colonel Powell that the C.O. relented and promoted Irwin to major and second in command. The new arrangement, with Cecil Clare as adjutant, worked well. 'In time,' Irwin said, 'since I wasn't quite so close to him and hadn't got to carry out his orders . . . we got on very well indeed.'

While waiting to leave Codford for the port of embarkation Billie began a diary.

July 25th 1915

I am starting this diary today, because today my valise [canvas kitbag] was packed & loaded, which is the first thing which has actually affected me, in our move. Some of the Division has already gone, most of it, in fact, including the General who went this afternoon. I thought I'd just note down just what I took in my valise & what is on my back.

In my Valise is, my flea bag, which Stanley gave me, it's not been washed since I joined, in November! Also a tunic, a pr. of knickers, 1 pr. of ordinary Tommy's trousers, 1 pr. pyjamas & carpet slippers, 1 pr. boots, 1 pr. socks, (Amy), 1 shirt, 1 set of underclothing, 4 handkerchiefs, 1 collar, odd note books, an F.S.P.B. [Field Service Pocket Book], a prayer book, a razor strop, & 1 pack of cards. Not much, but I'm trusting to you, Mother, & the G.P.O. Well, that's gone & is now standing on a waggon in the rain weighing 37 lbs. (not the rain, or the waggon) just 2 lbs more than the regulation weight! Now on my back, in pouches, pack, haversacks, etc. is, or is it, are:- Fleece lined Burberry with shoulder straps, gym shoes, 1 set of underclothing, 1 pr. socks, a towel a mess tin a scarf, a waterproof ground sheet, a complete holdall, & a housewife [sewing kit], washing & shaving things, 1 pack of cards, compass, revolver, vaseline, glasses, 3 knives, knife, fork, spoon and tin opener, 3 boot laces, safety pins, medicine case, three books of poetry, Shelly, Keats, & Omar, & the Minstral Boy, 4 I should have said, essence of beef tablets, notepaper, etc. 50 rounds of ammunition, 10 rifle & 40 revolver, wire cutters, trench periscope, notebooks, maps, pencils & sketching things, steel mirror, air pillow, Bible, flask, pocket book, wrist watch, Onoto [fountain pen], M's photo, money belt, (£5 in notes, £2 in gold) water bottle, food for 2 days, Coy. pay sheets, oil bottle, megaphone, respirator & bread bag, a thick blackthorn stick, & matches, electric torch, 4 first field dressings & iodine bottle sewn in lining of coat (called an "ampoule" no one knows why), identity disc, cardigan waistcoat, Company roll call book. There may be some more I've forgotten, anyhow you see, I'm pretty self-supporting, & I reckon I could march my 20 miles a day easily, with that load. I'll try to remember to tell you the exact weight of it all later. I wonder how much I'll chuck away, after a bit!!

This afternoon I went to tea with Mrs Powell, & Mrs Maxse (general's wife) came in, she was charming & very interesting. I fancy I'll leave this now till tomorrow. I intend to send this home just before we leave our concentration camp "somewhere in France". This is a large F.S. (Field Service) pocket book. It may interest you to know that

I have never been so fit & healthy before in my life, also I am perfectly happy & not in the least bit worrying about any single little thing.

There was little to do, apart from strolling round the camp, 'to prevent us getting too fat & lazy', while some of the officers struggled with the intricacies of a French map. At last came the moment of departure. The second section of the battalion left Folkestone on the evening of July 27th, arrived in Boulogne the following morning and 'staggered up a huge hill' to Osterhove Rest Camp on the outskirts of the town. Kitchener's men had landed in France at last.

NOTES

As few of Billie's letters survive from this period, details of the 8th East Surreys' formation and its first months come mostly from other sources, notably the *History of the East Surrey Regiment, History of the 55th Brigade*, an Imperial War Museum interview with the then Lt.-Col. Irwin in 1973, the memoirs of P.G. Heath and *The New Army in the Making*. Heath had been a clerk in the city of London before enlisting in the 23rd London Regiment in August 1914. In November 1914 he gained a commission in the 8th East Surreys. 'There is a little book about now called "The New Army in the making" by an officer,' Billie told his family on September 15th, 1915. 'The officer is Capt. Mitchell of our B. Coy. He was one of the most brilliant professors, at the London University. It's only a little booklet, but it's most awfully true & describes our life at Purfleet & Codford to a T. I don't know what a T is, do you I wonder?'
1. Middlebrook, p.19.
2. 1 Samuel 15, v.32-33: Agag, king of the Amalekites, a nation slaughtered by Saul at Samuel's command, was spared by Saul, contrary to Samuel's orders. 'Then said Samuel, Bring ye hither to me Agag . . . And Agag came unto him delicately. And Agag said, Surely the bitterness of death is past. And Samuel said, As thy sword hath made women childless, so shall thy mother be childless among women. And Samuel hewed

Agag in pieces before the Lord in Gilgal.' A better known text then than now, it would seem, for references to Agag's walk (no doubt he realised his likely fate) appear in other letters and memoirs of the period.
3. Sir Ivone Kirkpatrick, *The War, 1914-1918*, unpublished account, IWM 79/50/1.
4. Maj.-Gen. Ivor Maxse, 'Notes on the New Armies by a Divisional Commander, No.1', Maxse papers. IWM 69/53/5.
5. Lt.-Col. H.H. Hemming, *Preparing for War*, unpublished account, IWM PP/MCR/155.
6. Lt.-Col. T.M. Banks and Capt. R.A. Chell, *With the 10th Essex in France*, (Gay & Hancock, London, 1921) pp. 21-2.
7. '18th Division Brigade and Combined Training 1915' and 'Training Instructions, 18th Div.', Maxse papers, IWM 69/53/5.
8. Maxse papers, IWM 69/53/7. Shoubridge was Senior General Staff Officer of the 18th Division.
9. According to J.M. Mitchell, the Army allowed every man per day

1¼ lb bread	2 oz sugar
1 lb meat or	1 oz cheese
pressed beef	1 oz jam
2 oz bacon	¹⁄₂₀ oz mustard
½ oz salt	1/36 oz pepper
½ oz tea	

which meant that one brigade

needed 5½ tons of food daily. The antipathy shown by some French towards British battalions billeted in their villages seems quite reasonable in the circumstances.

10. As lieutenant. A 2nd lieutenant received 8/6d a day plus 2/6d field allowance.

11. Allied landings had taken place on the Gallipoli peninsular at the end of April in an attempt to open the Dardanelles and allow supplies through to Russia. The attempt failed and all surviving troops were evacuated at the end of 1915.

12. This was more of a compliment than it appears, as Mr. Schooling, an actuary by profession, was himself a writer, contributing to *Punch* and to *Blackwood's Magazine*. He was a more interesting character than appears from the letters – he was a member of the Magic Circle, for instance.

2 KEEPING IN TOUCH

'Letters <u>must</u> be very welcome out here,' Billie wrote two days after his arrival in France, adding plaintively, 'So far I think I am the only person in the regiment who hasn't had one!' [22] Three weeks later, after receiving a batch, he was thanking his family 'so very much for all of them, they are such a help.' [34]

The effect on morale of regular and frequent communication between England and the troops was recognised by the authorities. The mail service – to France, if not to places further afield – seems to have been well organised and astonishingly efficient as a result. Despite the volume – an average of 500,000 letters and 60 to 70,000 parcels, 100 tons of mail in all, were crossing the Channel daily by midsummer, 1915[1] – and despite the fact that name and regiment were all that were allowed on the envelope, delivery never took longer than four days, and was often shorter. Letters posted in England before 9 p.m. on Thursday, July 29th, for instance, reached the 8th East Surrey Regiment in Picardy by 5 p.m. on Saturday, the 31st. Mail was regarded as so important that it was even delivered to the trenches. 'Our letters come up with the rations at night, to a village behind, which is called the "Dump",' Billie reported from the front line, '& we fetch up the "grub" etc. in tins and boxes slung on long poles.' [29] Mail travelling in the opposite direction was less trustworthy, in Billie's opinion. During his first tour at the front he sent his own letters down the line with the medical officer. 'That is safer than the ration corporal & more likely to arrive.' [29]

The quantity of letters mattered as much as, if not more than, their quality. 'The post has just come in,' Billie told his mother. 'I had <u>five</u> letters, you, Elsie, Tom, Howard and who do you think has written again. Quite right (7 sides closely written too)! Naturally I'm feeling awfully bucked, more so than usual. It's awfully good of you all.' [33] On this occasion, of course, it was doubtless Muffie's letter that gave him so much pleasure, but there were other times when he gloated over a quantity of letters. Howard agreed. 'It is a heavenly sensation to sit down with about ten letters in front of you & work solemnly through them.' [26th February, 1918]

'Your letters have been delightful,' Billie told the family, 'but when you

forward one on to me, like Miss Ulph's for instance, never put it inside one of your envelopes. You evidently don't realise the tonic there is in the sight of an envelope.' [38] He and Aunt Annie kept up 'quite a regular correspondence,' for that very reason. 'You see we both know the value of envelopes.' [56]
He was not above using blackmail, if need be.

Yesterday I sent F.S.P.C.s to all the Uncles and Aunts whose addresses I know, & to everyone I could think of. It's a wonderful thing, a F.S.C.P. It costs nothing, takes no time, & gives no mental energy, it is in fact the essence of laziness, the ideal of the wordless correspondent & the bored nephew alike. From it may spring a parcel, a letter, anything! Should this little paper seed, as it were, (to carry on the metaphor) fall on stony ground, & not produce some packet in the course of a week or so, be certain it turns bad & rots & that awful disease, a prickly conscience, sets in, in the heart of the recipee! [27]

On this occasion at least one seed fell on fertile ground. Five days later Billie reported the receipt of 'an awfully jolly letter from Abbot, my tutor, in answer to a F.S.P.C.' [31]
Letters were valuable for keeping in touch. 'We do see the papers now & then,'[2] he said, on August 22nd, 'but I'd love to have your own opinions on things like the National Reg & the War Loan & the recruiting, the nos. of slackers on the river etc. You wouldn't believe how awfully interesting things like that have suddenly become to me.' 'Don't forget my request for news,' he reminded them a week later. 'We do get some here on the telephone, & a few sheets of Foolscap come round every day, called unofficially the 'Corp Daily Liar'. It's chiefly to keep our spirits up, judging by its remarks.' [38]
Domestic details were even more welcome. 'That must have been a topping trip to Abinger & I enjoyed the Kipper incident immensely. I love to hear of things like those. As you won't get this till about 8 days after you wrote, it's rather trying for you to spot which letter I'm answering. Still there won't be many notable kipper incidents.' [80]
Elsie's letters were 'splendid', Amy's voluminous ('Next time you write a book like that . . . '), and at least one of Doff's was 'most entertaining when I'd pieced it together & sorted out the various items.' [42] As for Muffie, hers were so frequent and so lengthy ('She has written me some ripping long letters' [25]; 'Another huge letter arrived from Muff to-day . . . I had one yesterday too' [159]) that bundles of them had to be sent back to Tennyson's House to be stored in Billie's bureau for safe-keeping. Now that he was in

France, doing his bit, attitudes had changed in the Schooling household. 'It's rather ripping, but do you know old pa Schooling has quite turned round,' Billie reported on August 7th. 'She [Muffie] says 'Poppar' Schooling quite likes me now,' he added, three days later. By the end of the month he was telling his family that 'Mr. Schooling now actually packs my parcels!' [38]

Parcels from Hastings seem to have been almost as frequent as the letters. 'Muffie sent me some magazines, a tin of sparghetti (with instructions luckily) some fly ointment, 1lb of pep. creams & some Hasting's Hun Poison (Homemade Cocoanut ice). She is a brick, isn't she.' [32] 'I had a tremendous parcel from Muffie today, sausages and every conceivable thing, cake, choc. & a plum pudding etc. etc.' [38] 'Some parcel,' he said of another. 'She is topping and I don't know what I'd do out here, without her.' [26]

Billie had received parcels from home even before leaving England. 'Thanks most awfully for all your letters & parcels & socks & watches & things,' he had written from Codford the previous May.[3] No one knew what would be needed in the way of parcels on the other side of the Channel. 'I can get things washed here alright,' he said in one of his first letters from France, as if he had expected otherwise, thus conjuring up a picture of the entire British Expeditionary Force returning its laundry to England every week. (Howard did send his washing home from Sheerness for at least two years, and his mending and darning too.)

'Collect all socks & wash 'em ready,' Billie told his mother while waiting to embark. 'You will find if you get this various socks, shirts and hankies all suitable for my parcels.' [18] These were presumably the contents of 'that case full of oddments' which he had sent home, being unable to fit them into his valise.

'I hope you've already sent off my parcels,' he wrote, two days after setting foot in France, 'as I want the cigars badly, not daring to trust the local outpost, even if he kept them, which I doubt.' [20] 'Did Elsie get these cigars at Maunders or Woolworths?' he asked a week later. 'They asphyxiate the flies quite well, when I can deceive anyone into smoking one.' [26]

Within days he was overwhelmed by the goods arriving. 'Don't send anything more except the Nestle's milk & the cigars, until I send a service card asking for something, you know how,' he wrote after only a week on the Continent. 'We are as I told you in the lap of luxury . . . I have loads of choc. Punch, cigars & tinned milk, are the things [needed] & those weekly at present.' [22]

Clothing, food, toiletries, cigars and brandy were the staple items in parcels from home. Other items became important according to the situation. Candles were always necessary once he had reached the trenches, and

2: KEEPING IN TOUCH 35

mousetraps useful. Stanley was asked for a pistol to deal with the rats. [43] Reading matter was important and cheap novels much in demand, 'any 7d by George Birmingham or the Williamsons for preference.'⁴ [147]. So many officers received *Punch* that Billie soon asked for *The Bystander* to be sent instead. A parcel was welcome whatever its ingredients. One of the most comprehensive must surely have been that sent to Billie 'with love (?) from Monica & Irene.' It included 'matches gum & sealing wax soap, nails, string, pins, candles, tape, cotton, pencil, cigarettes & choc. Some parcel,' Billie summed up. [191]

The kind and quantity of food required depended on messing arrangements at the time and the nearness of the brigade canteen. Chocolate and sweets were always popular, butter and milk often needed. 'Any unsweetened tin milk will do, but Ideal is the best. I know you can get it at Fortnum & Mason' [165]. Sausages and meat, like the butter and milk, came in tins, expensive to send and no doubt the reason for one of Billie's letters. 'A ripping parcel came from you, potted meat & chicken etc. but if it cost 7/6 it was not worth [it] I think.' The cost had worried him from early on.

Evening of 4.9.15

. . . Your parcels have been simply ripping lately. I had a lovely one waiting for me when we arrived here, with fly papers, hair shampoo and studs etc., just the very things you want in billets. I'm afraid you must be spending a young fortune on them, Mother, if you like I'll send you a cheque to carry on with, because you see I've got the money and I don't see that it's fair for you to spend such a lot on me, when I'm earning ('some' earn) pay, more than enough to cover all my wants.'⁵ [42]

The larger quantities of food coming out from England were shared. 'We had haddock (8 days old) for breakfast, it came out in a fish basket without having a single bone broken. You might try that as an experiment will you? Some fish in a box, not bloaters, kippers or 'errings.' [165]

'A Kate & Sydney' pudding arrived from Billie's schoolfriend, Donald Campbell. 'It's still in its own recepticle and not mine, so I don't know how nice it is yet. We are going to sniff at it another 3 days, so as to get full value before eating it.' [99] One hopes that it was still edible when eventually served.

There were ways of improving the rations besides parcels from home. 'The other day we sent a fiver to the B.E.F. canteen at Havre & asked for a case of whisky & a weekly case of soda. Well, they arrived the other day, 12 bots of jolly good whisky & lots of soda, all for 52 frs! Pretty useful, eh?' [56]

Parcels also came regularly from Fortnum and Mason, 'so we dine well, considering.' [88] 'The East Surreys always did themselves well,' Lt.-Col. Powell told General Maxse.[6]

Articles of clothing were regularly requested. Socks, of course, were of the utmost importance to an expeditionary force that moved mostly on foot, but more important to Billie than socks – or so it seems from his letters – were kneecaps, presumably because of the fear of rheumatism. The family were so concerned about his health that when Billie was due for leave in the autumn of 1915 Stanley wrote from Gibralter on his way to Egypt, '[I] almost hope his knee trouble will be bad enough to keep him at home all the winter, he oughtn't to run [the] risk of crocking himself for life through Rheumatic Fever.' [21st November, 1915]

A friend of the family had made a 'splendid' kneecap while Billie was at the Staff College – 'I thanked Miss E. last night & begged her to make another' [2] - but kneecaps that were satisfactory in England were apparently not so in France. Poor Miss E.'s efforts were now spurned. 'Miss E's knee-caps are too thick & I must have the others as soon as poss.' [74]

A touch of desperation sounded in his letter to Elsie. 'If the knee caps you have sent are the rubber ones they won't do. I want something like pants & vest material to reach from calf to halfway up thigh, just covering all round the knee . . . My old knees are twitching in a most unpleasant manner. Please send out one pair of the thickest, long pants to be found in London. My tum tum, to put it nicely, is about 36 to 38 inches I suppose, in circumference. The censor, while passing this interesting detail, is glad of the opportunity of pointing out that this item is recorded solely with the purpose of aiding the purchaser in the difficult manner of deciding on what size her brother requires.' [80]

'The blank cheques etc. can wait a bit, but not the knee caps,' he wrote a week later, 'not even while they're being knitted. Rheumatism is my great danger & far harder to fight than 1,000,000 huns.' [88]

At last, but not until the end of October, he was satisfied. 'The knee caps are simply ripping, just as I wanted.' After that, references cease, presumably because a satisfactory source of supply had been found.

A request for gloves was more easily dealt with. 'Ring up Mrs. Ackerley & ask her where she bought Joe's, I want some just like his, please.' [88]

Billie received so much clothing during his first weeks in France that on October 10th he had to tell the family, 'never [to] send clothes of any kind unless I ask for them. My valise now weighs about 90 lbs & it should be 35 only.'

Misunderstandings occurred, as after his repeated requests for flannels. 'OF COURSE I meant washing glove flannels, but you weren't to know, I quite see. The others will do to sleep in, when it's cold, instead of or as well as pygies.' [37] And consternation was apparently caused by his remark that, 'Your 3rd parcel arrived yesterday, when I'd packed everything so I put it bodily on to the cooker.' [25] He wrote later, of another parcel, '[It] sounds excellent, but has not arrived yet. It will come, I expect, just as we're packed up to go 'up' tomorrow . . . It will go on the cooker! In case you are still in doubt about that phrase, it merely infers that it will be carried to the trenches on the Kitchen, travelling, G.S. 3rd pattern, Mark VI!!!'[7] [80]

By September he had a cooker of his own, a Tommie's Cooker[8] that he had asked the family to get from the Army and Navy Stores – 'I'm not asking for anything I don't really want.' [29] – which was 'a great & roaring success. I've made myself & two others as well cocoa the last 4 nights on duty in the trenches, & by Jove, my old 'brewing' hand, from 'study days' had not forgotten his cunning.' [42]

Billie was definite about his wants. Shampoo had to be bottled ('and for Elsie's benefit, my hair is about ½ an inch long, as we have the clippers over our scalps as often as possible' [51]); shaving powder had to be Colgate's, 'a tin of Colgates Rapid Shave powder.' [57] 'The only 'crab' to it was you sent Colgates Shaving Stick, not Powder,' he said of one parcel. 'My pleasures out here are few, and lathering a real brushlike & mud-sploshed chin with the powder is one of em.' [179]

Sometimes he must have driven his family frantic. 'Do send out the braid and stars I asked for on that list AT ONCE,' he wrote on December 20th. 'Hurry up the braid and stars!!!' he urged on the 23rd, but on January 8th he was telling the family, 'If you haven't already sent them don't send any braid and stars.' This letter was apparently ignored, for two weeks later he wrote that 'the braid was alright, but the stars were bright & should have been dull. However I burnt them & now they're all right. Thanks.' [137]

Tom's responsibility was to keep his brother supplied with 'indellible pencils,' which Billie acknowledged. 'I'm writing this with 1 of Tommy's ripping pencils. They are great, thanks old boy no end.' [34] Envelopes were always needed ('cheap ones of course') and requested more frequently than writing paper, which is surprising when one considers the length of some of the letters.

Despite Billie's request to his family, to 'number clearly all my parcels then I shall [know] which I get & which get lost,' [29] the parcel post seems to have been very reliable: no reference was ever made to anything missing. Eight to ten days seems to have been the usual time between an item being requested and being received. Even one which had to be ordered took very little longer.

Evening of 4.9.15
Please send at once
1. <u>2</u> protractors (a short 6 inch ruler, flat, marked with various scales
    & measures
2. One pair of folding (if possible) dividers. If you can't get folding
    ones, get ones with the points protected.
    I lost both mine which I brought out and they are indispensable.
    You can't read & use a map without them – & I live in a seething
    ocean of maps, French, English, artillery, aeroplane, Ordinance
    Survey, field sketches. [42]

'I'm so glad you ordered good ones,' he said on the 12th. On the 15th he
recorded their arrival. 'The dividers & protractors are a great god-send,' he
said two days later.

Articles as indispensable should surely have been available through military channels. Military equipment was not always adequate, however. Siegfried Sassoon had to buy his own wire-cutters from the Army and Navy
Stores for the attack on July 1st because of the inadequacy of army ones.[9]

References to the contents of some parcels are intriguing. 'Thank Auntie
for the rabbit,' is one. Was the rabbit alive? Dead? A mascot? Edible – chocolate, perhaps? It is impossible to tell. Even more puzzling are the letters referring to Shirley More and her ball.

Billie had been an enthusiastic theatre-goer, particularly to musicals and
revues. 'I should like some p.c.s. of Shirley & Unity More,' he told Amy in
August 1915, 'the latter is an Hippodrome flame of mine, who is now at the
Alabama in 'Shell Out.'[10] The next mention of Shirley More is on October
10th. 'I shall rub the ball in the mud & send it back with an <u>appropriate</u> letter
and ask her for a signed photo! Just for fun and then send it to Muff.' [80]

'A parcel containing the celebrated ball from Shirley . . . arrived today,' he
reported the following day. [81]

'I've not had an answer from Shirley yet,' he said ten days later. 'I sent her
back that ball with a long letter. However I've met someone who knows her
well, & says she's a most ordinary and uninteresting married woman, off
the stage!' Before he could finish his letter the post came in,

bearing a card from Cox's saying my pay is being paid in all right,
AND a huge photo 12' × 8' [he must have meant 12″ × 8″] of Shirley
with a little note saying she was charmed by my letter & kind
remarks. Wow! Wow! Don't be too shocked. It's a jolly good photo,
but she looks in it what she is, a robust wench of some 40 summers.
However the spirit is right. Now what we do is to tear it up, all but

the face, & send one piece to each of 7 or 8 other actresses, asking them to replace their photos which have been hit by a shell!!!! SOME DODGE!! Aren't we terrors? [90]

The Unity More whom Billie mentions was a popular actress, dancer and singer, at twenty-one just two weeks younger than Billie. Shirley remains a mystery. There is no mention of her in theatrical reference books, so no way of knowing whether she was Unity's mother, or an elder sister; no way, either, of finding out more about that 'celebrated ball'.

The traffic in parcels was not entirely one way. Travelling in the opposite direction were the souvenirs, ranging from the delightful – 'I found these two daisies today, they're the first I've seen & they struck me as being a nice peaceful sort of thing to send from here' [138] – to unpleasant relics of war.
    There were presents too, of course, a fruit knife and fork, bought from one of the 'two pretty and charming sisters' who ran the buffet outside the divisional headquarters at Heilly[11]; a cockerel-crested whistle, sent 'To Mother with love', for calling the dog[12]; pin cushions for Muff and Doff. 'I see, too late, that I've addressed the pin cushion I wrote 'Muff' on the box of, to Doff & vice versa, mais cela n'est egal!' [127]. Not a present but a more pleasant souvenir than most was a chocolate box tin 'given to the troops by the Colonies named on the lid (I can't remember who). There were about 50 boxes per Battalion & I managed to pinch one. The Queen didn't give any-thing as the Army was too big.'[13] [136]
    There is no indication of the family's reaction to the battlefield debris that kept arriving on their doorstep, often with technical detail provided. 'One [souvenir] is an A.P. (ask Howard) (armour-piercing) <u>rifle</u> bullet, for firing through brick walls or iron plated loopholes. I've only <u>its</u> steel inside, not the nickel casing. An ordinary bullet, of course, has a lead tummy, so to speak.' [40]

I've sent off a match box containing two German rifle or machine gun bullets which I picked up on the grass in No Man's Land the other day. The interesting part about them is that they have no gro[o]ves from the rifling of the barrel on them, proving that the barrel was worn quite smooth. They probably went through the air turning head over heels instead of spinning with the point first, both apparently hit a stone with their wrong ends first. You'll notice they are shorter than ours; a wee bit fatter (.01 of an inch to be exact) and more pointed. [100]

There was a French aeroplane dart – 'They drop hundreds of them at [a] time. It has been made into a pen, by the blacksmith here. Aren't they horribly deadly.'[14] [54] Most unpleasant of all, however, must surely have been the inside of a gas shell, sent to Elsie from an unhealthy section of the front line. 'Don't burn it,' Billie warned, 'as I'm not sure it won't make you all cry.' [124]

In July 1915, however, Billie had yet to set foot on a battlefield. With the battalion's arrival in France his journey to the front had just begun.

NOTES

1. Hansard, 9 June, 1915.
2. 'We get the Daily Mirror, Sketch, & English Daily Mail one day late in billets & 2 days late when we're up.' [56]
3. Billie's watches suffered a high casualty rate. '[They] are all going,' he wrote on September 17th, as if that were noteworthy. There are a number of references in his letters to watches being damaged, and to others being received in his parcels.
4. George Birmingham was a prolific Irish writer of serious historical fiction as well as light comedy and farce. The Williamsons were a husband and wife team who wrote bright and amusing romances.
5. M.Ps made numerous complaints in the House of Commons about the cost to families of sending parcels to men in France. Their requests that the rate should at least be reduced from the foreign to the inland rate were always turned down by the Postmaster-General. The Army simply had not got the transport available to cope with the increase in numbers of parcels that a reduced postal rate would bring.
6. Maxse papers, IWM 69/53/7. So Lt.-Col Powell said, when describing the lunch served up in Montauban Alley after the slaughter on July 1st, 1916, of Heidseck 1906 and cold tongue. However, Powell, who had not been present on July 1st, was writing from hearsay. The battalion War Diary states that 'L/C Brame turned up with a bottle of

champagne to be drunk in Montauban "on der Tag". This was sent round from officer to officer . . . all E.S. officers engaged in the attack who had not been killed or wounded,' which is rather different from the full-blown lunch that Colonel Powell implies. Ackerley said that East Surrey Regiment officers had been told to take a bottle of whisky or rum with them when they attacked on July 1st, with which to celebrate the expected victory. (Ackerley's whisky bottle was shattered during the advance by an exploding shell.)
7. In army parlance, a cooker was a travelling field kitchen, wheeled and pulled by horses or mules. Billie amused himself a number of times by listing things back to front in army fashion. Heath referred to one occasion when, after a particularly wet tour in the trenches, Billie sent an indent back to the quartermaster at battalion headquarters requesting '200 – Brellas Um.'
8. Small stove, made from solidified paraffin wax. It produced very little heat and was used in places where ordinary cooking was impossible, i.e. in the front line.
9. *Memoirs of an Infantry Officer*, pp.52-3.
10. *Shell Out*, a revue, had in fact opened that month at the Comedy Theatre.
11. Heath's description of the sisters. He went on to describe the buffet as a 'superb teashop.' Billie always

referred to one of the sisters as the
Elephant Flapper, or the E.F., for
what reasons one can only surmise.

12. See entry dated 4th August 1988 in
the visitors' book at Carnoy
Cemetery.

13. Such presents from the monarch to
the Army were traditional. There is a
chocolate box in the Regimental
Museum of the Queen's Royal
Surrey Regiment, which was given
by Queen Mary to the East Surrey
Regiment at Christmas 1914,
presumably the last year she did so.

14. Darts were the forerunner of the
modern cluster bombs and were
dropped from aeroplanes in large
numbers on both sides. It was quite
usual for relics to be turned into
more useful items – bullet casings
into pencil holders, for instance.

Roll of Officers

HEADQUARTERS

Commanding Officer	Lieut-Colonel H.G. Powell
Second in Command	Major C.C. Clifton
Adjutant	Capt. O.C. Clare
Machine-gun Officers	C. Thorne[1]/A.L. Holberton
Quartermaster	G. Baines
Transport Officer	J.J. Thorley
Medical Officer	E.C. Gimson
Scout Officer	P.B. Frere

COMPANY OFFICERS

A   Maj. A.P.B. Irwin*
Capt. T. Flatau[2]
Lt. J.R. Ackerley*[3]
Lt. R. Heath
Lt. R.H. Rhodes
2nd Lt. N.P.E. Wrightson

B   Capt. G.M. Place
Capt. J.M. Mitchell
Lt. R.E. Soames[2]
2nd Lt. J.C. Drane
2nd Lt. H.G. Eley
2nd Lt. G.H.S. Musgrove[2]

C   Capt. C.S. Pearce[2]
Capt. W.P. Nevill*[2]
Lt. G.B. Clare
2nd Lt. P.G. Heath
2nd Lt. A.E.A. Jacobs[4]
2nd Lt. E.J.H. Twigg

D   Capt. C.L.J. Bowen
Capt. B.B. Paull*[1]
2nd Lt. C.J. Cadge
2nd Lt. E.C. Hetherington[3]
2nd Lt. G.G. Morse[3]
2nd Lt. M. Thorne[5]

*   not yet gazetted
1. killed 30 September 1916
2. killed 1 July 1916

3. wounded 1 July 1916
4. killed 8 August 1916
5. killed 27 September 1915

3 TO THE TRENCHES

28.viii.15

I wonder
Try to guess
Hard to say

Dear Mother etc,

'Ici nous sommes'. I trust the sudden burst of a foreign tongue won't disclose my whereabouts to any lurking Teuton.

We've no news, not that I could tell you if we had, so I'll give you a description of our wanderings. Après le petit déjeuner – sorry I simply can't controll it, j'ai packé mon pack. My gear weighs some £500 I should think by the feel of it, older soldiers tell us it will grow on us in time. I sincerely hope mine is past his prime & will start to shrivel up at once.

We left the Plain [Salisbury] in silence, no excitements of any note.

We reached 'what's the name' about 11 p.m. a 6½ hour journey from Thingummy. A dear little turbine two sector (1000 stand up) whizzed us over. Most of us lightened the load we were carrying without undoing our packs! You follow my meaning. I did very well really & felt quite fit all the time.

It was quite interesting watching our little destroyer escort sneaking along like a beetle – not a glow-worm.

No submarines bothered us, which was a great disappointment as I had hoped we might fire at them, I don't suppose!!

It was practically light when we landed. It was awfully like going out to winter sports, except that there were only sentries lounging about and no crowds.

Oh I forgot. At Guildford a Band turned out & deafened us while we paused and chatted to various maidens, who had been seeing troops off all day long. Most interesting. I sent a note to Aunt Annie by another officer this morning, and she saw him and I am to go down to the Hospital to dinner to-night. It will be topping. [19]

Aunt Annie, Matron of a base hospital in Boulogne, wasted no time in reporting back to her sister on Billie's arrival.

The Western Front, Autumn 1915

28th   *Boulogne*
I have seen Billie, he passed (with the Regiments) the hospital this
afternoon about 3 p.m. I was on the steps & he shouted out to me he
would be down later, he came about 6 p.m. & we went out in the
town. I thought him looking simply splendid, so much older too,
doesn't he? We went to the shops & he made one or two purchases, &
then at 7 p.m. we went to dinner at the Hotel Duvaux. Elsie will
remember we had tea there with Major Isacke, & Kennerley Rumford
came in. We had a lovely time together & such a nice dinner with
topping champagne! Billie's treat all of it, & then he went back to
camp, he had to be in by 9 p.m. he expects to leave tonight about 2
a.m. I have come straight back to hospital to write to you at once; the
Regiment is splendid, such a fine set of men they looked as they
marched past today.
    Bill was in great form, & so delighted to be out, dear old boy. I may
see him again if they don't go tonight, but I think they are almost sure
to . . . The Camp Bill is in is about 2 miles out of Boulogne. I walked a
bit of the way back with him tonight.

Next day Billie gave his own description of their evening together:

29.VIII.17
I met Aunt Annie at her hospital and we sallied forth. I got another
wristwatch, which is still going. Auntie paid for it, so I gave her
dinner. We split a bottle of Veuve Clicquot, the very best champagne
in [Boulogne], over a very nice little dinner. It was awfully jolly seeing
her like that. In the afternoon the C.O. took the battalion for a march
through the town and the men loved it. I got back from Aunt Annie at
9 p.m. on Wednesday and we were to have stayed where we were, by
way of a rest, however, after about a 100 contradictory orders
probably for the benefit of spies we quietly slunk off at 2 in the
morning. Now we're in billets, a jolly little village [Bertangles] about
20 miles from that mysterious place, The Front, if anything a little
less. It's quite cosy, and we've joined up again with our transport &
our valises! Of course we can't guess at all what our next move will
be. I'm looking forward to a little eye shutting to-night but I did get
about forty seven winks on the floor of the train. We went 1st, and
really have been very comfy. All the arrangements for us at the port of
disembarkation were really marvellous. We had tents and even

blankets, all the men as well . . . I've got some top-hole looking eggs
for our tea & I hear there's some bacon about; you really might be
staying at the Ritz!!! When the wind's right you can hear the guns, so
what is left of the population tell us. Only the very old men are left
. . . There are bullet holes in the walls of the houses in this place, but
very old ones. And nothing has happened here for months and
months. All our Company officers grub together at the Company
H.Qs, where Pearce and I sleep.

It's awfully jolly and everything is so toppingly managed. We
passed the place where Elsie used to come and sketch this morning,
and all over the place there are large English camps. Also we passed
every five minutes long long trains of empty trucks, waggons and
horse boxes, going down. There will be no weekend leave, I hear!

So bye bye
  with very best love
   from *Wilfred* [19]

Like so many others, Billie's diary was short lived, his entry for July 25th
being both the first and the last. 'The C.O. has told me my diary if I'm
allowed to keep it will never pass the Censor,' he had told his mother while
still at Codford, 'so it will have to wait till I can get some one to bring it back.'
[18] Such infrequent reports were not likely to satisfy a family anxious for
news, and Billie realised within two days of his arrival that he would not
have the time to keep a diary as well as write satisfactory letters. After all,
there was not only the family but also Muff who 'has to have a fair share of
my pencil lead.' [21] He had to ask the family to send his letters to them
down to Muff, 'as really I find I can't write two. I have to censor about 200 so
you can understand.'

ICI

VOILA

VOICI

Ne pense pas

July 30th

Dear People, nations and languages,

Hail! I've such a lot of interesting (I think) odds & ends to tell you
about, & of course I want Muff to know them as well, & [as] I've not
time to write two lots, that I [am] sending this to you and a carbon
paper copy of the newsy parts to Muff. The same letter in fact with
the extremities adjusted. Let's hope I shan't mix the envelopes! [20]

He did mix the envelopes later to his eldest sister, but only as a joke. 'I hope you appreciated the letter in the 'wrong' envelope,' he wrote then. 'I might have made it much better only I didn't think of doing it till the last moment!' [80]

'If you keep [these letters],' he told Elsie now, '& number each as you get them ('you' means any of the family, of course) I think it will give a fairly connected yarn of my wanderings.' [21]

His wanderings began only a few hours after he had said good-bye to Aunt Annie. 'Suddenly at 1 in the morning they whisked us off into a huge train, where we found our transport & everything (which had come by another route), & away we went through Abbeville etc. to B – s.' [56]

The quality of billets was always important from the point of view of morale, but varied enormously. 'I've got a piano in my room, room mark you, & a jolly comfy bed too, but it's got so many teeth out, that no one cares to play on it, thank heavens,' Billie said, of his new abode at Bertangles. [20] 'Now & again, when interest is flagging, I oblige with my world renowned rendering of "Les Batons de Beouf", f.f.f.f. (or chopsticks) & occasionally, God save, etc., so you see we are well looked after. The piano is not govt. issue although it looks like it.' There were problems – 'We're dreadfully hard up for good drinking water, just here, but we get on all right, chiefly with boiling & lemonade & various other deadly concoctions' – but the officers on the whole were reasonably comfortable. 'Of course we luxurious officers have our box from Fortnum & Mason, of dear old Piccadily.'

The men, in barns and sheds, warm but not clean, were not so fortunate.

The great thing about these billets is that they're not so healthy as they might be. I've spent the whole morning trying to devise every possible improvement. You see with no disinfectant & no drains and a lot of men the difficulties are enormous. Don't think we've come out, not prepared for this, of course we've every possible method of controlling it, but it is hard. After each meal there are heaps & heaps of bully beef tins, biscuit crumbs & perhaps fat off bacon, eggshells etc. & everything has to be burnt or buried. The flies here are legion. I've never seen so many before. They send you fairly crazy. Kill that fly is not the only remark I've heard about them![1] [20]

I do wish you were here [he wrote to Elsie, the artist, on his second evening in France], it's so awfully pretty. There's a topping view from here & about 4 miles away there is a lovely old cathedral ['I can see Amiens' was the coded message]; away on my right I can see a little wooded hill with a dear little village snuggling on it. There's a charming old wind mill too, just loping round as if he thought he

ought to have finished his day's work too. The rest of the view is only
French, because of the inevitable rows of solitary trees (that's rather a
'bull', but you know what I mean), otherwise I might be on Leith Hill,
or old Holmbury Head. Where is the war? I can't see it, except in my
own puttees.[2] But just a second. About a dozen Tommies[3] (always
spell them with a capital, you would if you knew ours, I am not
complaining that you don't, old thing, at all; I'm only suggesting it)
are helping an old couple to load a huge hay waggon. And now a
long, long supply column is trailing up with our grub & perhaps your
letters. (Some chaps got letters today, dated the 28th. I hope you've
got my address right.) Now & then a dispatch rider goes simply
roaring past. It's topping for them out here, as the roads are splendid
near here & their horse power is their only limit. Occasionally an
aeroplane blows over and some of our officers saw one getting
'hotted' with shells nearer the trenches from a tree with glasses. (The
tree hadn't got glasses). The Sun has lived up to its August reputation
and can conscientiously report "all correct", to the church spire when
he goes off to bed each night, away among the trees just behind me.

The butterflies here are quite fascinating, after ours too, quite a rare
English one has just gone past as if he had bought the place, or was
the Kaiser of Butterflies. However pride always comes before a nasty
jolt, and now a swallow is hot on the poor beggar's trail. There's a
glorious smell of new hay & clover, in fact I can't remember a more
peaceful evening. [21]

To-day is as usual, bright and sunny [Billie wrote on August 1st],
and being Sunday, after church parade, we are all taking lunch in the
travelling kitchens, and going down to a river about 3 miles off to
bathe, quite a picnic. The whole battalion is going, combining exercise
& pleasure with cleanliness & also getting the men out of this none
too healthy village. [22]

Though the division was still some way from the front, life was not without its excitements, as Billie recounted on July 30th:

Today, while I was working out the men's pay, in French money, I
heard a plop, plop, of a rifle, so I hopped out, (most of the men were
out on a route march) to see what was up. The French who have been
through this place, about a week ago (& between ourselves they left it
jolly dirty), were evidently tired & had chucked away a lot of
ammunition into a garden, where our men had lit a fire to burn

rubbish. This was now exploding all over the place, while the man who had lit the fire, was hunting about just near it for other cartridges. Of course I hoofed him off quick, out of the way & posted a sentry to warn anyone coming that way. A little later a French woman brought me her little boy, who described "furioso" that a bullet had gone past his arm by one inch. I took it "cum granio", on the 6th repetition, this time "tres lentement si vo plait" by which time they were cooler & more subdued. A few well chosen words from "Helps to the Helpless" or some such list of inanities, soon did the pacifying trick. [21]

Paying the men proved to be a more difficult operation than might be expected. In his previous letter Billie had written of the Field Cashier, 'apparently a mythical gentleman [who] was to have rolled up today & changed our money & given us pay for the men, so I collected all the money I could carry for our coy. & took it up to H.Qs to change but the dear lad had missed his connection at Cologne or somewhere & I'm still (5.15 p.m.) carrying it all.'

'We pay the men here in 5 fr. notes, & I usually contrive to lose 2 or three each pay day, which I'll have to make up sometime, I suppose,' he wrote on September 15th. 'I often have to go about with 1600 frs. on me, in 5 fr. notes, as an opportunity for paying may not synchronise (I think) with the visit of that adorable bird, the Field cashier, so no wonder a few go 'west.' I suppose that expression has reached civilian England by now. Anything lost or mis-aimed like a bullet is said by Tommy to have 'gone west'.

New Army battalions reached the front in stages. 'From landing town I trained to Bertangles for a week, then to Lahoussoye (?) two nights. Then on here to Derncourt (?) [Dernancourt] a little south of Albert. We go up tomorrow night for four days,' was Billie's coded account of his travels. His mother was still having difficulty deciphering the dots. 'I gather from your letters that you didn't know when we went,' Billie wrote to her on the August Bank Holiday. 'I told you quite clearly, & Elsie deciphered it and put the date quite plainly on a letter which was correct. We came over on Tuesday night, and have been over nearly a week now.'
He had been more sympathetic earlier in the same letter.

Another thing Mother, just between ourselves, that I want to thank you for, is for being so jolly, or rather brave (but that's conceited on my part to think that) when you said good-bye; because I know you thought it was dangerous out here, but it's not really of course, especially where we are likely to be when we do go 'up'. So don't

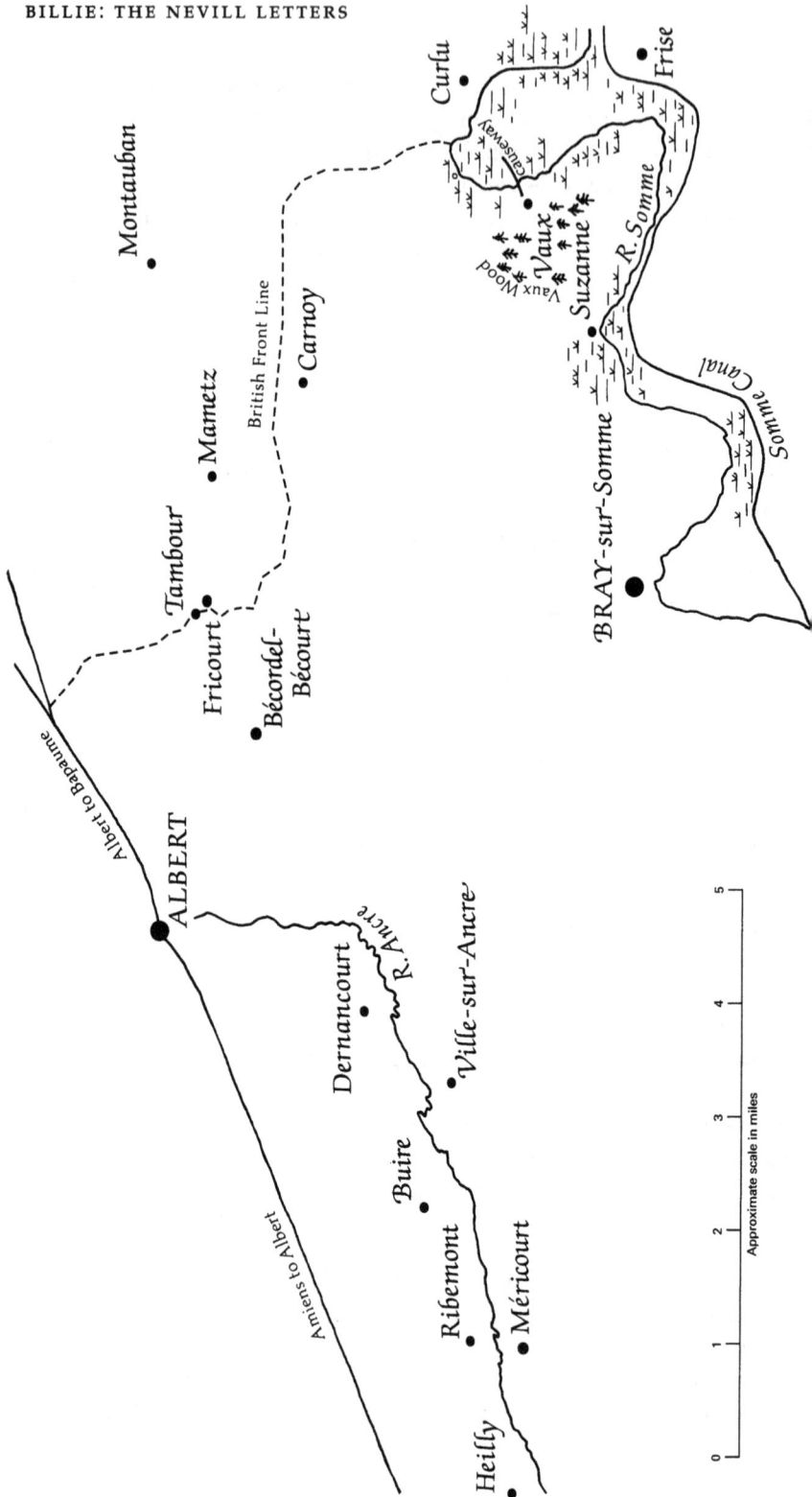

Montauban

Curlu

Frise

Causeway

Vaux

Suzanne

Vaux Wood

R. Somme

British Front Line

Carnoy

Mametz

Somme Canal

BRAY-sur-Somme

Tambour

Fricourt

Bécordel-Bécourt

Albert to Bapaume

ALBERT

R. Ancre

Dernancourt

Ville-sur-Ancre

Buire

Amiens to Albert

Ribemont

Méricourt

Heilly

0   1   2   3   4   5

Approximate scale in miles

worry a scrap, I shall be home on leave soon, I expect. Not that you want leave out here, in a picnic like this. You know you do miss a lot by not being able to come out. It's the greatest fun imaginable and I wouldn't have missed it for worlds. By crossing I've already earned the medal, although of course I've not seen a Hun yet, nor am I likely too, I'm afraid, for a long time. Don't ever worry about people called snipers. I think in England one is apt to picture our Tommies crawling in terror of a sniper. Not a bit. We're as good & better than all their snipers, & if one shows himself, he gets 'it' – hit. It's the "Jummuns" who'll do the crawling round in terror, when we get near 'em.' [22]

He qualified his enthusiasm a little in a letter to Elsie. 'Of course all this is awfully novel & interesting at first, but I can see it will pall after a bit.' [21] 'It's quite an experience, you know,' he told Amy, 'sort of "off the beaten track" a bit & consequently very entertaining.'
He wrote again to Elsie on August 5th,

not a letter like my others have been, but a kind of list of odds and ends, which may interest you. This is addressed to you, but of course, everyone will see it who wants to.
   The first thing of interest is that I was "gassed" this morning. Several officers from each regiment went to attend a lecture on gas, asphyxiating shells & liquid fire.[4] It was most interesting and ended by us all putting on our helmets & going & standing in front of a gas cylinder which was hissing out the gas. You simply couldn't sniff it, even in a room at close range. Regiments can now stand a perpetual 5 hour gas attack without any effect at all, and when the Bosches stroll across expecting to find 'em all done in – you can't see them for dust when they get 30 rounds rapid fire in their tails. In the front line near here they have shelters sometimes under 30 or 40 ft. of solid earth. Jack Johnson proof. Which is jolly.
   On a front of about 12 miles to a depth of about 2 miles there are 200 miles of telephone wire. Any subaltern in the front trench can turn the fire of 16 guns, two miles behind, on to any target he likes in 2 mins.
   Nowadays behind your entanglements you often have 30 ft. high rabbit netting to stop bombs. On iron post this is very hard to cut and almost indestructible by ordinary shell fire. The trenches are so safe that you almost get punished if you do happen to get wounded. For instance, Brother Bosche the other day jerked over 620 coalbox bombs in 24 hrs. – result 2 killed, 3 wounded!!!

In one place the French had a charming little communication post, in a valley, to keep in touch with some advance line, when lo and behold the Bosches flooded the whole blessed valley. Shell fire to a Frenchman being like water to a duck's back so the French calmly & without any fuss built a fresh island with boats & odds & ends in about 20 feet of water. The post is still there, quite fit in a rain of shells.

Cheerho now. I've got to censor heaps of the men's letters now. Cheerho, yrs awfully,

Bill [24]

'We leave to-morrow night for billets nearer up'[5] was part of the coded message in his letter to Elsie, a move he described to his mother two days later.

The great thing that struck me about our move up, was the way the men loved it. They were getting rather fed up with our old billets. I've never seen 'em so cheerful. We pushed off about 7 p.m. and it was about 1 a.m. when we reached here. You know French villages have about 10 roads running into them instead of straggling along one main road like ours do. On the way we passed a park of motor transport, all covered over with hay, so that from above you couldn't possibly spot them. Lots of the houses we passed had been shelled and really I'd have loved to have taken some of our slackers through them . . . And then in the midst of all this you come across one of these great crucifixes the French love so much. All the time on our march last night we could see the flash lights, and searchlights, star parachuts etc. of the trenches, so we had our noses the right way, and that helped a good deal in carrying Mr. Pack who was very heavy. But when you know every step is putting you nearer to settling your account with Brother Bosche, you can go on for miles. Last night it fell to my lot to take the names of those who fell out of the march. It's not a nice job & very tiring as you're perpetually stopping and then, when you've hoisted the wretched fellow on to an ammunition cart & got his rifle & equipment up too, you've got to catch up your place in the column; perhaps 3 to 400 yds away, by then. Now & then you would look up & find yourself slogging beside huge great motor lorries, miles of them all standing there waiting, you only hope, crammed with food. Finally we reached our billets and got settled in at last. I had to take a guard out to block one of the roads into [the] village and by Jove, I felt sorry for the wretched men on guard, as I was nearly

dead myself. You see we had a night alarm, the night before we left
our old billets. I was in bed in pyjamas at the time, but I was on the
road with my equipment on & dressed in 2 mins. You get into a habit
of bustling here. About 3 a.m. after a cup of lovely nectar (milkless
and 'stewy' tea) and a glorious 'dog' or ration, a curious case of
euphemism (look it up Muff!!) biscuit, I coiled up on the floor (stone)
of a farmhouse, head on air pillow and coat, shoulder on spare shirt,
& 3 spare prs of socks under my hip bone, with a lined burberry over
me & slept the sleep of the person who nowadays does all his work &
moving by night & has all his routine work to do by day.[6] [25]

'One thing that positively hits you in the face, about France,' Billie had
written the day after his arrival in the country, '& that is that every single
young chap is away in uniform. They take the war quite differently to us.'
[20] He remarked on it again, during this march. 'No one left, except the
very, very old people and the absolute kids. Not a single young man about.
It's a grand example to anyone . . . Every house you go into here has its
photos of people at the Front & its "hatred" of the "Sacré Bosches".'
   Two nights later 'we made another of our silent midnight bounds up to
the trenches, this time we landed about 4 miles short.' They were now at
Dernancourt, two miles south of Albert, between the rivers Ancre and
Somme, and site of the East Surreys' headquarters. The new billets were
'not nearly so jolly as the last, but passable, being one bare 10 by 15 room,
dining-room, bedroom and office for six officers.' [26]

I'll try to describe our billet. It's a big yard, with sheds all round, and
the house, a little shop & farm combined, stands back away from the
road, on one side of the yard, with a jolly back garden and orchard,
where I'm writing now. I'm afraid our advent has rather disturbed the
domestic arrangements, as a casual glance disclosed (through the
window of the next room) an enormous bed, with a row of about 7
heads on its two pillows. Light hair and dark, grownups and babies,
all jammed pell-mell into this enormous bed. The kiddies are terrible
at pinching the everlasting 'souvenir'. In the first shed (our door is
always open & is on the road side of course) are about 15½ huge
Belgian hares. I like them no end, as they are the only quiet members
of the community. Next door is a whopping great donkey, apparently
doing a life sentence of solitary confinement, under protest. He's got a
grand contralto & bass voice suitable for 'Drake is going West, Lads'.
But unfortunately I've not got the music with me. He wakes up about
3.15 a.m.!! So do we!!!! Then a mysterious being gets up about 4 each

day, & works a sqeaky pump-handle, as if his life depended on it, and
then washes aloud just under my window, dear soul. After this he
walks in wooden shoes across the cobbled yard (I could tell him a mile
away now) and lets loose, not the Americans, as Lewis Sydney says,
in Push and Go[7] (ah me!) but a bevy of full throated ducks, who at
once dash for my pump trough, and bathe fortissimo, singing an early
morning hymn the while. This starts off the poultry generally & the
day with all its glory is fully started. With the <u>sun</u>, blushing from its
morning dip in the majestic ocean (I don't suppose) come about 17¾
billion flies & gnats etc. That caps it, and no more sleep is possible, as
the flies wake the men up, & for about an hour my pump handle flies
up & down. Like Mother and Elsie going to catch the 'bus, &
forgetting an umbrella, or a purse, or the tickets etc. etc.!!!! I rather
like that little picture personally. [28]

Despite the nearness of the front line and the sound of guns, Billie was
able to describe his surroundings as 'another of those charming little back-
waters from the war, which make it so hard to realise what the war means &
is,' [27] but the front still beckoned. 'We're simply dying to see these curious
blighters [the Bosches]. I hope they'll show their noses a bit, but they are
such rabbits, we may not see a 'pickle haube' for days yet.'[8] [25]
    Normal practice was for the officers and N.C.Os of new battalions to get
instruction in trench duty from experienced hands over a period of four
days or so while the men remained behind. In the case of the East Surreys,
two full companies were sent up together to be instructed by the 1st Bedford
Regiment. A and B companies were the first to go.

They went up last night in a blinding thunderstorm, poor old chaps
[Billie wrote], we send them up food each night to a little village (now
a mere stone heap) & they send down & fetch it up the rest of the
way, (it's nearly all bully and biscuits up there) & the waggon slinks
back before it gets light. We heard a nasty bombardment about the
time they were due to arrive there last night, but at present have no
news of any casualties; we shall hear tonight from the food party all
about them. [27]

The following day, while waiting to take his turn in the trenches, Billie
approached the front line.

Yesterday I was allowed to take a party up about ¾ of a mile behind
the trenches to learn some tips from the 'Sappers' [Royal Engineers],

who were making wiry devilments and contraptions. It wasn't very
exciting, but I had the pleasure of being in the middle of what you
have often seen in the papers as 'an occasional or intermittent artillery
duel.' I was only about ¼ of a mile just in front of one of our guns,
and by Jove, when he went off I knew it. I was standing up on top of
a hill looking round when off he went in the valley just below, firing
right up over my hill. First of course, I heard the shell come.
"Prwwtt" & then "Boomsh". I sat down then. And then came the
answer. It really was ripping. You couldn't hear the bang of the gun
which was probably 4 miles off but just the shell, very high, & just
overhead, looking for our gun. It's like a very soft whistle and chirrup
of a canary combined, and in this case I heard each one for about 6
seconds. When the shell goes off it is quite a small explosion
compared to the sound of the gun. These of course were only about
18-36 pounders I should think. Still it was very pretty . . .

That evening Billie came under more direct attack while out digging.[9]
After 'a glorious day in baking sun' he and his men fed at 6.30 before marching off 'with our tool carts to the 2nd line trenches to dig.'

Always, about 7-9 or 10 each night, the thoughtful huns specially
arrange a few surprise packets for all the working parties, ration
parties, & ambulance parties, who like burglars do their various jobs
at night. The trench we were on was on the top of a hill, just through
a little village, about 1400 yds from the 'Brethren'. The Company (D)
that dug there last night, or rather the night before, were sniped by 3
or 4 enthusiasts the whole time, as they very foolishly smoked in the
open. I shall always remember last night as being my first time under
any sort of fire. It was also my first introduction to star shells &
fireballs. It was most awfully pretty to watch, very like an ordinary
regatta display. These shells go up something like an ordinary rocket
(they have them as well, of course, just bursting into a cloud of small
stars) but they keep solid so to speak, all in one very bright lump,
magnesium wire I think they're made up of. Some of them are
attached to parachutes, which are folded round & the thing is fired
out of a catapult or something like that. This kind hang up as long as
3 or even 4 minutes sometimes. They lit us up, even where we were
right back, and a few (say 2 every 5 minutes) bullets did flit about our
heads. Nothing to write home about really, but merely interesting.
Most of them were ricochets, which [make] a sound like the drone of
a bee. It's very amusing to stand up and watch. Suddenly there's a

little flicker of light in front and the next second a bee goes past at about 2000 feet per second. One little chap went past about 1 yard away, with a perfectly dinkie little "Zip". About 5 seconds afterwards you get [to] hear the 'plop'.

The great thing, or rather 'Set Piece' of the entertainment was a captive observation balloon (exactly like the one over Barnes Common way, sort [of] sausagy looking) which had come down to roost for the night, and was getting 'hotted' by the Brethren. Poor old thing, he couldn't hide from those star-shells, they lit him up a real treat, every now & then, & then you see a terrific flash, quite near him, & later the dickens of a boom-crash, probably from an eight inch howitzer, at the outside. They've no 'heavies' near here, nothing that is, to send a telegram about. (N.B. Can you tell how it's a howitzer? Sorry!) It was about a mile away, I should guess, this balloon thing, & I don't think they got it.

Nothing else of great interest happened. We got home about 3 this morning, all safe & sound, except one man, who got a pick about 3 inches into his, well – he was bending over at the time, shovelling. I soused him in iodine from his ampoule, and put on a 1st field dressing. My first & I hope my last. Then a good dose of brandy & he's quite alright to-day, only stiff. [28]

'I'm looking forward to seeing Brother Bosche in the flesh soon, & hitting him there soon,' [23] Billie had written at the beginning of August. His request for permission to go up with A and B companies into the trenches was refused and he had to wait until it was his own company's turn. At last, three weeks after the battalion's arrival in France, he reached the front line.

> There-at-Last
> Thanksbe[10]
> 14.8.15

Dear People,
. . . Last night I led the Company up to the trenches, a filthy job. I wish you'd let the L.C.C. know how bad the roads are in this borough, I mean the flooring over and the drain for the rain water. It really ought to be seen, I shall write to the Times if this sort of thing goes on. Well, we got [there] alright and finally landed here round about 12. Our way up was illuminated by the usual fireworks and the occasional drone of a 'rico', or a 'spent'. On closer acquaintance I find a bullet from about 250 yds away, makes a neater little 'Zip' than one from a mile or so, which is more of a hiss. The Regiment (1st Beds),

who are teaching us for these four days, are most awfully kind to us &
mother us splendidly . . . I'm in a dug out with Pearce and the other
Coy. commander, who's teaching us, they both have beds, but the
floor is quite jolly & dry. Our roof is about 12 ft thick. There are
crowds of mice here, the little dears ['send me 10 mousetraps,' was
the *cri de coeur* at the end of this letter], and rats, they keep a cat in the
regiment for them, a sort of Government Service Trench Cat, Mark
six. But the War Officer under-estimated its duties, & omitted to issue
50 extra stomachs! On Hill 60, they had heaps of cats but they used to
frighten the sentries at night so, by jumping on 'em from behind, that
they don't issue cats now, worse luck. [29]

Let us talk of Freddie [he wrote the following day]. You don't know
Freddie, do you? Freddie is the mouse who 'keeps' just north of our
dinner table, in the wall. He's a dear little chap & diets entirely on
currants & tallow, sort of like mother at Harrogate, he's so regular; &
he's careful not to spoil the wick or eat the tiny dry stalks. But you
must see him at 'dejeuner' or 'fif-o'clock tay', to know and appreciate
him. I can always tell when it's 'Our Fred' who's on my neck or
nibbling my hair (he eats hair as one would drink coffee & liqueurs).
Other mice are silly and bite string in half, or chew into air pillows
(Elsie's is still in nightly use) or rattle paper at night. Of course it's
only want of thought and I know the little dears don't mean any
harm. [30]

Mothered they might be by the 1st Bedfords, but the East Surreys had to
take their turn with trench duties. Minimising the inconvenience and discomfort – 'Night duty in the rain is tiresome, but no worse than running for
the post on a wet night' – Billie described to his family how he had pulled
the legs of the Germans during his night on duty.

I ordered no firing at all. Usually each sentry fires off once every five
minutes or so. The Bosches of course thought after a bit that we were
crawling up to trim their entanglements and scrag them, and started
firing off into the ground in front (no man's land) with great éclat. Still
no reply from us, so they sent up heaps & heaps of flares and star
shells etc. and blazed away for the rest of the night. It was simply
killing to hear & see them, or rather their recochets & light . . . I grieve
to say that I 'ducked' from a bullet. It has annoyed me intensely as I
had not 'bobbed' so far, and most of us had. However no one saw me;
it was in this bally 'commy' trench they are sniping. A bullet hit the
parapet about a yard to my left front as I was walking up, showered

me in mud and ricocheted with a loud purr just across my face, and
landed about 6 inches off my right ear with more dirt. My own silly
fault entirely, it was a chance shot from a rifle, aimed by day and
fixed. I shall stoop there till it's dug down a bit deeper. One of our
officers, Cadge, of another company, got in the way of a 'wizz-bang'
and another man stopped a 'stray' rifle bullet, both are quite all right
luckily. A 'wizz-bang' is a 3 inch shell, fired at very close range and
burst by a short fuse on the parapet. You don't hear them whistle like
a big shell from some distance back, they just wiss and explode, hence
the name. [30]

'The trenches are the greatest fun, & I'm longing for our next trip,' he
wrote at the end of his four days up, adding, 'The great attraction is not
having breakfast till about 10 in the morning.' [32] 'I suppose you'll want a
description of those mysterious things, the trenches,' he said, on his return
to Dernancourt.

To look at they are exactly as if a gang of navvies had tried to lay a
drainage system down without a foreman, a ruler or a plumb line.
Ours happen to be in chalk and you can see nothing but heaps of
chalk everywhere, thrown up apparently without rhyme or reason,
not in the least in one straight line, but waving about all over the
place. In some places you can throw a stone across No Man's Land
lefthanded, in others you might fit in a ¼ racing track straight. These
two distances may be only 200' apart laterally. Where it's close, the
land is pitted & scarred with mine craters. In No Man's Land you may
see perhaps an old plough, or a cart (overturned probably) or a
harrow, just as they were left months ago. The whole place gives the
impression of absolute desertion, peace & quiet: a sort of 'dead land'
you might read of in some novel about Central Africa or the Incas of
Mexico. That would be the impression of a casual observer, & that
casual observer would get a wrong impression. All those trenches
lead somewhere, each has its particular object, every bend & curve is
made to serve some special purpose. Inside they are kept daily in
perfect condition, the drainage system would rival London's itself. All
the traffic is controlled as if by policemen, time tables are kept of the
time to get from say 'Roberts' to 'Drake'. The routes are marked
carefully to various places & every trench is named and very often
numbered as well. There are wells in the trenches, cook houses,
officers' messes, arm racks, gratings for drainage, every possible
comfort & convenience in fact. Also there is ample bomb-proof cover

for everyone. And yet there is nothing that cannot be improved, so work is always going on somewhere. [33]

Seventy-five years later it is still possible to see where the chalk was thrown up, apparently without rhyme or reason. In spring, before the year's crops have grown high enough to act as cover, the white lines of the trenches meander for miles across the fields of Picardy.

NOTES

1. 'The flies are chronic,' Billie said, on another occasion. 'They have reveillée one hr before we do, & they're never late on parade!! The Blighters!' [26] And Elsie's cigars were no good as fly-killers if Billie's fellow officers refused to smoke them.
2. Long strips of cloth wound spirally round the legs from ankle to knee. They originated in the Indian Army where they were worn as protection against snakes.
3. 'Notes for Divisional Commanders' Conference', dated 4th October, 1915, state, 'The use of the word "Tommy" to be absolutely barred. The term is never permitted in a good regiment.' (Maxse papers, IWM 69/53/6) Not an order that ever seems to have been obeyed.
4. The Germans had used gas for the first time at Ypres the previous April, and liquid fire in July.
5. 'To go 'up' or 'down' simply & solely refer to the front trenches & to the 'rest' camps or billets,' Billie explained to Amy. [27]
6. Five days later he was writing that it 'should be noted that my hip-bone takes just 20 minutes to worm through my straw & rest for the

remainder of the night, on the finest floor for dropping watches, crockery, etc. on which I ever hope to meet; it's a regular Parlourmaid's Paradise!!' [28]
7. A show in London.
8. These were the German full-dress helmets of patent leather with brass badges and spikes.
9. C Company was digging communication trenches in Bécordel-Bécourt Wood at this time. Digging was a continuing chore in the underground world of the front line. New trenches had to be dug (it took 450 men 6 hours to dig 250 yards), and old ones maintained against the weather, shelling and mining. The chalk soil in the Somme area was comparatively easy to dig when dry. In the wet it turned into glutinous mud which stuck to every surface, making it impossible to keep trenches clean.
10. Christian Carver, the Artillery Forward Observation Officer attached to the East Surreys, who became a friend of Billie's, headed his letters similarly as he approached the front: 'A Bit Nearer', 'Further up still', 'In the Firing Line at last'.

4 TRENCH LIFE

Back in billets you get what exercise you can, after you've had your sleep right out. Everything is inspected & deficiencies replaced & repairs done. The men are all bathed as often as possible. In the afternoon you write, & censor letters and slack about, go round and practise your french in some 'epicerie' or 'estaminet', read magazines & laze generally. About 4 or so the post comes in & then you probably answer some letters which won't go till the next day. Then tea, plenty of lovely French jam and hot bread; a read or a short stroll & supper, perhaps at some other company's mess. And so to an early bed (?) about 9 o'clock. [33]

There was a good deal of toing and froing between the messes of the four companies. 'I had breakfast with D coy. this morning, it was quite a rag. We started with tinned peaches, then sardines & finally eggs & marmalade, all on the same plate of course. It quite reminded me of Dover.' 'I see our Mess waiter-cook-manager (a charming Tommy called Potter) mawling two fowls, who, 10 mins. ago, were in the prime of life, one of them already has that peculiarly naked indecent appearance, which a plucked fowl always presents . . . John Bowen (see the list of officers I gave you) is coming into dinner with us tonight. Hence the murder of the poultry.' [27] The meal offered Billie by A company on the other hand was obviously inferior – 'rather dull & no gravy.' [43]

On August 22nd, 1915, the battalion moved up into trenches east of Albert for their first tour of duty. For the next few months they would spend eight to fourteen days in the trenches followed by a similar period in billets in the rear. At this time the line held by the British ran from the Belgian sector just north of Ypres southwards to meet the French sector near the river Somme. The 55th Brigade which included the East Surreys were, in fact, taking over a part of the line from the French, the sector beginning at La Boiselle and running south to a point opposite Fricourt, a village almost entirely in German hands. This particular sector was considered a quiet one, having seen no large scale attack for some time. Most activity there occurred either underground or in the sky above.

Mining went on throughout the autumn and winter – 'people trying to blow each other up on each side,' as Irwin put it. Activity in the air was more seasonal. Though Billie would later be dismissive about the Royal Flying Corps, that summer he was impressed. 'Our airmen are all over the place & the Bosches waste hundreds of rounds on them,' he wrote on August 9th. 'Yesterday there was an air duel right over the village. The "Gummun" got his 'iron ration' in about ¼ hr.' 'There are an enormous lot of aeroplanes round here, I think a fresh fleet must have be[en] attached to our army R.F.C. H.Qs,' he wrote on another occasion [27]. Describing the delights of billet life, he said,

After tea there is nearly always some aeroplane fun on. Last night a 'hun' came over and got 'hotted' proper. His armour plating shone in the sun & he looked like a little silver dart in a perfect blue sky. You might have been at Brooklands, if it hadn't been for the white puffs of smoke from the shells, all round him. [33]

The brigade history makes life at this time sound positively civilised. 'Shells outside the trench system were hardly known. Neither side shelled the transport, and shelling never began before 8 a.m. so that all could have breakfast comfortably before setting down to the day's work,' though it does admit that 'the wire was bad; sentries of both sides fired steadily all night; the trenches were nowhere more than 700 yds apart.' Billy acknowledged his easier situation on hearing of a visit to Twickenham from two cousins on leave. 'I should think they were awfully interesting and if they were through Hooge, well – ! Of course they've had a pretty thick time of it, while I've only been beanfeasting at present.' [42]

The impression given by the brigade history is deceptive, however. The line might have been quiet compared with other sections of the front, but danger was ever present. From August 22nd, when it took over its sector of the line, until the end of the year, the 18th Division suffered 1,247 casualties.[1] Wiring parties, night raids, shelling and sniping all took their toll. During their four days of instruction in August, for instance, C and D companies of the 8th East Surreys lost one man killed and three wounded, a subaltern, Cadge, being one of the latter; during the battalion's first tour of duty two were killed and thirteen wounded. Later in the year there was also the weather to contend with, but Billie, waiting to go up on his first tour, was full of enthusiasm.

Same old orchard
22nd Aug. 1915

Dear Family,

. . . To-night we are going 'up' for a good long spell, I'm glad to say,
as it's far nicer 'up' than 'down', I think. Pearce has gone on to get the
hang of the line we're to hold, and I have to take the company up this
evening. I've been on the hop looking after things the whole morning,
it's incredible what a lot there is to see to every time we move. I
needn't say how I love it all, and I'm sure it's doing me a little good,
looking entirely after 200 odd men, I say entirely because Pearce is
away today, in the ordinary way, of course, I more or less understudy
him . . . I simply love having to run the coy. in his absence; as long as
you don't let people come & hustle you, you're alright; once [you] get
excited & try to think of 8 things at once & you may as well go home.
To-night I know I shan't get a wink of sleep, so after this I shall lie
down . . . The weather is simply glorious thank goodness, as the
'commy' trenches will be nice & dry. The serg. who 'stopped' the pt.
of a pick that night is better, but can't walk far, however, I've
managed to smuggle him up somehow. Also I'm getting up my
Tommies great coat & my fleece lined Burberry & a pair of Tommies
Trousers, so I shall be warm at night alright. Also our long expected
box from Fortnum & Mason's Piccadilly has at last turned up, a
fortnight late, so we are well off for food & we've laid in good stocks
of food here & a standing order for fresh milk, wine & eggs daily to be
sent up!! Thank Heavens we didn't go to the Darders. They say
there's a war on there. When I'm 'up' I'll write when I can, but I'm so
afraid of alarming you and giving the impression that there's any
danger that they may not be long letters. [34]

Anxious as always that his family should be able to picture his surroundings, Billie's first letter from the front line on the outskirts of Fricourt could
scarcely be considered short.

This bit of trench is quite the most comic I've ever seen, in some parts
it's about 30 yds from the Huns, so we have to keep a pretty cute
look-out just there. Our line just includes the outskirts of a little
village which is held by the Brethren, all except the bit we've got . . .
it's a very interesting sector, with the trenches creeping in & out &
through & under the ruins of these cottages. There are wells here
which are pretty useful as you can imagine. Also there is an old
estaminet and a little railway station, as the line runs through ours &

the Huns' trenches. (N.B. the service is not working as smoothly as usual). There are some old coaches on a siding in 'No Man's Land' which are now what are known as 'shell-traps'. They are in worse repair than the S.E. & C.R. [South-Eastern and Chatham Railway] so you can imagine the state they're in! There are some waggons on the road, upside down now and surrounded with 'Hunny' sand-bags, not 'honey'. There's a cemetry just behind our fire-trench, with about ½ a little chapel-mortuary place. A nice handy little rest camp, as I heard one of the men say! But that's a horrid thing to say, & you might think there was some danger. I assure you again there's no danger at all . . .

Our parapet is very odd in places as it is 'revetted'[2], or supported, with bed-steads, sideboards, table legs, cart-wheels, bricks, fenders & any old thing you can think of. Our dug-outs this time are too killing for words. In one of them there is a lovely case of stuffed birds, a beautiful 4 poster bed, and some nice chairs, a good big table, towel horse, ivory wash-hand stand etc. & endless bric-a-brac. They are all furnished magnificently from the cottages here and are jolly cosy. The beds are a great treat. Company H.Qs is a wonderful place, but I must be very careful how I describe it, as I don't want this, supposing it got into the wrong hands, before it ever left here, to be of any use to anyone.[3] We're hidden away, quite snugly in a little dip, we've got our signal section dug in next door, a room for our servants & messengers & a store place, this is all for Pearce & I. Also we have a space about 30 yds. square where it's safe to walk about which is topping. If we were here for a month I'd certainly ask you for a Badminton set, as we could play toppingly. French Cricket is suitable & in vogue.

On the left as you come in is a marvellous 'paper-flower' white bouquet in a gilt framed case, worn by all brides if they are not already widows, & evidently a family treasure; next to it is my "duty roll" of officers & a time-table of the times a messenger takes to get from here to all H.Qs of companys & our platoons, in wet or dry weather by day or night. Next again was a huge full length mirror. With some heartsearching this morning I took an entrenching tool & scientifically smashed [it] into pieces suitable for periscopes for our sentries by day! I've kept a good lump as a mirror of course. The frame has already been bagged to frame the air hole of one of the other dug-outs! Then there's such a jolly old book shelf, what's on it now? A candle, Punch, a tin of butter, a bottle of "Vin Ordinaire", a megaphone, 2 smoke helmets, some fags & baccy of Pearce's, my hold

all, some powder bombs for dispersing gas, if it's used, some lights
corresponding to their star shells, Newnes Summer Annual, The
Morning Post of 5 days ago, and a water bottle, some Nestles milk, a
shaving brush & two periscopes; that's about all I can see sitting down
here at the table. We've got a hat rack & an umbrella stand next to this
& then comes a map (from aeroplane photos) of the German trenches,
so accurate that you can follow every 'traverse' & bend in them. Then
comes the thing, my bed, save the word! It was (about the time of the
Norman Conquest) a decent Godfearing piece of Early Victorian
furniture, in solid iron; something like a racing bob-sleigh &
something like a combined 'reaper-binder' with a dash of the
thrashing machine thrown in. However it missed its vocation I should
think in its youth, anyhow it's lost its springs now, and their place
has been somewhat inadequately filled by a kind of barbed wire
entanglement, the product of the brain of some genius in the way of
an officer's servant. The mattress missed its connection about 9
months ago & is now above me on the roof full of earth, poor soul . . .
Two of our chairs have backs; the third is only used by visitors (once)!!
Another bed (?) and another table, littered with red-covers, mags;
plates, message forms for the telephone, glasses, a revolver, Pearce's,
some biscuits, and a place laid for an officer on duty now, who will
get some bully & tea when he comes off, & I go on in about ½ an hour
now (it's now eleven p.m. & I'm writing this by two candles' light,
hence any bad spelling! Odd coats & haversacks, mouses-traps, or
mice trapses, or whatever they're called in the plural, rats, sticks,
boxes & bottles litter the floor. The roof was only designed to conduct
the rain into certain well defined areas on the floor and the post of
gutter is now a sinecure. The Hun side is sandbagged, this is a hut
not a dug-out, but occasionally one strolls through. We shutter the
windows at night to screen the light . . .

We've caught nearly 20 mice today, so what tonight's bag will be I
don't know.[4] This is one of the things that matter, that & our supply
of candles. I've got 14 now of the latter, so we are all right, thanks
largely to you and your parcels . . .

On our parapets there are some tiny trees planted with posts & wire
round them, so funny, planted I expect by some kiddies last year &
still here. The most striking thing of all is right bang in No Man's L.
Namely a big crucifix, with some trees round it. All the trees end
about 5 ft from the ground now and are splintered with bullets. Some
wire entanglements near it have been shelled. But there stands that
crucifix, absolutely untouched, neither the cross nor the figure have a

scratch so far as I can see with glasses! It is most extraordinary. I don't
want to be journaleesy, but really the text in Joshua 1.9 is wonderfully
born out.[5] That incidentally is my favourite text, and that's how I
happen to know the reference . . .

Today [August 24th] I've about found my 'trench-legs'! It's
extraordinary how clumsy one is at first. You see these commy
trenches are very rarely more than 3 feet wide, & the floor has drains,
gutters, gratings, catch-pits, etc. You simply bump into the wall every
time. Now this morning I noticed quite a difference, I can swing
round corners at full walking pace without knocking at all. It's quite
an art . . .

I should love to show you over our bit, it's so funny in some places.
In one house the whole side wall has gone over, leaving a dining &
bed room exposed. The dining room is quite bare, even to the bell,
wire & pull, which are out along one of our underground listening
posts. A basin is up there standing with its jug, all correct, just
waiting for peace, when it will carry on as if there never had been a
war. I wonder if we shall. [35]

Yes [he wrote to Elsie four days later], the trenches are awfully hard
to describe. You see, I knew all the ground work, or rather book
work, about the trenches before I ever left England, so I leave that
out, although you can't know it, & only give you my impressions, so
in the end you only get, as it were, a peep at odd places, and not a
thorough picture of the whole thing. I enclose one or two rough
plans, to give you perhaps a little more idea of what the actual trench
& its windings are like. This is probably stale. It's only an idea, but is
just the sort of thing an aeroplane sees. You notice none of the
'commy' trenches run straight back, as then the Huns, who may be on
higher ground, would see people moving. The Huns are of course
beyond the barbed wire. This is not our bit of course, but it's the same
type. Only the red one, the fire trench, has the fire step, the rest are
all about 7 feet deep, by 3 wide, roughly. We've had a good deal of
rain lately, but we can't complain, as it's been a ripping holiday so far,
after our really strenuous time on Salisbury Plain . . .

I foresee a chance of changing my socks and washing my feet very
shortly, when the post has gone. They got soaked two days ago &
have been ever since. You know how after a wet walk you look
forward to changing your socks, well I've been wandering round this
dear old quagmire, called, by a curious euphemism, a trench, for
about 50 hrs on and off . . . I've decided that babies who object to

baths should come for a week or so to the trenches! Why our nice
ones would foster the desire for soap and water, even in Tom's
obscure attic!

Even in the front line a certain amount of social life continued between the
four companies of the battalion.

I've now had a wash, a shave & dinner. Bully beef stewed and dog
biscuits today.[6] The potatoe party got lost[7] & didn't roll up till we had
finished coffee! We had coffee today as the Brigade machine[-gun]
officer came in to dinner as well as another company commander,
John Bowen, so we were quite a jolly crowd, as Pearce & I are feeding
our Regimental machine gunner, C. Thorne, a topping Cambridge
Rugger blue. [35]

To an outsider Billie's attempt to allay the anxieties of his family often seem
more likely to have increased them.

24th Aug. (still) 1915 (curiously enough)
About 3 this morning Eley of B. Coy. made his platoon fire 5 rds rapid
into the village in front. I nearly died with laughter at the result! Every
hun for about ½ a mile each way hopped up & let off his gun. The
flashes are awfully pretty to watch on occasions like this, and the air
seems alive with bullets, and the drone of the ricochets is like a hive
of bees chanting a vesper. Also the dear things kept about 3 star-shells
in the air at a time for about 5 or 10 minutes on end. But I mustn't
write like this, or you'll think there is some risk about this. Of course
there isn't.
　Yesterday afternoon I sat out in some long grass in 'No Man's land'
for about 10 mins. listening for digging in a hole there. Great fun,
quite safe except for about 7 yds where you want to leg it to the hole
with some vim. Coming back I got about 4 shots round my tail as I
bolted back, but the poor souls are too slow. As I say, if you're careful
& think of everything before you do it for about 10 mins. & allow for
everything you can't come to any harm. Luckily I'm far too frightened
to do anything rash so I'm all right. Of course in attacks you've got to
run a certain amount of risk, but in trench warfare, or 'waiting' it's
dead safe! [35]

　Last night [he wrote a couple of days later], or rather this morning,
I was on duty, in command of about 500 yds of fire-trench, & solely
responsible for keeping the Huns out, which sounds awful, but

means nothing, from 11.30 p.m. to 5 a.m. We were rather bothered as
Brother Hun was lobbing grenades at us from a curious contraption,
most of them missed the trench, naturally, but I disapprove of the
Hun doing this, as these things make a colossal row & shake the
ground a bit, & the pieces simply burn round your ears, so to stop, I
got through to a howitzer battery on the telephone & gave him the
spot off the artillery map, & presently along came a couple of "express
trains" & Hunno was quiet after that. It was a treat to hear our two
shells come slowly shrieking & whistling up & then swish as they fly
overhead & land – crash. A blinding flash, smack in their trench, & a
terrific report, some of the pieces actually came back into our trench,
about 200 yds away. Pretty accurate shooting from over 2 miles & at
night! We were not troubled again for a bit! [37]

The fine weather, which had been 'simply glorious' when C company
marched up the dry river bed that formed the communication trench to the
front line, lasted less than a week.

I'll tell you about last night [Billie wrote on August 29th, describing
the break up]. Harken:- I was for duty from 7.30 pip emma till 11.30.
Well, about 7 o'clock I had supper, soup and sardines à l'huile, 'pain
aux communication trenches', vin very ordinaire with a stiff glass of
water. One of Stanley's 'fly-killers' finished the meal. I looked out &
saw that the weather which has been topping was going to bust up
some, so I wound my waterproof sheet round my good old fleecelined burberry, filled up the cracks round the neck with dirty hankies,
stuck a collection of star shells in my pockets, and a revolver, seized a
smoke-helmet & a stick and sallied forth. At 7.30½ it started.
Absolutely blinding rain, lightning like a thousand starshells all in
one, and thunder that put the guns in the shade. It was so black you
had to feel your way along the trench and your elbows were knocked
to bits (that is a discomfort you don't reckon on till you've lived here
for a bit). All the time the rifles kept on plopping, with now and then
a shell, of the 'hun' variety, shrieking over into some village probably
looking for our transport; rifle grenades added to the merry din and
really I don't know when I've heard such a ghastly row. Our drainage
system, good as it is, couldn't cope with the water and we soon had
every facility for bathing, just like any South Coast watering place.
However I didn't come over here to paddle; as I heard one of my
sergeants murmur, as he came round a traverse with a strong breast
stroke, and double kick (à la Annette Kellerman[8]), "The Lord never

meant me for a duck, and I make a —— bad one!" After about ½ an
hour we were skin soaked. It was wonderful! I could picture Violet
Lorraine singing "Dear Old Saturday Night" at the Hippodrome and
wondered how she'd like this breed of Saturday night. I expect
Shirley was there too, singing 'Chinatown' & 'Mavourneen O'Shea'. I
had a shot at them myself. Yes, I know it sounds like 'frightfulness'
but the storm drowned it, and no one was hurt luckily. After about 3
hrs. it got a bit lighter and the rain stopped, but by then most of the
gratings over the drains had become loose as the floor was now a
quagmire, and now & then, lest one's interest should flag, one foot
would retire into a yard or so of water, giving your other leg a lusty
twist, just to keep things going, as it were . . .

Now all this sounds rather unpleasant & it is in a way, physically
anyhow, but there's a marvellous feeling all the time, of the [men]
sticking it out. I suppose it's what a novelist would describe as the
fighting spirit. Anyhow it more than makes up for any discomforts.
Then the Huns are 'for it' just as much as you, and certainly haven't
the 'go' of our Tommies. [40]

The bad weather continued, as a result of which the East Surreys' relief
from the trenches on September 3rd, a night both wet and dark, took longer
than expected. It 'was timed to take place at 9 pip emma and we got away at
1.30 ack emma and into billets 7 miles away at 5.30 so we were hanging
about for 4 hrs. in the 'commy' trenches. I can tell you we were pretty dead
when we did arrive.' [42] 'I won't dwell on our crawl down from the
trenches to these billets, it just won't bear thinking about,' Billie wrote, three
days later. 'My only remembrance of it rain & mud & then mud & rain
again.' [43]

'No rest for the wicked, or us!' he exclaimed, the day after their arrival.
'This morning we were routed out, about 5.30 to dig! My aunt! It was the
pink edge, after a solid fortnight, the last week mostly in rain.' There were
compensations, however. "Some' Billets, Clean Straw, No rats!' he headed
his letter. 'Quite a nice place too,' he said, 'the only drawback being the
owner, a poor old woman at least 50 (even in the shade) who is very touchy
about mud on her floor and tallow soap and red wine on the tables, which is
of course all in the day's work.' [42] The billets this time were at Ribemont
on the River Ancre, six miles south-west of Albert.

I'm just near the place Dorothy mentions [in a recently received
letter]. The name is that of one of Mrs. Bull's sons. Not Fred. Rather

cute! Well, I'm about 3 miles east by south of that in the trenches and now in billets I'm about 4 miles west by south of the same place. This town, now an utter ruin, possesses an enormous monument, à la Nelson's Column, and on top in Nelson's shoes there was an enormous gilded statue of the Madonna. A beautiful aiming point for the Huns which they soon used. But although they got a direct hit on it, & knocked it over, it has not fallen to the ground. It's an extraordinary sight, which people come to see from miles round, like this [he drew the statue]. No one knows how it stays up there. There must be some very strong iron stay, pulling it back from the feet. My drawing is really exactly like it! It's far more remarkable than that crucifix in N.M.L. With the sun full on it as I saw it, from about a mile & a half away, I think it was one of the most wonderful sights I've seen. It's an enormous height, towering above the chimneys & quite fresh looking gilt.[9] [42]

The most striking feature about Ribemont, the village the East Surreys now occupied, was the absence of

the everlasting crucifix on the road leading into it, its place being taken by an enormous notice saying "English beer sold wholesale" & "Also jam, fruit and fresh butter and milk". It cheers you up no end after a march. It's supposed to be the best billeting town (with the place where the hot baths are) in the sector. It's awfully clean and mouseless.

This morning I took the company down to [Heilly] for its hot baths. This excellent scheme is worked in the cellars of a big disused cheese factory. There are huge boilers and each man has a whole churning tub to himself, which is a huge thing. They provide clean clothing afterwards, if you want it, quite free of course.[10] It's all disinfected with stuff like you bath a dog with, and you smell like a dog after a bath exactly, only we don't roll in the garden! . . . There's a special place for officers. I put two officers on to this & retired with the doctor in charge, to the Divisional Buffet, across the road. 'SOME' spot! It is the conservatory of a big chateau there & is run by Madame & her two perfectly sweet daughters. I spent about 1½ hrs. there, buying those odds & ends[11] which will I hope arrive sometime or other & in a more or less whole condition. First I had coffee & cakes & then chose about a million cards. Then, chatting the while in that fluent French which has made my name a word to juggle with on the 7 seas, or in the five nations, I embarked on my first "Viskee et l'eau de soud." After 25 of

these, you could have juggled with my name from the Bermudas to
Bermondsey. Having spent about 3 mos. pay with allowances, I went
back and bathed while the other offs had their innings at the chateau.
The operations closed with a short stroll home along the river to
billets. [43]

The first night in the Ribemont billet had not been entirely satisfactory,
with six officers sleeping on a straw-covered floor while Pearce, the company commander, occupied the one bed that Billie had managed to find. Billie and a fellow officer decided to improve the situation.

The next (last) night Bertie Clare & I flushed a wopping great double
bed on the landing in the private part of a very nice butcher's shop.
We both slept in it last night. Clean sheets! It's just a wee bit
embarrassing when the family retires through your bedroom,
however, this is war time and after all we're over here defending their
blooming country, & they've got to lump us. That is a point of view,
which escapes most of the people one meets in Billets. If only I had
time I'd write the funniest book in the world about billets and odd
things . . . My new billet is on the top floor, & I'm there now writing
this, while Bertie is reading a mag in bed. It's too comic. Curtained off
from us are the butcher's two men-servant-boot & knife-boy-
assistants. They snored when we came up, but since we burgled in &
prised open the only window which lies in their half, they've been
quieter. On my left the ladies of the house are retiring, below me is
the staff of some 'lad' in the A.O.C. . . .

                                                                          8.9.15
   "Awake, for morning in the bowl of night,
   Hath flung the stone that put the stars to flight"
as Omar Kayyam's worst translater expresses it; or, as I should say,
   "Hop it, for Peachy with the water comes,
   His ghastly hobnails titulate my drums."
   Not really very good.
   It appears that neither Bertie nor I had a stitch of bed clothing over
us last night. All I can say is that I didn't, & the clothes were not on
the floor. [43]

September 10th marked the first anniversary of the 8th East Surreys' formation. To mark the occasion Billie sent home an account of the battalion's first
year. 'If you think it worth it, you can try to make a few shekels for the
Belgian Madames [the Nevills had Belgian refugees living with them at

Tennyson's House] by sending it to a paper. If they seem to want that sort of thing I could easily do some much better little sketches of life out here. This is just a sample not properly polished up. The local rag might like this sort of thing.' [50]

This morning a note came round to say that, on this momentous occasion, there would be no work in the afternoon [Billie wrote of the celebrations]. I expect this sounds pretty generous, but remember we're resting after 14 days hard! Well, the morning dragged along in that monotonous way a morning in billets has, with its eternal inspections and rapid firing practice. The afternoon was devoted to football but, as the ground was outside the billeting area, only those with the energy to carry rifle and equipment turned up to encourage the 22 drops of sweat who were racing about in 106 degress Fahr. and long trousers. At half-time a sand-bag full of apples masqueraded as a plate of lemons and contributed the one unassailably successful item – at any rate from the point of view of the aforesaid drops and the referee! Sand-bags, I may say, take the place of letter-boxes, socks, trousers, waste-paper baskets, carpets, travelling trunks and 101 other things which, in peace time, are really quite costly!

For 5.30 a concert had been billed, in the garden of the old Château now Head Quarters. The same old songs met with the same old applause, but you could notice a few eyes that used to laugh twitching a bit when it came to the old favourites, 'Keep the home fires burning' and so on. Capt. C.P.G's songs were as usual the pièce de résistance and, while he was 'on', it was easy to pick out the 'new drafts' from the old stagers when some time-honoured joke was brought out. Pte W. obliged with his celebrated 'Boiled Beef and Carrots' solo and Serg. O. was thinly disguised as the invulnerable Mother-in-Law and produced once more a few peels of joy – so low have we sunk!!! The proceedings closed, amid sighs of relief from at least some of the audience, with a few appropriate if pithy remarks by the Colonel.

Dinner, at the C.O.'s invitation, was a great success: Soupe au Cruet, Chicken de l'arc de Noé, Pêche in tins, all washed down with the red wine of France, this time called 'Graves', probably a curious foreshadowing the 'morning after'. No speeches dimmed the meal luckily and we adjoined to the Salon. I think if I tell you that, on the splendid cut-glass chandelier, there hangs, as an ash tray, a large French tin jam-bucket it will give you some idea of our appreciation of the magnificience of that room! Even our six weeks mud-stained senses shrank from dropping our ash on that floor! It has a carpet and chairs which I should call Jacobean, which not being given in my 'how to speak fluent French in 48 hours' I should construe as Louis Quatorze. And then the fun began. Picture us all, about 30 I suppose, squatting round the room, sharing five cups of coffee and smoking ration baccy and fags, except in a few exalted cases where the supply from home had not yet failed. There was, to an impressionable mind like mine, much food for thought in that crowd. The Irish Bar had lost our pianist and chief entertainer, while a big London bank is doubtless missing our only tenor. We are all much the same now, though some confirmed civilian still pulls off his cap when the National Anthem is sung, or commits some such military crime!

After Auld Lang Syne we crept back in the dark to our various billets, thinking for once of something other than the Hun and his ways. A thoroughly unwarlike day which did more good than 48 hours sleep or 10 months training.

Billie does not elaborate on his own thoughts during the evening but he had obviously been considering his future, for the following day he told his family that he had put his name down for a permanent commission 'in the real Regular Army!' [50]

Let me explain about this commission business [he wrote on September 15th]. You see the W.O. offer so many permanent commissions to present temporary offs. like myself [his captaincy had just been gazetted], beside the ordinary Sandhurst commissions. Well seeing as how I've forgotten everything, I suppose, by now, I thought I'd apply. I've got to stay for [the] duration anyhow so I may as well be permanent as temporary. If permanent, & I expect to be gazetted quite soon, I shall be a 2nd Lt. again as far as regular seniority counts, but I shall continue to hold any present temporary rank at Capt. as long as I stay with this battn; and I think they won't shift us to whatever regular battns. we get (I've asked for 1st East Surrey Reg.) till after the War. Now suppose War lasts four or five years more, then I've got 4 or 5 years' seniority in the regular regiment before I even join it, which would mean a great deal. I'd be able to live entirely on my pay. Also, I doubt if they will put us 'K's pups' back from Capt. to 2nd Lt. regulars as after all we've had commissions as long or longer than lots of them. Now the real regulars of Sandhurst days before the War like Campbell, will have to be promoted of course, as they will be quite seniors, as most of the Colonels will be over age &

resign & so everyone will shift up one. Of course it's rather a gamble, on the length of the war. [56]

Supposing the war goes on for 4 yrs [he said in another letter], well I'll have 4 yrs' seniority as a regular, before I ever join a regular Battn. I should be able to live on my pay as soon as I became a regular captain, which would not be long, if the war lasts for a year or 2. You see it's rather a gamble. If the war stops soon I should not have seniority enough to make it worth while staying a regular, so I should resign and go on with the schoolmastering idea, where there'll be plenty of openings. [52]

Schoolmastering was not the only possibility he had considered.

By the way I don't think you congratulated me on getting the Military Special, thereby getting half a degree, but perhaps I didn't tell you I'd done it. Abbot [his tutor at Jesus College] wrote & told me about it about a month ago. If I stop out here long enough, I'll get the other half, I think, so then I'll have endless careers & the whole world before me!!! I rather fancy myself as private secretary to some Lord or other. Earl Dysart can't write his own name for instance, & I could 'foot' some of his cheques with real pleasure.[12] [56]

There was one formality with regard to his application.

Last Sunday instead of taking the Church Parade I had to go to Divisional Headquarters to pass the New Medical exam for the Regulars. Need I say, I waltzed through it. I then had a chat with the celebrated Elephant Flapper of H . She was as charming as ever: by now I can understand everything that is said to me slowly & can answer and talk much better than before, somewhat naturally when you come to think of it. [61]

His commission came through at the beginning of November. 'I'm now a regular 2nd Lt. in the East Yorkshire Reg!! Never heard of 'em before. I'm trying to get transferred to 1st E.S.R.'[13] [95]

Meanwhile the battalion remained at Ribemont. 'Moves were frequently expected and then cancelled,' the regimental history reports, 'but good use was made of the period of rest for company training, etc.' Billie did a 'potted course of machine gun.' His company was instructed in the art of lighting braziers in the wind – good entertainment, apparently. He tested his mother's map-reading once more:

> This morning we marched down south through M to the next river at
> S, along the sweetly pretty valley to V where we turned up to M again
> & so home to R . . . I presume you can follow all this on that map I
> sent you. The wealth & prosperity of a villager here is judged by the
> size of the manure heap in his front yard. Some we passed to-day
> smelt very well to do. [57]

There was organised recreation as well as instruction. 'Today we are
having, or rather have had Aquatic Sports. The tub race provided the usual
laughter & sore skins for the specs and compets. respectively. No one got
across the greasy pole at all. The sun went out during the water polo match
and both teams froze to death nearly. I sheared off early,' he added, 'as I
wanted to write to Muff, since although I write to her as much as I do home,
I am in her debt in the way of letters, which is pretty good isn't it.'

There was football 'as often as we want it', as well as more intellectual
pursuits. 'To-night everyone is at an Auction Bridge Drive at Bn. H.Qs (thus
do we fight the Huns) but I squirmed out of it.' 'In fact,' Billy concluded,
'being back in billets is really ripping fun.'

Ribemont provided an ideal setting for billets though insect life was a
hazard. 'The orchard behind us running down about 300 yds to the river, is
simply alive with apples, I never saw such a crowd. We have great apple
fights . . . I've tried sitting in the orchard here to write, but along comes a
wapping gnat & sinks a shaft in your hand, or neck, or nose. My face looked
like a Belgian sand-dune, after it had be[en] shelled by our Monitors, after
my first attempt so nowadays I write indoors.' [56]

In Ribemont the battalion came into greater contact with the local population, giving Billie an opportunity to practise his French.

> I've quite lost my heart to Marie, a quaint little kiddie of 15, whose
> home is in the German part of France at Tourcoing, I think. N.B. I've
> told Muffie of this 'affaire' & she has replied with a glowing account
> of a similar case with a certain mythical Harry. This is our usual
> practice I may say. Doubtless Adam & Eve would have done the
> same, if possible . . . Talking of Marie, out here all the places are
> remembered by the name of the 'mamselle' at the café, or bazaar. For
> instance one might ask for H [Heilly] "Oh, yes, where the 'Elephant
> Flapper' lives." The E.F. is a great pal of mine. I bought your little
> knick-nax (?) off her. Then there is Rosamonde at the Cafe de la
> Jeuness at D [Dernancourt]. Another lady is known to half the B.E.F.

as 'the Cow', solely because she was once surprised in curling papers, by an early customer wanting coffee, on his way to dig somewhere! And so it is everywhere. One's flirtations with these damsels are invariably limited to creeping up very sheepishly & shyly asking if they've any Chocolat, or Carte-postales. And then having paid some ruinous price creeping sheepishly away again. The men are too killing for words. "Chocolat." The wretched girl hands them a packet of Peters or some make. "Non, les little round ones, silly, si'l vous plait." You'd die with laughing if you heard some of 'em. One corporal of ours poses as a bit of an interpreter. I heard him tackling the local butcher's wife for "quelque chose vite à cooker, vous savez, mais pas trop tough, vous savez?" He was handed a hunk of beef steak and seemed quite happy in spite of the 'trente sous'. They reckon everything in so many 'sous' here. I asked why & was told they only did it so as to be easy for les Anglais. I wish they wouldn't . . . The old lady of our billets is a Mlle Pitons. She always tells us she's a Mademoiselle & not Mme., as we all called her. I asked her if she wanted me to marry her, but she didn't jump at the notion somehow so I don't know why she persists in disclosing the fact of her old maidhood . . . My French, don't laugh, is coming on apace. I get as much practice as possible, what with Marie & the E.F. & one thing & another. [56]

On September 18th the battalion moved into fresh billets in nearby Ville-sur-Ancre, a village which could provide good accommodation for fifteen hundred and which was to remain their billeting town until the following spring.

We've only moved about 2 miles, à les (aux) Corbeaux, but that of course means all the collecting everything, cleaning up & loading just as if for a 200 mile trek. After a tender farewell to the aged hag who had been worrying us for the last 12 days or so, I discovered I'd lost my old blackthorne cudgel. Frantic search by everyone and at last my servant unearthed it and the Battalion pushed off . . . The sun was simply awful and although we only marched for about ¾ hr one man fell out with a slight stroke. On the way here we passed two simply ripping armoured cars! each mounting 4 maxims & one 3 pounder gun. They were so cleverly painted I hardly spotted them in the trees; their manned by Naval people in Khaki, sort of half breeds. The great sight however came later. We had just passed a notice on the road:– "Arrête Municipal. Vitesse automobile 12 klm (7½ m.) when along came one of our new Motor cycle Machine Gun batteries going at least 35 miles an hour, with their repair waggon and ammunition reserve all blinding along at the same pace behind. At least 25 side cars went past, not quite all of them had m-gs, but it was a great sight . . .

I've bought a lot more p.p.cs which I'll endeavour to smuggle home. I don't think it matters if the names are scratched out. ['I should suggest put all the cards I send home in one big Album,' Billie wrote, on the envelope enclosing this letter. 'I've sent off 4 packets of cards by the same post as this.'] The shop I bought them at, like many shops in these villages, is owned & run by refugees from A-t [Albert], which is no longer habitable for civilians. We had a terrible struggle about a room to feed in – as monsieur's old mother has such a weak heart she can't stand the smell of food!! Two interpreters & 1 oz of Players soon altered monsieur's views & apparently his mater is better now. Talking of food there is no English beer here, but the C.O. has written to ask the B.E.F. canteen to open a branch here so we may be saved. The idea is that this should be our permanent billeting town for the winter, & I shan't mind if it is. It's about 4½ miles 'down'. Monsieur here is a consumptive looking giant about 8 ft high & 4½ ft thick, rather an awe inspiring merchant, but I don't think he's in very good training poor old chap. There's a perfectly ripping garden here too, & the usual fruit supply. I'm afraid we shall miss our fresh meat from the butcher at R but we are going to send in every day and buy some. But it won't be the same after 2 dusty miles on a bycyle carrier, semi-clad in the Petit Journal!

I've got a room & bed all to my lonesome, this time, so I've no complaints. It's not a desperately exciting room, having only the usual enormous bed & miniature wash basin, seven old strip fly papers & a chest of drawers – 2 ft high & 1 wide. The mural decorations are one rosary, one wooden crucifix and two enormous pictures – one of the Madonna and the other a Calvary scene!!! so I ought to be pretty good, oughtn't I? My room opens into Bertie Clare's and both open into our mess room, which is jolly handy and means we needn't put our collars on before breakfast. The other officers are next door & next door but one. The village produces eggs, milk, tinned & fresh fruit & biscuits. We are making a barn into a big ante-room for the officers, where there is a billiard table & will be papers etc. There are incidentally no cues or balls, but this as I have said before is War, though it's mighty hard to remember it sometimes, which is a jolly good thing out here, I can promise you. My window opens on to the road & the church (intact) is just opposite. It strikes the quarters, that is the church clock does, & 10 has just banged out, so I think I'd better dry up & turn in. [58]

The battalion's return to the trenches was ordered, and then postponed 'owing to an inspection by K of K, who's supposed to be near here. Terribly hot, & means endless cleaning & elbow grease.' [60].

'Lord Kitchener expressed himself as being much pleased by the appearance and steadiness of the two battalions,' the regimental history reported (the 10th Essex was inspected at the same time). Maxse, too, was pleased. 'Everything is going exceedingly well for us just now,' he wrote home to his wife two days later. Billie, however, was unimpressed. 'He [Kitchener] was looking awfully worn out and judging from photos had aged enormously.' [61]

By now Billie was becoming restless. '<u>Still</u> in billets,' he headed his letter. 'I'm very fed up with Billets, you get so fat and lazy,' he complained. [61] 'That of course is an enormously difficult problem, how to keep fit, both in & out, particularly out, of the trenches. We're all as well as anything, but we couldn't march now with packs half as far as we could at Codford.' [56]

'The air just now is electrical in the extreme with the wildest rumours but I really mustn't breathe what is, after all, only my guess at the truth,' he had written three weeks previously, on September 7th. Presumably suggestions of the coming push had been circulating. Now the Battle of Loos was about to begin, thirty-five miles to the north of Albert. 'The real advance has started,' Billie wrote in code in his letter of September 22nd. 'We may not be in the show here at all. I hope we shall.' On September 26th, the day after the battle began, he told Elsie

that ours and the French really big pushes are a tremendous success at <u>present</u>. In one place the front line is captured on a front of 41 miles!!! This is true. I mustn't tell you more, but this general news can't matter. Stand by for excellent news, but I'm afraid heavy casualties. [64]

His forecast of heavy casualties turned out to be only too true. One of those caring for them would be his sister Amy.

NOTES

1. *The 18th Division in the Great War*, p.16.
2. Revetment was the means of

stopping the side of the trench from falling in, either due to enemy action, the weather or normal wear and tear. Pit props, brushwood or sandbags were the more usual forms of support, but anything suitable found in the area was utilised.

3. Billie's anxiety about security seems a little strange, considering how much the enemy knew of the English disposition in this area. On August 1st, two days after the 18th Division had landed in France and long before it reached the front, Billie told his mother that 'The other day the Bosches threw notes into the trenches near here, which are in several places 10' apart, notes saying they were glad to hear the 18th Division had come up behind!! We with our secrecy! Isn't it wonderful.'

4. 'We snaffled 8 mice only last night but that was because we didn't bother to reset the traps.' [24th August]

5. 'Be strong and of good courage: be not afraid, neither be thou dismayed; for the Lord thy God is with thee whithersoever thou goest.'

6. This sounds preferable to the lunch that awaited him on his return from the trenches, 'a lusty hunk of timber-wolf, followed by some yellow lumps of a soft fruity material floating in a general modicum of fluid, tasting partially of cafe-au-lait & partially of Tinned Wiltshire sausages. The whole made palatable by a portion of ration bread of about the same consistency as a skating rink. To wash this down was some "Vin Vinegaire" or something, (the bottles of ale all being dead.)' [43]

7. 'Some potatoes grow flourishingly in one of the gardens here, & when cooked will repay the belly-slink over the parapet of the 'commy' trench, which is required to pluck them. Do you pluck or gather spuds?' [35]

8. An Australian aquatic performer, who first appeared on the London stage in a tank at the Hippodrome, and was an instant success. She was apparently a very powerful swimmer.

9. The basilica in Albert, dedicated to the Virgin Mary, had a tower at the top of which a gilded statue of the Madonna held her Son up to God. The statue had been knocked horizontal by a German shell in January 1915 and was secured in this position by French engineers. It remained, as a landmark and an artillery observation post, until the Germans overran Albert in 1918. It was then knocked down by the British to prevent the Germans from using it in the same way. Although Albert lay in a hollow, the tower was tall enough to enable the statue to be seen from some distance away.

10. Billie was later to complain about the unnecessary amount of clothing provided by the Government. 'Although we only had an easy fortnight up, our coy. alone (220 men) has had 150 prs. of puttees, 100 coats, 100 trousers, 150 hats, etc. etc. all new, mind you, 300 odd shirts & N. socks & about 50 prs. of boots. It's simply ridiculous, you know, they don't want them a bit, just a few do of course but it's absurd the way they shower things on us. The inhabitants live on our leavings like Lazarus (rather apt).' [56]

11. 'I've sent off . . . a little knife and fork, fruit, prs. 1, marks V. They were not for sale really but I soon wheedled them out of madame, from the buffet at the Chateau near here.' [49]

12. The previous week he had reported that 'Earl Dysart has just sent me £10 for the Men's Fund!' – presumably through a secretary. [41]

13. The 1st and 2nd East Surreys were both Regular battalions, whereas the 8th was a Service battalion, i.e. made up of volunteers, with some Regular officers such as Major Irwin and Lt.-Col. Powell to train them. (In November 1915 Maxse complained that several battalions in the 18th Division had only one officer who had done any soldiering before the war.)

5 NURSING IN FRANCE

Amy's decision to become a V.A.D. can only be regarded as quixotic. At thirty-six, she was eight years over the age specified by the Voluntary Aid Detachment for recruits, she was not physically strong and she does not sound to have been a very confident nurse. Muffie had told Billie that 'she simply couldn't hang about at home & do no war work,' and Amy, with a brother in the Army, the Royal Flying Corps and the Royal Naval Reserve, may well have felt the same. However, there were other ways in which she could have helped in the war effort. Nursing in England, for instance, rather than in France, would have been both easier and more comfortable. Conditions in the base hospitals across the Channel were primitive. No. 24 General at Étaples, the hospital to which Amy was sent, was still largely under canvas in 1915; the construction of replacement huts went on throughout the wet and windy winter of 1915/16, making the area one large building site. Conditions there were unpleasant enough for the younger V.A.Ds, let alone one who by the standard of the day was approaching middle age.

It is hard not to conclude that Amy's decision was due to Aunt Annie's influence. Ann Beadsmore Smith, Mrs. Nevill's youngest sister, was a formidable woman. Trained as a nurse at St. Batholomew's Hospital in London, where she became a ward sister, she went out to South Africa at the outbreak of the Boer War and spent three years nursing there with the Army Nursing Service Reserve. On her return to England she stayed with the Reserve when it became Queen Alexandra's Imperial Military Nursing Service, and by 1915 she was one of the Service's most senior matrons. She was extremely capable, an excellent nurse and an able administrator. Her skill in nursing had even been acknowledged by the Kaiser, after she and another sister had nursed his staff surgeon back to health following an attack of pleurisy during a visit to England in 1907. Kaiser Wilhelm presented each sister with a brooch as a token of his gratitude. It was not, one imagines, a gift much worn after 1914.

The first general hospital to the British Expeditionary Force landed in France on August 12th, 1914. Aunt Annie followed four days later and was matron of a hospital outside Boulogne until the summer of 1915 when, soon

after seeing Billie, she moved to the newly set up No 24 General at Étaples.
'I never knew her to be cross or ruffled,' a nurse who served under her
wrote of her later. 'She dealt as happily and easily with generals as with
orderlies, and had a wonderful sense of humour. She was handsome,
beautifully turned out, an example to the nursing staff in every way.'[1]

Despite her apparent composure, however, Aunt Annie was highly
strung and, as so often happens, it was her family and those closest to her
who suffered. She was running a large hospital in difficult conditions, dealing with dreadful casualties; it was no wonder that the strain sometimes
told. People in positions of authority tend to be isolated; Aunt Annie may
well have felt lonely. In such circumstances it must have been tempting to
put pressure on someone as sweet-tempered and willing as Amy to come
over to France to act as companion and confidante.

Whether Amy's enlistment was due to Aunt Annie or not, she still had to
fulfil the requirements of the Voluntary Aid Detachment – spend time working in a hospital in England, gain certificates in first aid and home nursing,
provide a reference from 'a magistrate or person of position' (Aunt Annie,
possibly) and have an interview with a matron, normally of a large training
school. Only then could her papers be sent before the Selection Board. It all
took time, and there is an indication in Amy's letter to her mother that on
the other side of the Channel Aunt Annie was becoming impatient. In an
attempt to hurry matters along Amy visited the Detachment Headquarters
at Devonshire House in London. Mrs. Nevill was staying with friends in
Kent at the time; Amy wrote to her at once.

D.H. Evans & Co. Ltd.
Reading Room
Aug 24. 15   *Oxford Street, W.*
My beloved family,
    Isn't this too sickening. This morning I spent ages at Devonshire
House. They say to my great relief, I have done all I can, & it's so
difficult to make them understand in France all the rules & regulations
for sending out V.A.Ds. The only thing I can do now is to see Miss
MacSwinney tomorrow morning, it's the only day of the week she is
in Town, & get her to find out if I have passed before the official list is
out, & if I have to send in my Selection Board papers at once, without
waiting to actually receive the Certificates. I have to take certain
papers to her tomorrow, so just writing isn't any good. I'm getting
very nervous about my exam on Thursday, I know I don't know
anything about it . . .
    I did a lot of business at Devonshire House everyone was most

1   Billie, spring 1915

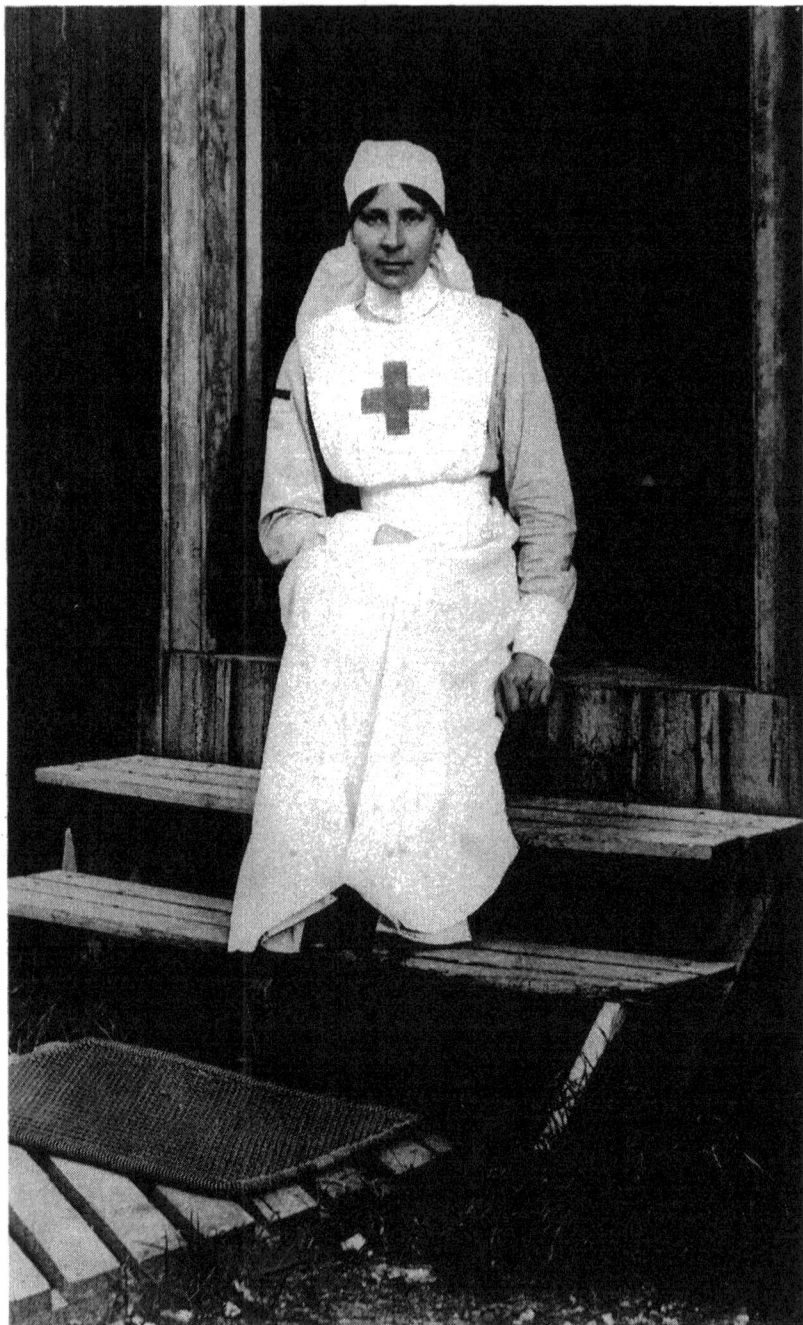

2   Amy, July 1916

3   Kitchener's appeal

4   A.P.B. Irwin

5   Billie, Howard, Mrs Nevill and Elsie, May 1916

6 Officers of the 8th East Surrey Regiment, 1915

Left to right:

Top row: Soames – Twigg – Morse – Wrightson – P.G. Heath – Frere
          C. Thorne – W. Nevill – Holberton – Hetherington

2nd row: Cadge – Paull – Thorley – Gimson – Eley – R. Heath
          J. Ackerley – Davis – Rhodes

3rd row: Flatau – Mitchell – Pearce – Clifton – Col. Powell – C.C. Clare
(seated)   Irwin – Bowen – Place – Brill

4th row: Jacobs – Drane – Musgrove – M. Thorne
(squatting)

(Photograph: Elliott and Fry)

7   Major-General Ivor Maxse, by Francis Dodd

8 Field Service Post Card

9 Muffie Schooling

10 P.G. Heath

11 J.R. Ackerlev

12 The Basilica at Albert

13 Heilly Château – Headquarters of the 18th Division

14 Aunt Annie

15 Nurses' club at Etaples

16 Captain Gimson

17 Marlborough Thorne

18 Collecting wood from a ruined house

19 Alcinie with Hetherington and Pegg

20 Janion, Billie and Paull

21 V.A.D. kitchen at Étaples

DRAWN BY R. CATON WOODVILLE

THE GAME.

A company of the East Surrey Regiment is reported to
have dribbled four footballs, the gift of their captain who
fell in the fight, for a mile and a quarter into the enemy
trenches.

On through the hail of slaughter
  Where gallant comrades fall,
Where blood is poured like water,
  They drive the trickling ball.
The fear of death before them
  Is but an empty name;
True to the land that bore them
  The Surreys play the game!

On without check or falter,
  They press towards the goal;
Who falls on freedom's altar
  The Lord shall rest his soul.
But still they charge, the living,
  Into that hell of flame;
Ungrudging in their giving,
  Our soldiers play the game!

And now at last is ended
  The task so well begun;
Though savagely defended
  The lines of death are won.
In this, their hour of glory,
  A deathless place they claim
In England's splendid story,
  The men who played the game!
                              TOUCHSTONE.

"ON THROUGH THE HAIL OF SLAUGHTER ... THEY DRIVE THE TRICKLING BALL":

22 "The Surreys Play the Game!" by R. Caton Woodville, which appeared in
    The Illustrated London News, 27th July, 1916. (The caption was incorrect and
    should have read 'Montauban' and not 'Contalmaison'.)
    "The Game" was published in the Daily Mail on 12th July, 1916.

THE GERMAN TRENCHES UNDER A HAIL OF SHELLS.

ST SURREYS CHARGING TOWARDS THE GERMAN TRENCHES AT CONTALMAISON

23 Vaux

24 Cornelius Thorne (Photo: Vandyke)

25 No. 2 Stationary Hospital, Abbeville

26 Front-line trench on the Somme

27 The ceremony at Kingston Barracks. *(Daily Graphic*, 22nd July, 1916)

28 Ackerley, photographed by WPN   29 Billie's headstone

30 Group photograph by WPN. Ackerley, second from left; Capt. Aveling, second from right.

kind, & the Matron, a Miss Fisher, took a great interest in me, & very kindly gave me my official interview then & there on the spot, which she explained she had never done before, you always had to wait to see her until after you had your Certificates. She said my two months at St. Mary's would be a great point with the Selection Committee, & said I was also to say I had a little French!! I told her it was about two words & she said never mind quite enough! & also that I could cook a little, hope I shan't be turned on as Cook in Chief to the Hospital!! I am going straight home now to work at my Home Nursing.

Billie had offered Amy 'anything which will be useful to her' from the belongings he had sent home from Codford. Once in France he chose to send letters of medical interest to her rather than to any other member of the family. [18]

Mr. Savory & Moore gelatin medicine is a great success. Twice I've stopped headaches, from loss of sleep, with phenacetin & caffeine, & last night dosed one of our sergeants with quinine, with great success. We're near a railhead here, which means that after that point motor supply columns take grub & ammunition up from the railways. They take it to the refilling point, where the Divisional Train meets them, sorts out the stuff into the various Brigades of artillery & infantry & carries it, in large horse drawn waggons, to the 'collecting points' of each regiment. The regiment sends back its transport and carries the stuff up at night, to the end of the long communication trenches, dump it down, go off & collect any odd casualties that have been missed by the R.A.M.C. cars, or who were late, & bring them back & dump them at the 'collecting points' and notify the RamCorps. That is roughly how an army is maintained in the field. On our railway journey from port of disembarkation, for 8 or 9 hrs we were passing long empty (except in some cases for an occasional RAM corps carriage) trains of goods waggons, every 5 minutes, all on their way down to the overseas Base. [27]

Now, while Amy was waiting to embark, Billie wrote to her again, a letter that while appreciative and encouraging was not exactly cheering.

8 ESR
BEF
In F
You'll soon have the same I hope

Dear old A,

Thanks for your tremendous outpouring, most acceptable. This is only a note as you may not have the benefit (what side!!) of my home epistles much longer. I should like some p.c.s. of Shirley & Unity More, the latter is an Hippodrome flame of mine, who is now at the Alabama in Shell Out. I've now had about four different opinions of Quinneys, we must see it <u>when</u> I get leave[2] . . .

The idea about the V.A.Ding sounds sensible, you'll have to watch the tradesmen at first to see they don't get done down. It must be annoying having to wait like this, I had to for about 4 months, so I can sympathise really. I hope you're bagging everything of mine that could be of any use to you. You know it's very good of you to come out & lend a hand when we can't really help ourselves, I don't suppose you think that yourself, because you wouldn't, it's not like you to, but I & everyone always say however bad a time we're having, that the nurses have the worst of all; not a very comforting item of news . . .

Goodbye & good luck old thing, love as usual,

yrs ever

Bill [47a]

No doubt because of the battle of Loos, which began on September 25th and continued until October 10th, Amy's wait turned out to be shorter than Billie's. The base hospitals needed every extra hand they could get to help with the 50,000 casualties suffered at Loos.

<u>No time to read it through</u>

Thursday 30th [September] 15

My very dearest Mother,

24 General Hospital
B.E.F.

This is really the first moment I have been able to write a line, & now I don't know where to begin. Aunt A. says she has sent you a line so you know I'm here. The journey was a great success, but you know we were the last to cross, & for two days there has been no packet over because of submarines . . . It was a beautiful crossing but I believe very cold. I went straight below, as I felt a little sick before starting. Aunt Annie was much too busy to meet me, or rather us, but a Miss Woodford, a territorial sister met us, she was very nice indeed . . . We all had lunch at the Louvre Hotel & then 25 of us left in a huge Motor Lorry arrangement to this place, some to 24 Gen. some to 25 & some to 26 . . . Directly we started on our 23 ml drive, it began to pelt,

we left soon after 4 p.m. & so it kept on the whole way, very
depressing. The Home Sister met us here, Miss Foster – very nice
indeed – and we are all in little huts. Aunt Annie had made my half
look ever so nice, with matting on the floor & a strip of carpet, 2
packing cases, one on the top of the other to make a cupboard, & two
of the cloths you sent out over them as covers & curtains, flowers, a
coathanger on a nail & a looking glass hung up, also an easy chair! It
really looked most comfortable, and a lantern.

We then all went over to the Mess Tent & had tea, in the pelting
rain, the rain was all through the sides of the tent, & everywhere was
soaking. Our luggage then arrived & after having 3 blankets served
out to us, we went to our huts to unpack by one candle light. The
chair had to be ousted, as it entirely filled my room, & the box holdall
& camp kit could not fit in with it. The first thing I did was to get my
bed out & made up, so as to have somewhere to put things down. I
did not do much unpacking that night as Aunt Annie turned up &
after a great talk we went over to dinner. When she is in for meals I sit
by her. Aunt Annie has been absolutely sweet to me so has everyone
else & I am very happy & very well quite truly, I feel heaps better &
haven't had a pain or ache at all. Aunt A gave me her eiderdown as a
mattress, insisted on my having it, & I truly was glad, also she gave
me a pillow. That reminds me, I do want a nice pillow more than
anything else, if you could possibly spare one, the one provided is
very small & hard, about 3 pieces of straw in a hard green canvas
case![3] We did not sleep awfully well as we are almost on to [the]
railway line. The line runs parallel with our row of huts and is
without exageration as close to my bed, & on the same level, as the
front of our house is to the little piece of our garden on the other side
of the road. Trains passed all night, & in passing welcomed us with
loud piercing shrieks . . . Aunt Annie has a pair of wading boots,
which she vows she never wears & does not want: they fit me
beautiful[ly] & bath parade is a grand sight, fortunately I am quite
close to the bath rooms, only about as far as from our house to no.21. I
wore the wading boots my combs, nightie, dressing gown mack &
hood. I stepped out of my hut into a huge puddle & got to the
bathroom very cold, had a tepid wash & came back. The next morning
was worse, the wind howled round, & the rain just fell, & I paddled
to the bath again. After breakfast we were interviewed by various
people & at last sent to our wards. I have a dear of a Sister & one
other Red Cross girl quite nice. It's most interesting & delightful . . .

I have absolutely no time to write a line. We are rather busy & I am

not having my regular times off, & the bits I have Aunt A likes me to
be with her. She is so perfectly nice to me, & everyone is so friendly. I
have had heaps of callers, which has also used up my spare time.
Today I'm changing my hut & am going to be nearer Aunt A & with
her delightful little secretary Miss Gordon, quite a nice change & a
bigger hut. Each day a bit of this has been written. Today I'm only off
for 1 hr, & tea first with Aunt A & a friend of hers & then the mess tea
with girls I'd promised to have tea with, have used up the precious
time.

I am absolutely happy & love being in the wards, the orderlies do
all the heavy work, & the whole morning I'm helping Sister with
dressings. You see the wounds are bad, & they take two to do them
always & that's my job. Today I was able to get everything ready for
Sister by myself. From 1.15 to 3 I am on quite alone, with one orderlie,
the men are mostly asleep & I get dressing[s] etc. ready for the next
day . . . My Sister is Sister Knight and we are great friends already. In
fact I seem to have dropped into the midst of delightful friends. Of
course it's because Aunt A is so tremendously popular here.

Crowds of very best love,
    Amy

To Miss A.A. Nevill   Sunday
24 General Hospital, B.E.F.   *UP*
Cheery oh,

Welcome to the B.E.F! The finest thing anyone ever belonged to!
I'm afraid you'll be most awfully busy, but you won't be handling me
yet a while. Aunt A & I have kept up a good stream of letters so it'll
save me a stamp! I wonder how you like it, I know you'll be up to
your eyes in work for a bit now, but we have strafed the old huns a
good deal and they're very peevish about it.

I've been up a week now & am suffering from sore feet, please
nurse. It's nothing, only from not taking off one's boots for so
long . . .

Good-bye old girl, I spent 2 hours helping in our regimental aid
post the other night. We see em first hand & – well – I won't describe
'em, & so I can sympathise with you in your beastly work. It's ripping
to feel you're just behind me.

With VBL to you and AA,
    Billie [71]

'I feel as if I had been here ages,' Amy wrote, less than a week after her first letter, 'quite settled in a way & yet not quite enough to find time for letter writing.' [3] Lack of consecutive time for letter writing continued to be a problem throughout her stay in France, except while on night duty, and meant that her letters were far less frequent than those of her brother, seven to his fifty-six in the three months to the end of the year.

An additional reason for the infrequency of her letters was the matter of censorship. All letters in France had to be censored, by the company commander in army battalions, by the matron in the base hospitals.[4] Billie censored his own letters, Amy's had to be censored by her matron – Aunt Annie in other words. 'I just hate Matron censoring my letter,' Amy wrote, later in the war, when she and Aunt Annie were no longer together, 'not that there is anything in them, & I don't mind a stranger reading them but Matron, nice as she is, it's horrid, & has put me dead off writing.' [21] If that was the effect of an unrelated matron how much worse it must have been to have to submit letters to Aunt Annie.

There were special green envelopes, the contents of which did not have to be censored by an officer or a matron on the spot, but might be opened by a faceless censor at base, but green envelopes were regarded as a privilege and only intermittently available. 'You say always have an envelope addressed but that's difficult,' she explained. 'I like yours to go in a green envelope & they are doled out about one a week, no not as often as that, sometimes it's three weeks before we get them.' [6]

Time available was another factor. As second in command of his company, and later in command, Billie had more control over his time than did Amy over hers. 'The labours of the day being over,' he wrote to Elsie on his third evening abroad, 'I've strolled out to a field behind my cottage, to have as it were a 'papery' chat with you.' [21] Amy's free time depended on the amount of work in the wards, and was in any case at Aunt Annie's disposal. There were also various duties she felt obliged to undertake, as well as the need to get to know her colleagues. She tried to explain the difficulties to her family:

I think about you all, all day but I find it so difficult to write. Of course every evening I spend with Aunt Annie & we haven't finished talking yet! also everyone is so awfully kind to me, & our little set of V.A.D. & three or four awfully nice military pros meet for great supper parties in the different huts, & naturally just at first I don't want to refuse to go. I don't mean I don't enjoy them, I do very much & they are such nice girls, but I could then write letters, however that won't go on for ever & when I know them better I can say I want to write. [3]

Sometimes it seemed as if the only time available to her was in the early hours of the morning.

We came back early [from a half day spent in Paris-Plage] to write letters in the warm Club room, but found so many people to talk to they did not get done. I know three girls in the Sick Sisters' ward, & had also been asked to visit them, so that took up time. I then went to a hut supper, instead of mess as I had a hot bath, & we had a good meal, real turtle soup, with Oxo tablets in it, & Pati de Fois Gras paste & biscuits & jam, & then were just settling to letters when callers arrived, it does seem so impossible to get them done. I left early & came to sit in bed to do them, & ran in to say goodnight to Aunt Annie, & we then talked, her saying all the time write, which was quite impossible of course, until just on 12 I fled to bed, & here I am as fresh as a daisy writing at 5.45. [4]

There were misunderstandings. Instead of addressing a letter to the family she addressed it to Stanley alone, as he was about to embark for Egypt with the Royal Flying Corps – 'flitting Pharaohwards', as Billie put it. [91] 'You have, I know, every right to be furious with me,' Amy said. 'Now the time is flying & I don't realise how long it really is since I did write. I felt sure Stanley would be home & concluded you would open the letter, as it was a family one.' [4]
Her letters had always been long. 'Your tremendous outpouring,' Billie had described one, adding, 'Next time you write a book like that, number the pages, please.' [47a] He wrote again, 'Amy, I don't like to have to speak twice about the same thing, nor do you, but again an enormous letter & the pages not numbered! As a matter of fact they happened to be in order this time. I shall have to ask you not to write if this occurs again.' [51] Now her letters were written when she could, a paragraph at a time. Occasionally there was as much as ten days between the beginning of a letter and its posting. It made for disjointed reading.

'I am truly ashamed of this letter but it's all I can manage. I have refused to spend my time off with anyone today so of course first Gordon, Aunt Annie's sec. & my hut companion, wanted to pour [a] misunderstanding with Aunt Annie into my ear, & then on my way here another girl, Miss Adams taking her first walk out from being in Sick Sisters, tracked me down, & I am having tea with another girl here at ¼ to 4, & have to visit Sick Sisters before going on duty again at 5, such is what always happens.' [5]

The homesickness from which she suffered must surely have been aggravated by the presence of her aunt and the reminiscing in which they in-
dulged – 'Aunt Annie & I are always talking about you all,' she told them at
home. [5] Stanley's departure from England provoked a particularly bad
bout.

I am thinking about you all so much tonight, & wondering where you
are, if you, any of you, have gone to Gosport to see Stanley. [They all
had.] I should so love to be with you & am really very homesick
today. I have come & shut myself in Aunt Annie's hut, she is out to
dinner, it's the only place I feel I shall not be disturbed in. [5]

It is clear from her letters that Amy was greatly put upon by Aunt Annie.
There is nothing to suggest that she was not working as hard as any other
V.A.D. in the hospital – '[Aunt Annie] says A is topping & works hard all
day & is frantically busy & v. happy,' Billie reported home on October 15th –
but whereas the spare time of other V.A.Ds was their own, Amy's was at
Aunt Annie's disposal. Yet Amy rarely complained, and then only at particularly outrageous behaviour on Aunt Annie's part. Presumably, in line
with the social attitudes of the time, she took it for granted that she should
be at an older relation's beck and call. There is never any reason to doubt her
affection for her aunt.

Everyone naturally loves her [she reported to her mother on October
5th], & we are delighted to have each other. On the whole she is very
well, looks better than she has done for ages, & is a trifle fatter, but
gets rather tired, one or two nights has gone to bed really early, I'm
glad to say, & I have been in to talk to her in bed. [3]

Whatever the demands of Aunt Annie, however, there were undoubted
compensations for Amy in the relationship, quite apart from the use of
Matron's hut as a place of refuge in times of unhappiness. Aunt Annie had
prepared Amy's quarters before Amy's arrival, and given her equipment
and clothes. Now she introduced her to hospital social life. 'I have an afternoon off today . . . Aunt Annie is fetching me & we are going up to the
Nurses' Club to tea. Aunt Annie has installed me [as] a member.'

The Club is rather a jolly place, it's run by some elderly Red Cross
people. They have a very nice big room, full of easy chairs & fires,
really warm, all the papers, & plenty of books, then there is another
summer room, no fire at present so we don't use it. Then there is a

large room, also warm for tea. All the hospitals in this part use it, I have not yet quite discovered where one hospital ends & the other begins, & have several times got lost. Tea is supplied at cost price, and is very cosy & good. [5]

Another benefit was the fact that, as Matron, Aunt Annie had access to transport, allowing Amy to visit further afield than she could otherwise have done.

On Wednesday I had a ½ day, & went with another girl, in the motor Aunt Annie uses, with her "John" & Colonel Martin to [Boulogne] where 7 Stationary is. We had a delightful afternoon, but were most awfully disappointed Aunt Annie at the last moment could not come with us . . .
     Yesterday I had off from 2 – 5, & Aunt Annie suddenly said she could motor me into the dearest little place about 4 mls away . . . where the golf links are, & we would walk back or get the train back, 'we' being another awfully nice V.A.D., a Miss Cliff & I. [3]

Of all her outings, the most enjoyable was 'a huge spree' Amy shared with Aunt Annie early in 1916.

Colonel Raw took us in the faithful John's car & we went to see the most wonderful hospital for the tubercular children of Paris in the world. It really was most interesting, & afterwards we had a nice little time on the beach by the sea, Elsie I believe knows that bit of coast, it's not far from where she & Howard were one summer when Aunt Annie joined them. The women going out to dig for worms for bait, just as the sun was going down, & the fishing fleet coming in. We had a great day, out to lunch & tea, & all in the mood to thoroughly enjoy it. [10]

But in the dreadful weather of that autumn and winter perhaps the most important benefit to Amy from her relationship with Aunt Annie was the physical comfort it provided. As Matron, Aunt Annie not only had a fire in her office, but a stove in her hut as well, making her room 'the only warm spot here.' [5]
     The effect of the bad weather at Étaples was made worse by the conditions of the camp. Though winter huts were being rushed up, much of the camp was still tented, and that not always securely. 'The mess tent was blown down the other day,' Amy wrote on October 10th, '& between the mess tent

& our huts our winter quarters are being built, at present the whole place is strewn with boards, it's like playing a huge game of "spilikens" to try & walk over the boards without falling.' [3] 'Our floor is soaking wet, it gets a little dry by the lamp & is then soaked again by the rain the next minute. They have now, fortunately, succeeded in shutting the side of my hut up. The bottom half lifts up on a hinge, it was open when I arrived, & then refused to be shut, however by a great deal of digging etc. it has shut.' [4] This was on November 4th, when Amy had been in France for almost six weeks. Two days later she was reporting the first fall of snow, four inches of it in one night.

Occasionally we wonder, how we keep so well & what you would say to see us strolling along to our baths, in a sharp frost with only nighties & dressing gowns on, & then after a hot bath back to our huts. What I really don't truly love is getting up in the morning, no hot water, dressing with frozen hands & then going over to the mess tent, just like an ice well, it blew down the other day [it is not clear whether Amy is referring to the incident she had mentioned three weeks before or to a second occasion] & for two days we had to mess in the skeleton winter huts in the course of construction, walls roof & a floor but not a window in the place, & yet we all agreed it was more comfortable than the tent! Oh for a blazing fire again, to warm feet sometimes. [5]

Bad as conditions might have been in the hospitals, however, they were much worse for the men in the trenches, a fact of which Amy was only too well aware. 'Poor old Billie, of course we are in the height of luxury to him no doubt, the men just love being in hospital these either soaking wet days or freezing cold.' [5]

There are two girls here I have made real friends with [Amy told her family, sounding positively schoolgirlish]. One is called Miss Adams and the other is a Miss Cliffe, one is ugly and a ripping good sort, one of the best, and the other is just adorable and very pretty, and I love them both, we are a team and do everything together . . . It's hardly stopped raining for the last 10 days until yesterday, when I had my ½ day, I went with Adam and Eve, as my two friends are called, to Paris-Plage by the train. We caught the first one in we could and had our hairs washed. The man in his effort to speak English to me asked me very politely "to take my hair off"! [4]

Hours off-duty were not always so entertaining.

Sunday, Monday & Tuesday we spent our off time doing up bunches
of flowers for the cemetery, every grave or rather every man had a
bunch of flowers put on his grave, over 500 of them & on Tuesday
several, about 20 of us Aunt Annie of course as well, took them up,
on a wheeled stretcher, & we carried them up in baths it's a good 20'
walk, & had them all on the graves by 6.30 a.m. & then went into a
service at the Mortuary Chapel. [4]

There is no indication why Amy wrote so disappointingly little about her
work in the wards. Perhaps she did not wish to upset her mother. Perhaps
the family had heard more than enough from Aunt Annie in the past. It may
be that the circumscribed life of women generally was the reason for Amy's
dwelling on the more trivial details of her life – or perhaps she thought it
was such details that would most interest her family.

Tell Elsie I don't know what I should do without the two green bags.
They hang up in my tent, one with collars & belts & the other with all
sorts of oddments. I do wish you could all just come over & see Aunt
Annie & me, it would be so much nicer to feel you knew what our
quarters were like.
. . . My bed was a difficulty it was so difficult to get warm but now I
have managed it, & think it'll do for the winter. I purchased a <u>very</u>
<u>large</u> cotton padded quilt for 17 frs. it sounds a lot I know, but it <u>is</u>
cold at nights in our huts. I must tell you [about] my bed, first I have
the mattress then a folded army blanket, then half the quilt, then half
the rug, then the rug & quilt are folded over me, & I have the two
army blankets, & dressing gown & for the last two nights I've really
slept well, & now I have my pillow I'm absolutely happy.'
    I have purchased a waterproof bag to carry my towels to the bath
also to put my nightie into & clothes when I'm there, as the bathroom
is a big cemented floored shed with six cubicle baths & some lavs, the
floors are often very wet & I can't bear to put anything on them & the
small creatures, only clean country friends, are rather abundant, so
I'm glad of my sack. [3]

By now the family at Tennyson's House must have been spending a considerable amount of time and money sending parcels to their relatives serving overseas.
    'Thank you my beloved for your kind offer to send me anything,' Amy
wrote on October 5th, 'a surprise parcel at intervals – Maids of Honour etc.
would be a great joy but I have everything I want.' Maids of Honour were

regularly included, being popular not only with Amy and Aunt Annie ('we ate them over her office fire' [5]) but also with Howard and Billie, the latter on one occasion eating three dozen at a sitting. [65]

Food was the most popular item in parcels sent to Amy. Meals provided for the nurses were basic, often cooked by V.A.Ds with little experience of cooking and certainly none in cooking for large numbers. In the Army, officers of a battalion, like those of the 8th East Surreys, could club together to pay for regular hampers to be sent out from Fortnum and Mason, but few nurses could afford such a luxury. So potted meat, turkey, ham, cake, butter and cream regularly came out to Étaples from Twickenham – anything to improve the diet and provide for the supper parties that were held in the huts. 'We've had such feasts lately, I really shall get fat,' Amy told them at home when acknowledging the arrival of one of their 'beautiful' parcels. 'Fancy Amy getting fat, 'ow 'orrible,' was Billie's reaction to that news [136]. He sought confirmation of the dreadful fact from his sister, telling his mother three weeks later that Amy 'denies that she is obese now (it is obese isn't it, & not obscene, I never can remember).' [149]

There were more mundane wants, of course. Hands suffered badly from hospital work. '[They] are just awful, finger & thumb tips all cracked & it's so difficult to keep them smooth in the least. I would love you to send me a really warm, easy to slip on pair of gloves, some lined woolly ones, not expensive ones but as warm as you can and grey in colour.' [4] Cuffs and underclothing wore out and had to be replaced ('combies and knickers' were even given as Christmas presents); an urgent request was made for the much needed macintosh hat that had blown away in the wind.

Then there were items that should surely have been provided by the hospital. 'What happened about the 6 lbs of permanganate of potash, were you able to get it? Aunt Annie rather wants it.' [3] And the following spring, writing from No. 2 Stationary Hospital in Abbeville: 'I would love a tin of knife powder, yes I mean it Knife powder please, we can't get it, here, & there are 50 knives to clean 3 times a day & sometimes more, & as many paper serviettes as you can send reasonably. My wants are rather strange I know, ordinary washing soda is another!! think of the dusters to be washed, & not a scrap of soap to be had & the saucepans & pots, oh, you should see our kitchen, today for example after 34 trays – absolutely the limit . . . Our kitchen is about the size of the pantry – no, larder – at home not a scrap larger!' [19]

Larger items were sometimes offered by friends and relations. 'Before I forget Aunt Annie has been given a typewriter so don't bother but how nice of the Percivals, we do so want a gramophone, there are about 2 for the wards, but there are such heaps of wards, we have to take it in turns.' [3]

Two letters later, the gramophone had arrived at Boulogne. 'We are so excited,' Amy reported. 'Colonel Kiddle has been asked to clear it & it will be sent on here as soon as possible.' [5]

Lastly there were various items that Amy requested from time to time for her living quarters. In this she was no different from her fellow volunteers. A present-day reader of letters and reminiscences of the period is struck by the way in which V.A.Ds newly arrived in France instantly set about improving their domestic surroundings.

My new hut, that I'm sharing with Miss Gordon, Aunt Annie's secretary is a little larger than my first one, & we have made it really quite comfortable, the only thing we want is a little more of that casement cloth Mother & I got at Breach, we can quite well do with another 6 yds, Miss Gordon & I were going to share it, so if Mother wouldn't mind getting it, I will send a postal order when it comes. [3]

It is almost as if by recreating home the V.A.Ds could blot out the horrors of the wards in which they worked. But Amy did not talk of horrors.

I am in an acute Surgical ward, with a very nice Sister, Sister Knight, she is so awfully good to me & anyone more patient with an idiot it would be impossible to find. The work is very light compared to St. Mary's & I never feel tired, although quite busy enough . . .

I'm in one of the wards where we only take the worst cases, & poor dears, they are bad. I can't tell you about them, but they are so good, & I'm awfully happy in the wards, we have not been so busy this last week, & that's why I was able to have a half day. I either get from 10 – 1 in the morning or 2 – 5 in the afternoon or 5 – 8, today it's 5 – 8 which means you are off from 5 for the rest of the day.

. . . We now have two trained nurses in our wards & myself, the dressings were too difficult for untrained people, & the responsibility too great for me, or the other V.A.D. to be left by ourselves when at any moment anything might happen, as ours were the worst cases, as soon as they can be moved, & are out of danger they go to England. [3]

We have had a busy time in the wards again [she wrote on November 4th], I was not able to take my times off, we had two very sad deaths. How I wish they would hurry up with helmets, our head cases are too terrible, & we had an amputation in yesterday, such a boy. We got a man home yesterday, who was not wounded, but he'd come in sick. He had 4 brothers killed at Mons, & the other brother has both feet off, so instead of his going to the convalescent Camp they fortunately let him go home. [4]

That man was indeed fortunate. Later in the war, when the shortage of men became acute, he would have been kept on the French side of the Channel, despite the sad family circumstances, and returned to the front as soon as he was fit.

As for the helmets, Amy would have been surprised to learn that two weeks previously the House of Commons had been assured that 'some thousands of helmets have already been issued.'[5] 'I know no reason why the troops should not be wearing the steel helmets issued to them,' the Under Secretary of State for War replied to a question in the House on December 9th. It is true that the first helmets had reached the 18th Division in November 1915, but they were only issued as trench stores, 6 per company of up to 250 men, which meant they had to be handed from sentry to sentry, providing protection for only a few. It was not until June 1916, just before the Battle of the Somme, that each man in the division had his own helmet. The East Surreys received theirs in time for Easter.

We totter round the village in steel helmets [Billie told Elsie on April 8th], & generally look a bit barmy, as the man who designed these helmets evidently had a massively developed brain, & fitted himself out against the Zeppos. [175a]

Everyone has a steel helmet now [he wrote to the family four days later], and I suppose you'll be pleased to hear I always wear one in the village. You want one there for the tiles and odd rafters which float down when you cough too loudly. [179]

As the letter was headed 'Back in the Wood', and later mentioned a 'Bosche' raid the previous night with 'an immense quantity of old iron in the air' this was another occasion when Billie's reassurances about his safety were only likely to cause his family greater concern.[6]

It has to be said that the helmets were not always welcomed. One divisional commander refused to allow them to be worn, considering that their use would encourage his men to get soft[7], and Raymond Asquith, returning to France after leave in May 1916, wrote to his wife, 'One fearful addition to the honours of War since I have been away is the steel helmet which we all have to wear now, when in the shell area. They are monstrously tiresome and heavy and I suppose if idiots like Pemberton Billing had not asked questions in Parliament about them we should have been allowed to go on with our comfortable caps.'[8] Their efficacy was doubted by some. One battalion of the North Staffordshire Regiment had their heads shaved before being sent into action on the Somme. When asked why, their Medical Officer, the only man allowed 'to keep his wool' as he put it, replied ominously, 'Head wounds galore.'[9] In fact the use of helmets reduced head wounds by seventy-five per cent.

NOTES

1. Helen Dey, obituary of Dame Ann Beadsmore Smith, *Q.A.R.A.N.C. Gazette*.
2. *Shell Out* & *Quinneys* were both London shows.
3. The Army had problems with pillows too. Billie had one provided by Elsie, but on October 19th wrote asking for another, 'fairly big and not rubbery water-proof as yours Elsie has perished in places & is no longer pneumatic.'
4. All officers hated censoring their men's letters, though Harold Macmillan was one of many who remembered it as a valuable experience for the insight it gave into the working class. 'It is a fearful nuisance, and I hate sort of prying into other people's affairs but it has to be done,' Howard told his mother in October 1914. 'Don't imagine this is an interesting job,' Billie said, in September 1915, and gave an example of the sort of letter he had to censor:

    No. *5270 Pt. Atkins,*
    No. *7 Platoon*
    B.E.F.

    Dear Ruth,
       Just a line hoping this will find you as it leaves me well at present Thank Ada for the chocolate Don't send any more gramaphone records as they would wake our officers even if we had a gramaphone Remember me to Jack I mustn't say any

more you know.
    Your Lonely
       Bert XXXXXX
P.C. Don't forget to remember Uncle Dick to send me some Woodbines.
'You know the sort of thing,' Billie finished, 'it palls after a few hundred – also you have to lick the envelopes up afterwards which is adding insult to mental injury!'
5. 21st October, 1915. Despite such assurances, *The Sphere* was only able to reproduce one small drawing of the proposed new British helmet in its November 13th issue. The French had been much quicker with protection for their men. On November 20th *The Sphere* devoted six full pages to drawings of French troops wearing their steel helmets in action.
6. R. Caton Woodville's drawing of the football incident on July 1st in the *Illustrated London News* shows all the East Surreys wearing steel helmets, except for one officer who bears a strong resemblance to Billie. However, the drawing has a distinct *Boy's Own Paper* flavour to it, despite the assistance the artist received in its preparation from one of the East Surrey wounded, so too much reliance should not be put on its accuracy.
7. Middlebrook, p.38.
8. Jolliffe, p.263.
9. Martin, p.85.

6 NO DANGER AT ALL

Billie was constantly reassuring those at home about his own safety. Their confidence in such reassurances, however, was disturbed by the talk of some wounded 8th East Surreys at a local hospital.

How awfully interesting that Miss Cheetham should have some of our chaps in her hospital; lucky beggars they are. Of course it's all rot about my being too venturesome. It's only because I will have the sentries at night looking over the parapet the whole time and not bobbing up & down, as you can't possibly get accustomed to the dark like that and watch properly, and secondly I won't tell anyone to look over without doing so myself and, if necessary, with new draft men for instance, talking to them a minute or two till they get confidence. But that's nothing at all. I'll take jolly good care of myself, as much as possible you can bet your shoes (I forget if ladies wear boots). [51]

He reassured his family again, several weeks later:

My invariable rule is:– Unless you're directly helping to kill a German don't run the tiniest chance of getting killed by a German, unless some order necessitates it. [88]

Nursing the wounded gave Miss Cheetham some idea of the needs of those at the front. 'Miss Cheetham sent me a piece of soap & a towel, a trifle suggestive, I admit, but very welcome, not that I'm short myself,' Billie later reported; 'and a box of 100 cigarettes which was rather a brick, as I don't smoke[1]; still I didn't have to go far to find 100 places to put them!' [74]

The final straw, as far as the family's peace of mind was concerned, must have come with a letter from Billie describing an incident ordered, foolishly one would have thought, on the night of a full moon.

Last day in billets
26.IX.15

Dear Familio,

. . . Three nights ago I had a rather quaint job, namely to inspect our barbed wired carefully on a front of about 200 yards. We started about 1.30 a.m. and no sooner over the parapet than the dear old moon came out & lit the place like day. The Huns are about 150 yards away here. Half an hour before we started, there had been one of the heaviest thunderstorms I've met. Picture the mud! Some moisture. Owing to the moon, all the work had to be done absolutely flat on one's stomach. Old tins, bottles & stones let alone the wire itself, all contributed to the fun. After about an hour, ___ it all noted down, its thickness, condition etc. Half a mile down a lake (commie trench) and 5 hours rest on a stretcher which I found in an old dugout and up again this time to make an accurate map of the trenches themselves. Then a 5 mile march home and when we got home we were told it was the wrong piece of front!!!! It wasn't our mistake or anyone's really, but the plans had been altered. The result was that we had the same job the next night but one. That is last night. Last night it was distinctly interesting as I had to lay a row of pegs, visible by day to us, but invisible to the Huns, on an accurate straight line (done by prismatic compass) at night; all this clear in front of our furthest advanced wire. Now getting the straight line is easy enough, but what is nasty is being in front of our barbed wire, as there are only a very few twisting ways through it and very hard to find at night. Also of a party of six, I was the only one armed, & that was my revolver! Just before we started I was warned to look out for a protective row of German snipers, guarding a party of Huns who had been seen mending their own wire which had been shelled a bit in the afternoon. It was a cheery bit of advice, wasn't it?

It took us just an hour to cover 400 yards this time, you see you've got to steady the compass every 10 yards to make certain you're going straight. Then each peg must be looked at from both sides to ensure being properly placed. A star shell landed about 3 yards from us & blazed, it seemed for hours, just by my side. I have never lain so still and flat in my life. I suppose 40 pairs of German eyes were watching that shell, & at that spot, I didn't know of an opening in our wire to bolt to for at least 200 yards. We waited a minute or two but no one appeared to have seen us, so we carried on. I managed to hit off the opening in our trenches to about 2 yards which was not bad work when done purely by compass. I expect this sounds a bit more

dangerous than it is. With picked men and great care, you're quite
safe, provided you don't have bad luck. I think we did pass a German
about 15 yards away. But we were 6 to one & he couldn't tell that we
weren't all round, so lay jolly low himself. It was rather funny as we
only had one revolver between us & our entrenching tools. Of course
we left him alone, it was a curious situation & of course it may not
have been a Hun at all but I must say it looked like one. We went off
home after collecting our kit which we'd left in the trench, as you
don't want anything that rattles on you. I'd arranged for cocoa with
some Sappers [Royal Engineers] at a village about 2 miles back so we
breakfasted there at 11.30 pm and went home. Considering it didn't
stop raining during the whole trip from billets up to the trenches &
while we were at work & back again you can imagine the state we
were in. I'm now in borrowed clothes as all mine are soaking. I got
into bed at 2 this morning. The C.O. sent for me this morning &
asked me the names of the men who'd come with me, & this is a dead
secret, I hear he has recommended me for a Military Cross. Of course,
you're not to mention this, as it's only a recommendation & may lead
to nothing, but I know the Divisional General said he'd try to get me
something. Of course it's absolute rot, fussing about it, as officers go
out patrolling most nights, it's only generals & people who never go
near the firing line, who think anything of it.

You remember I told you about my Captaincy, well that took five
months & people you told must have thought it was only a rumour,
so don't go spreading this about as I should feel such a fool, if it
comes to nothing, which is quite likely.

I managed to get into [Albert] the other day, where that Church is
with the falling statue. It leans right across the road, and fairly makes
you stare. I bagged some bricks off the wall and a piece of white tile
from the roof (I think) of a little porch. I'll send you each a piece . . .

Cheery Oh, now, remember dead silence about the M.C. please.
    With crowds of love to you all
        from
            Billie
P.S. I am also sending you a tin on a hooked wire, as I found it on
some advanced trip wire, the other night. It's got a bullet hole in it &
had a few pebbles in it.[2] [65]

I think I've got that old M.C. alright, [he wrote two days later] but
don't breathe a word to anyone outside the family yet. I hope to hear
definitely fairly soon. Anyhow I know the Divisional General is very

bucked & has promised to try and get me something. As I explained
to you, it's all rot to fuss about a little show like that, but the ribbon
looks very pretty on a tunic!!! [67]

Unfortunately politics mattered as much as deeds when medals were
being handed out, as Billie recounted a week later:

The Colonel told me yesterday he was sorry but I was not to have the
M.C. Our Brigadier & Divisional General both recommended me, but
the Army Corps Commander[3] said no. Because, so I was told by the
C.O., he wanted to give all the decorations he could to his old Regular
Division in his Army Corps!
    So that's that. I'm now what's called, 'noted for future occasions'.
Which I hope doesn't mean that when the next peculiarly villainous
job is going, I shall be for it! Never mind, better luck next time, it's
something to be recommended by the Div. Gen. [72]

The award of decorations seems to have been very arbitrary to the non-
military mind. The following year the recommendation that Captain
Gimson, the battalion medical officer, be awarded the V.C. for his courage
and devotion to duty on the first day of the Somme would also be down-
graded, in his case to the D.S.O. The reason given was that a similar recommendation had already been made on behalf of another medical officer in
the division but Major Irwin thought the reason was quite different.
'General Maxse, who was commanding our division, came up next day [i.e.
July 2nd] and found me writing out a recommendation, and in particular
Gimson's recommendation for the V.C. He told me that it wasn't sufficiently
journalistic and he wrote it for me. I think that's why he didn't get it.'[4]
    Irwin, who commanded the 8th East Surreys on July 1st was, like Gimson,
awarded the D.S.O. for his part in that action – rather oddly, one might
think. 'I was given a choice. I was told that I could have a brevet majority or
a D.S.O. and I said that I'd rather have something I could pin on my jacket
than a brevet majority and that's how it happened.'
    The rejection of Billie's recommendation did not mean that decorations
were never awarded; several Military Crosses were won by the battalion
during the winter of 1915/16, including one within the next fortnight. For the
first time Billie's resolute good spirits failed when describing this incident.

We're all rather depressed to-day as young (M) Thorne was shot dead
last night, out on a patrol. The man with him came back and said it
was about 5 yds from the German trenches so volunteers were sent

out to find him. Two parties were seen & machine gunned back into our trenches without loss, but a third party went right to the place & couldn't find him. Finally his brother arrived (C.Thorne), and although the senior officer present had forbidden any officer to go out, he hopped out & searched till he found his brother in an old shell hole & picked him up alone & carried him in, & then absolutely collapsed. Poor chap, I'm glad I wasn't there.

I liked young Thorne awfully, he was one of our very best subalterns, and is an enormous loss to D. Coy. Old Thorne his brother, the old Cambridge blue may get the V.C. for it, but I don't know, it was an awfully plucky thing to do, though every officer present volunteered at once but that was of course stopped. [66]

Young Thorne had gone out on patrol with the intention of bombing a German sniper and of finding whether certain craters were held by the enemy, at a point where the front lines were no more than ninety yards apart. The ground was pitted with shell holes and torn by explosions, making it difficult to locate anything or anybody, and was covered by machine-gun fire. Cornelius Thorne, hearing what had happened, came at once to the scene with his servant, 'and went straight out into the open, fol-lowed by Pte Hine, neither of them making any pretence at taking cover.'[5]

Thorne received the Military Cross – 'It's a small consolation, but I'm jolly glad; his people will be so pleased' [74] – and Private Hine the Distinguished Conduct Medal, both awards being presented by General Monro, Com-mander of the Third Army, the morning after the battalion's return to Ville-sur-Ancre at the end of the tour.

It had been an unpleasant tour, quite apart from the loss of young Thorne.

The rain is very reliable & has hardly failed us 3 days. I'm in borrowed trousers as all my bags got soaked before we came up & are now in my valise, soaking everything else in it, way back in billets . . . The rain is awfully depressing. [66]

I wonder if you realise [Billie asked three days later] what the weather means to a colony of people living practically entirely in the open, in ditches so to speak, for 8 or 10 days on end. [68]

Besides the rain, the battalion had also been subjected to a considerable variety of artillery fire from the Germans during this tour, which they were too short of ammunition to return. It was four weeks before Billie was able to write that 'We've at last got some trench mortars, and now we give the Huns

a copy of his own Hell <u>when</u> we can get the ammunition.' [85] In spite of this
there seems to have been a ridiculously schoolboyish attitude about the
situation.

We have rather a sporting crowd of huns opposite, as when we
shell them they crawl out the next night & put German flags in the
shell holes! Also this morning they stuck up a white flag of sorts and
big dummy man, we all blazed at it & they signalled the shots,
bulleyes, inners & magpies, with another flag!! Several times they've
put up targets for us.[6] [68]

I'm afraid you've been a bit starved lately for letters [he wrote on
October 2nd], but I've been <u>fairly</u> busy, you see, I'm writing this just
100 yds straight from the German firing line, in our Coy. H.Q.s dug
out. We are sapping out twelve odd mines from our trenches and
these turn out 1500 sand bags a day[7], which we have to carry away
and pile up in odd places, the trench here is very narrow & bad and
close, so there's a lot to see to. I expect we'll be relieved from here in
about 3 days now, and I hope we'll go back to where we came from,
as it was a ripping billet. Pearce and another officer are jawing away
hard so this is a bit disconnected. Our dug out is haunted by Artillery
F.O.O.s (Forward observation officers) and mining R.E. officers, <u>and</u>
the tunneling coy., so with ourselves we are a crowd sometimes, it's
nice and sociable of course, but worries me to death, if I want to write
or sleep. The trials of responsibility!! I don't 'arf suppose! [69]

5.10.15   *Still Up*
Dear Fam,
    Just a note. All's very well & happy. It's been raining this morning
and I am afraid it looks as if it may keep on a bit. Still it's not so cold.
We had frost three or 4 nights. This morning the Brethren elected to
jerk over four rifle grenades & four sausages, small. We at once
replied with 4 rifle grenades (2 slap in their trenches) and 6 shells
from the artillery. There has been a respectful silence ever since! Last
night we bombed two of their advanced listening posts, where we
heard scratching about with shovels. Yesterday P.G. Heath
harangued them in German through an enormous megaphone. Told
them their officers were afraid to tell them the truth! That 8 Zeps had
been brought down over London! That the English had taken Ostend
and Antwerp! the French had taken 200,000 prisoners!! finishing with
a string of the most awful oaths he could remember! We got no

audible reply but the wind was in our favour. And I don't suppose
they had a megaphone handy.
. . . Cheero and love to all, we're going down in two days
  Billie [72]

Reports of air raids on London had provoked a somewhat muddled dia-
tribe about the war effort.

The Zeps seem to have had a great time in town that was only four,
wait till you get about 40 at a time, then perhaps London will realise
what war is, and buck herself a bit because she's not making half the
effort that France is, & yet she's doing <u>more</u> I think, but she jolly well
ought to, having done nothing but crow about her power & resources
for years & years, now's the time to really use them. England is of
course the one hope against 'Hunnism' now, and I hope she'll realise
it. [56]

London seems to be getting a little idea of what W A R means [he
wrote on September 26th]. You'll soon get used to wondering if a
bomb's coming on your nasal organ at night. It's quite an exhiliarating
feeling, I assure you, after a week or two! Better paint out Tennyson's
House on the doorway!!

When at last the tour ended, Billie announced his return to billets with a
postcard – 'Am feeling much better after a ripping hot bath & change. I <u>had</u>
been afraid to sit on the ground for fear of making it dirty!' [73] – before writing at greater length.

In the same Billets
V.s.A.
10.10.15

Sunday
Dear Mother and Everyone,
   At last I can have a nice, long, uninterrupted(?) chat with you all, so
make yourselves comfy and listen.
   At the moment I'm in charge of 2 cooks, 1 groom and a puppy we
found, all that is left of the company at the moment, as we are the
"Battalion on Divisional Duties," and are scattered all over the place,
doing odd jobs, such as packing transports, digging, loading coal,
unloading supplies at Railhead etc. etc. What was left had Church
Parade and are now enjoying hot baths in an old mill here. I had my
hot bath the first night after we got back and – wow! – as

Umslopagaas (in Alan Quatermain) would probably have said – it was good. They put in some sheep-dip solution, which is guaranteed to kill everything!!!!!! Sorry! This morning I was able to go to an early service in an old schoolroom. It's the first time for 3 months I think, and the fact that I was the only one of "this congregation here present" made it none the less impressive and helpful!

News is very uncertain particularly on our front, in the North [he wrote on October 3rd, as the battle of Loos continued], & our own chance of a show seems to be dwindling, rapidly, worse luck, but I suppose you'll be pleased! [70]

Of course as you know I've not been very near all the recent fighting, but I have experienced 'a certain liveliness and considerable artillery activity'! In fact during the last three days of our last 12 in the trenches C. Coy was having a pretty rotten time of it. We were heavily shelled with those inventions of the Devil, trench mortars. They chuck a variety of eggs, varying from a thing about the size of a 3lb jam pot to an aerial torpedo, which has 250 lbs of explosive alone in it! The advantage about them is that you can see them in the air, of course you can't see the shells, but you can hear them. Everyone calls the trench mortar's (miner-werfer) egg (miner) a sausage, and I'm sending you home a piece of sausage skin! These sausages are fused and do not explode on percussion like an H.E. shell. They may go off in the air, or they may land with a thud and go off in 2 or 3 seconds. I'm sending you the nose caps for the fuses of two which landed just near me. They're mostly 60 & 80 lbs in weight, some are 112, and the aerial Tor far, far more of course. They're not built on the right principle luckily for doing damage, as they are too inaccurate for that, only one in a shower of 20 land in the trench, usually. The idea of them is purely frightfulness, as they make the most colossal noise and the concussion is enormous. Pearce for instance was blown down some steps into a dug out, Bertie Clare was chucked through the door of his, I had my cap pressed over my ears by one that went off in the air, & so on. We had three afternoons running of that, and very very few men hurt, though everyone was shaken a lot, some pretty badly. I'm as right as rain myself, but I don't smoke or anything, so I ought to be alright. One notices on those occasions who are the men you can trust & who are the other sort. There were precious few of the other sort. Perhaps you get some idea of the shock when I tell you that a candle was blown out in a dugout 100' from where one landed.

Added to this Pearce & I knew that the Germans had pierced our protective mines and were only 6 ft from the trench and had stopped digging and were charging up to 'blow'!!! Our own Mining officers had told us in the afternoon and said they hoped to be able to charge up and 'blow' first. This would of course blow in the German gallery from behind and cut all wires and fuses, which is the object of counter mining of course. Knowing it was a race as to which blew first, it was a pretty tense afternoon, and one had to lie quiet about it, even to the other officers as once that sort of thing gets round everyone gets most awfully jumpy. It was our last night up and we were mighty glad to be out of the place, I can tell you. Our sappers (some of the bravest men on earth) won the race by simply superhuman efforts and exploded their little countermine quite successfully, thereby cutting off the big German mine. A jolly fine performance . . .

While I'm on the subject about these sausages you can see them coming and hear them too, they make a low hum in the air. Nearly all go off after they've fallen about 2 or 3 seconds. The distance you can run in those 2 secs. would astonish the Olympians. When a big one lands in the trench, which is only about 1 in 20, they do do some damage and men often get temporarily buried. They gave us about 300 one afternoon!! The safest thing to do is to look over the parapet & watch for them and then you can see where to run for safety. It's pretty exciting and when you see two at once you don't want to hesitate long where to go to. A dug out is an absolute death trap as you may so easily get buried, and men will collect in them, naturally. It's like putting all your eggs in one basket. I think the worst time I'll ever have was when one (a small jam-jar sized one as it happened, but I didn't know at the time) landed plum on the roof of our dug out. Pearce and I were both in. It fell with a dull thud and that next two seconds, or was it 2 hrs. was pretty quiet. And then she went off just the other side of 3 ft of earth and timber from our heads. I never heard such a row in my life. We looked on the roof at daylight next morning and there was just one row of timber and about an inch of earth left over our heads! I must confess I felt a bit jumpy myself, even after we got back to billets the first day . . .

I think I've dilated enough on sausages now. Our artillery answered them with as much heavy H.E. as they could spare, and by jove it sounded grand to hear it whizz over & fairly crash into the German lines. Nice thoughts for Sunday, and I've been to Church, I should say service, twice!!

After that first day's sausaging we issued the men with rum to

steady them a bit and by jove they liked it. It took me 2½ hrs. to issue
it to the Company! Each man has an egg-cup full and it has to be
drunk at once in the presence of the issuing officer and it's some job. I
visited our further crater listening-posts[8] (where a cough means a
bomb) with this beastly tin hanging from my mouth, with the egg cup
floating in it, & knocking on the sides, as I crawled along in utter
darkness in the mud, up a tunnel about 2'6" square! Oh it's a great
game this.

It was very interesting seeing one's underclothes again when we
got here, and they hadn't altered much!!!! That shampoo is great stuff!
The hot bath was glorious, the second really epoch-making event
since we left Codford, of the quiet nights. The first event being my
other hot bath, at H [Heilly] about 5 weeks ago. I should think my
sleeping bag thought a stranger was crawling in!! After 12 really good
days you don't like to sit on the grass for fear of making it dirty!! I
must knock off for lunch now. I say, I hope I'm not frightening you at
all. I'm as fit and happy as ever and not a bit fed up or homesicky, so
don't worry a scrap, please. If you worry I shall, so there . . . [74]

Some time previously he had complained about the effect of binoculars.
After going up the line

you soon start rings round the eyes, & little headaches, chiefly from
looking through glasses . . . Could you get me a smallish telescope,
about £3 or £4 and send it out very carefully. When I get it I'll send
back my glasses, which you could easily sell for £4 anywhere, they
cost £5.10 and are awfully good, but not so useful in trenches, for
looking through loop holes & crannies, where you can only get one
eye. That's important & I meant to ask before. I don't mind if you
spend £5 on a good telly & I'll pay the difference from what you get
on my glasses. I'd like that soon. Don't forget I've got to carry it so
keep it light powerful & strong. [56]

At home, meanwhile, Stanley was equipping himself for Egypt. 'Of
course Stanley can have my camp equipment,' Billie wrote, 'but he'll get an
allowance of £17.10.0 for it himself; & I might want mine.' [66] 'I'm so glad
[Stanley's] getting on all right, tell him not to call anyone above a Brigadier 'a
fool' to his face!' he advised in his next letter. 'It's not done! . . . Re glasses. I
paid £5.10 for them & Stanley ought to pay £4.10 I think. They're very
powerful. This money must be a cheque (or cash) to Mother & of course,
Mother, you'll keep the change towards parcels. I'm the bloomin' millio-

naire of the party now-a-days.' [67] He wrote again two weeks later, on
October 14th.

Of course I don't want more than £4 for the glasses, just as Stanley
likes, I ought to give them to him as it's for the great Show. It's like
taking war profits! I don't quite like the idea of sitting out here,
costing so much. I think everyone who could ought to hand in his pay
which he doesn't need now. Take my case, why should I be able to
save £70 odd, over & above what I've spent, & I've not cramped
myself a bit? I really think they pay temporary offs too much.
Anyhow, by way of keeping the money circulating in England instead
of lying at Cox's, here is £5 which I insist on you, Elsie & Doff, the
family in fact, spending on pure enjoyment. I should like, but I won't
insist on this, to picture you having a really nice little dinner
somewhere & then some good seats at some theatre you all want to
see. It would do you all good & I should like it, which is the great
thing. If he could come, I should like Nulli [Elsie's husband-to-be] to
join, of course. [76]

'I'm so glad you had a decent evening with me, so to speak,' he wrote two
weeks later, on All Saints' Day. 'I enjoyed it no end.' [92] 'I'm glad you had
Billie's little spree, or rather big one,' Amy said. 'It was just like him and
how we should just love to have been with you.' [4]
   His letters told of various activities during life at rest.

I go for my french lessons to tea with D coy, where there is a
charming little lady, who understands all we say and corrects our
more blatant howlers. Shrieks of fun and roars of laughter! Nowadays
there is a Divisional Cinema Theatre, offs. a franc, men 30 centimes.
Occasionally there are variety turns. I've not been yet but shall to-
morrow, if I can . . . Twigg went into Amiens yesterday to try & get
some whisky & failed dismally. So here we are with some shampoo &
tainted water. As a matter of fact there is biere Anglaise & Grenadine,
let alone vin ord.
   Really I'm in the lap of luxury and today the sun is out for a change,
there's a nip in the air and a distinct twinge in my knees. Also I've
had toothache for 3 days. But that's gone now & was the fault of
whoever sent me all those sweets. I forget whether it was you or
Muff, you I believe. [74]

Dear Ma,

. . . Roland Heath, now in one of the Tunneling Coys, has just arrived
on a Douglas, so of course I must have a spin. You don't mind, do
you? Last night I went over to the Div. Cinema. An A.S.C. convoy of
about 20 cars called at our billets & took us over & waited till 8 &
brought us all home. It was a change & really a fairly good show. [79]

Rumours were circulating about moves further afield.

They say we shall send some more Divisions from round here to
Salonica.[9] I should like to see Greece & all that, but I don't fancy
myself on the sea at this time of year. Too jolly dangerous! I wouldn't
leave my little muddy trench for that! I hope you all do realise that a
trench is the safest thing in the world to be in. By now you must have
got that quaint idea that it's risky out here, out of your heads. I'm
really not exaggerating. It's only now & then when you have to leave
the trench that there's any danger. The sweet-natured Huns touched
off a wopping great mine about 2 hrs after we'd been relieved from
our last bed of roses (don't forget the thorns) but luckily we had
cleared out from there as we were ourselves just going to countermine
them, so we had no casualties. We ourselves were well on the way
here at the time, luckily. [76]

'I don't think you need worry about the casualties up North, I think
they've done all right, and the posish. is now quite promising, so far as we
can here,' [76] Billie wrote on October 14th on the subject of Loos; two days
later he was giving his 'Smiling Senior Soeur' his view of the world situation.

I don't think I should be raising your hopes unduly, if I say that the
Germans are really at the end of their tether, and in a jolly bad way!
They may keep it up a little longer But they must cave in soon now.
You must, and I think you do, look at the thing in its proper
perspective. Don't be influenced by casualties, or wounded people's
accounts, don't above all things believe all you see in the papers.
Sometimes they are too optimistic & sometimes they are hopelessly
pessimistic. You'll hear a lot about a place called 'Pit (or Fosse) 8' &
whole articles on the Hohenzollern & the Kaiser William Redoubts.
They are all absolutely Pawn's moves in the game & I think you do
realise all that. Russia is the great thing. Without doubt the German
Staff staked their all on beating Russia in one enormous battle,
whereas the Grand Duke hopped neatly out in the nick of time &

buried himself in the wilds of Russia, thereby shortening his communications and making everything easier and safer. Of course the effect on the Balkans was nearly as good as if the Huns had caught the Russians napping, & wiped the floor with them, instead of hustling them off home again. I should say Bulgaria has put her foot in it this time pretty securely. Rumour has it that we are going to give up the Darders[10], which is excellent, if true, & means lots more shells & men for France, or Serbia. [80]

Two weeks later, on November 2nd, he wrote again about the general situation.

Do you remember my making some very optimistic remarks about the duration of the war a little while ago, well I still absolutely believe what I said then. Everything goes to prove that the Huns are getting fed up, more fed up than we are I mean. The only danger to my mind is that some near sighted and fat headed people will say 'oh anything to stop the War' and when Germany proposes terms of peace, jump at them & make peace, on the pretext that we've lost so much already & so many valuable lives. I do hope that won't happen. That's just what Germany will want, when she sees she's failed in the Balkans, as she's pretty sure to sooner or later, a decent 5 years breathing space to refit, and then she'll start again. If the people at home don't let us down, we can stick this indefinitely and smash the huns down every time we want to, à la advance in the North & Champagne, provided we've got the munitions. I do hope everyone is giving the munition workers the credit due to them for the success of our first bound in the North. People are a bit gloomy because we didn't clear through all the works etc. up there, at our first bound, which is of course rot. It was the strongest part of the whole line, which we completely smashed up. Of course there were a few mistakes, but most of them completely unavoidable. I do wish people at home could realize the enormous difficulties of a show like that. The food & water question is far harder than the ammunitions. Your own shells destroy all the road which you yourself want to use directly you're through, that's only one small point illustrating the sort of thing one's apt to overlook. If you don't destroy the road, then the hun can get food and ammunitions up and supports.

   There must be some very nice & delicate questions to decide in Serbia now. Whether to relieve the Serbians and leave Bulgaria or go for Bulgaria & leave the Serbians. That seems to be the posish. I hear the French are a bit peevish because we didn't, so they say, send more men to Serbia. [93]

[The Huns have] not declared peace yet of course [he wrote on October 15th, while still in billets] & so we shall continue to frown across some grass at a line of peculiarly dull looking muddy chalk. Such is life at the moment. With any luck the huns may hop out either in front & advance, or leg it for Berlin. Anyhow I should be interested to see a German, I have heard about, & from them, but not called in person. [78]

His only contact so far with the enemy had not been pleasant.

We found the skeleton of a German in his equipment, in the wood where we were digging. Rather gruesome, but I'm afraid I've been cured of squeamishness by now at unpleasant sights, not to callousness of course. You can't get callous about that sort of thing, but you can school yourself out of staring at people who've been hit, help them along a bit without feeling fainty, as I confess I did at first. [76]

He sounded somewhat callous, however, when describing one incident, though it was not one that he had witnessed himself.

The other morning it was very misty & you couldn't see across No Man's Land, when suddenly the mist vanished & exposed about 60 Germans all out putting up barbed wire well in front. They fairly bolted but there happened to be a machine gun opposite & he also happened to be awake, bagged 35 of them! Pretty good. The Bosches were awfull[y] sick about it & sausaged the place for about 3 hrs but did no harm. Rather a comic little incident on the whole. [80]

The battalion went up to the trenches again during the night of October 16th, after a tiring time in billets. 'That awful digging,' Billie had said at one point. 'Starts at 5.30 a.m. & we get back at 4 p.m. Rather a long stretch.' [79] 'On the whole I shall be jolly glad to be up again,' he told Elsie, 'as we've been rather rushed and hustled about this time in billets, in fact the men haven't been really rested at all as they should be. But we are going to a very 'cushy' part of the line this time, no mines or sausages & practically no rifle grenades or whiz-bangs, the huns being nearly 300' away. Not at all like our last tour, which was too exciting to be pleasant at times.' [80]

NOTES

1. 'I've become a most terrible cigarette smoker lately,' Billie said, six months later, 'it's a bad business, but I shall be able to shake it off when we get back to some other distractions.' [177]
2. Tin cans were hung on the trip wire which was strung ten yards in front of the trench parapet in order to trap any Germans who might approach at night.
3. Lt.-Gen. Sir Thomas Morland, reputedly one of the better corps commanders.
4. Interview with Imperial War Museum.
5. *History of the 55th Brigade*. There are a number of accounts of this incident, with variations – the fatal shot is described as going through the head by one, through the heart by another, while Christian Carver, the F.O.O. on whose bed the body was laid, said that the single bullet had gone through Thorne's shoulder as well as both lungs. All accounts agree that the elder Thorne adored his brother, rushed over the top oblivious of German machine-gun fire and despite their difference in size (photographs show him as the smaller of the two) returned with his brother on his back.
6. 'The Germans just here have been very comic lately,' Christian Carver wrote home on September 30th, the same day as Billie. 'After we had been strafing them a good bit, they put up a large notice with "Chuck it!" written on it . . . Yesterday they put up a row of 8 stones on their parapet, and a Sergeant-Major who is a crack shot, started knocking

them off from right to left. After he had done four, they picked up the rest and threw them at us.'
7. Saps were communication lines, in this case for laying mines. It must be remembered that in the front line all activity had to be carried out below ground level or risk a sniper's bullet. Generally speaking, trenches were dug down, while saps were dug outwards from an existing trench. All soil excavated for whatever reason had to be removed to the rear, as any sign of white chalk on the surface would alert the enemy to the digging. A battalion in the trenches consequently used an enormous number of sandbags, 'about 10,000 a week if it's busy,' Billie said. 'Our brigade had a reserve of 250,000 sandbags when we landed in our fighting sector, so we are well off & have as many as we can fill with the men available for filling. I believe in other places they use heaps more than that.' [43]
8. Listening posts were either in concealed or underground positions out in No Man's Land, or in mine galleries, in the latter case in order to listen for sounds of the enemy mining underneath.
9. Sent to assist the Serbian army which was being driven into the mountains of Albania with devastating losses. The allied force was too small and arrived too late to assist on this occasion.
10. The rumours, though accurate, were premature, as the main evacuation from Gallipoli did not take place until the night of December 18th, ten weeks after this letter was written.

7 A COLD AUTUMN

'If I think I shall be out here for the winter which I do think at present,' Billie had written the previous August, after only his second night in the trenches, 'there will be a lot of things I'll be asking for, in the way of warm togs.' Even in August the nights were cold; he was sleeping then 'in a great coat, a tommies one, Mother's scarf, on Elsie's pillow & my pack, and in my Jaegar cardigan & of course the rest of my uniform complete and fully dressed, but I don't truly burn with the heat about 3 in the morning.' [30]

No. 1   UP
                                                                18.10.15
. . . It's awfully cold. Please send: one very thick long-sleeved long in body high in neck, sweater. Must be dark colours. Sort of enormous seaman's jersey. This is very urgent. VBL *Bill* [81]

No. 2   18.10.15
About this sweater: it must be as thick as poss. as light as poss. with the thickness. Must go up round the neck almost to the ears. Must have long sleeves. Must stretch down at least halfway down thigh. Must be dark in colour. Must come out here at once. All in one piece and no buttons. [82]

Mrs. Nevill sent what was needed, as always. 'The sweater is just what I had pictured in my mind,' Billie wrote on November 3rd.

                                                                     UP
                                                                19.X.15
Cheer up Familio,
    I fear my latest Arctic callings may have chilled your kindly hearts. All is now fairly well.
    This tour, as the facetious Staff call our visits to the firing line, we are in an extraordinarily quiet part of the front. Nothing doing at all.

A sort of rest camp, about 230 yds from the Wily Willies and their soaring sausages. They always put the people in here after that hot bit I was in last time.

My dug out is at present in the hands of the builders & decorators in the shape of Peachy, the priceless (5 frs a week). He (the builders, decorators, candlestick makers etc.) is now papering the roof with sandbags to keep the mice from danger by falling down my throat as I lie, drinking deep of the 'cokey' fumes of my brazier. The book says "no braziers to be used in dug outs", which is the sort of slush they do volunteer from their armchairs beyond the base; however since the hand of man, or a whiz bang, has provided me with a chimney, I break this rule nightly. The first night I <u>was</u> a <u>trifle</u> cold & in consequence of that you received those wild p.c.s about sweaters, which I still stick to absolutely. One grey, four legged, enthusiast, did fall from the roof, bounce off my pillow and ricochet into a bucket of water, where he ended his career fighting bravely.

Luckily we've had fine weather so far and no rain – touch wood – (thanks) – but even then an open plate of bacon & eggs carried half a mile up a 'commy' loses some of that warm juicy consistency which should always characterise the Briton's invariable breakfast dish! . . .

I never slept a wink the first night up, but lay & shivered, silently cursing the Kaiser. Next morning I sent down to Jimmy i.e. Dr. Gimson, the M.O. (Doff met him in the train at Codford) who is the prince of sportsmen, and he pinched a blanket for me from somewhere.[1] No inquiries, please. Now the kindly & farseeing Govt. has issued one blanket per man to last the whole winter, so we use a few at a time & hope the war will end soon. Last night I slept for the 3 hrs which I was allowed for sleep, warm & snug, & shall do the same in future, I hope.

This afternoon – nerve yourselves for a shock – I washed my forehead and shaved!! I expect we shall be here about 10 days and I think that amount of washing, at 2 day intervals won't be too much to ask! If you take your coat off your cardigan's hair stands on end with indignation, so it will be interesting to see my shirt again when we get to billets once more. We can hear the Northern Bombardments when the wind's right [presumably at Loos, thirty-five miles to the north]. I should say those guns would shift some earth, if they landed in a trench . . .

Up here one officer off duty per firing-line-company goes down to a meal at Batt. H.Q.s where they can cook anything . . . We have enough whisky & soda to last easily, & I am O.C. Rum so rest assured

of my complete comfort . . .
Good bye floods of love
   Billie [83]

UP

20.X.15

Dear Mother,
    . . . I've been down to lunch at H.Q.s to get a hot meal, which was
rather spoilt, as a social outing, owing to casualties coming down
from that hot trench I was in before. [84]

UP (night) 20.x.15

Dear People All,
    I have been weighing over in my mind and I think, as you've been
so good about not getting nervous about me, that I will tell you about
to-day, and this morning in particular. Before I start I want you to
understand that it didn't happen where I am now but where I was last
time, about 400 yds along the line from here. I was on duty from 2
a.m. to 6 a.m.; at 4.30 our miners exploded a small countermine
underground where I was last time. I'd been warned by telephone of
it and it was quite a small affair, just a tremble in the earth where I
was standing in my trench, 400 yds away. Well all was quiet till at
5.40 I was nearly thrown from a sitting position on a ledge on to the
ground, the whole earth fairly rocked; I jumped up and looked over
the trench and saw – well – the most awe-ful sight imagineable. There
was a cloud of smoke, hundreds of feet into the air, all pink in colour,
as it was lit by a sheet of flame, – well – I can't give its height in feet &
that conveys nothing if I could. The tongue of flame was without
exaggeration, about the size of that big clump of five trees in the
bottom half of Marble Hill Park, Nr. Hammertons! I've heard since
that it was by far the biggest mine there has been on the Western
Front, the whole war, beating Hill 60 & Ypres into fits; and we've
several mining officers here who've been out mining all last winter.
My men were all ready for any emergency, & of course my place is
with them, much as I longed to go & help poor B Coy, so all I could
do was to ring B Coy up and tell them we were absolutely ready to
lend a hand and offering them men & extra tools for digging.
However they said they had enough men & tools. So I waited till my
duty was over at 6, dismissed the company to dug outs, except of
course the sentries, & slunk off to B. Coy. The trenches are bad &
narrow there and the congestion is awful when parties meet each
other. Having spent 7 days in those trenches luckily I knew my way

about. The B Coy. officers were all in front, organising rescue parties for our miners who were buried in places, & doing the work which was most urgent, such as clearing out the trenches where they'd caved in & also steadying the men who had to fire as the Huns sent out some parties to take the crater. The crush in front was hopeless, though they did some splendid work. Two sergeants of ours went down shafts & fetched up 'gassed' miners till they fainted themselves, they saved 5 lives between them & are up for V.Cs. I'm afraid the air pump men (not E. Surreys) left their posts in places, but these were taken by our men (B Coy that is) & ventilation was soon restored. Obviously I could be of no use in front so I went back to the head of the main 'commy' just behind the firetrench and there – ! As I said the B Coy officers were all in front; & here I found a mass of men all rushing about in the most utter confusion. Scores of miners in their shirt sleeves, a reserve platoon (50) of ourselves who'd been sent up in case the Huns attacked seriously, several parties carrying up extra ammunition, stretcher bearers fighting to get on the front line, orderlies with messages struggling for the telephone dug out. No officers near & no one cool at all. Well it was no good trying to sort them out and Capt. Place, the Commander of B Coy had wisely put a sentry to prevent anyone, bar casualties, going down the commy, as that sort of thing starts panic. I can only say, thank Heavens the Germans didn't shell us at once. I managed to get hold of a few sergeants & made them thin the crush out as much as possible to each side and made myself for an open space in the thick of it. This was what I found; two miners in shirt sleeves & trousers only, lying on their backs, kicking & fighting for air, hopelessly gassed. I felt like shooting them with my revolver, it was so awful. The stretcher bearers were simply carrying these poor chaps from the mine shafts in their arms to the stretchers which they'd left in the 'commy' as the fire-trenches are too narrow for stretchers to pass along. Well no one was getting these men down on the stretchers or anything, they just stared at them. I got hold of the worst of the two and smacked his face and told him he'd be as right as rain in two shakes and then someone helped me carry him to the 1st stretcher, another chap had his coat off in a jiffy as a pillow and two more started off down the 'commy' to the M.O., carrying the stretchers. The other man was in an awful state, groaning etc. and then a third was pushed through the crush & left sort of collapsed against me, while I was trying to tell the 2nd he was quite alright & he would be better in a minute. Just then a party came up carrying boxes of ammunition & asking where to go with it. Well that wasn't exactly a nice situation as you'll agree, with two huge men probably (as it happened actually, I'm afraid) dying in your arms. However to make matters worse, the Huns did start shelling and the first one just cleared my head and almost caught the ammunition party. One advantage was that the crowd vanished, except a few who stayed. Now as I told you, when the Huns shell you, they put them all in the same place roughly. The Ammunition party vanished into a recess & left their boxes in the trench! Well I didn't fancy having 1000 rounds exploding at once in my face, as they would have if a shell hit the box. I knew the corporal in charge of the ammunition & called to him to move the boxes into better shelter at once, which he did, & then came to me & we got this third man, now practically dead, on to a stretcher. They stopped shelling us then mercifully, though luckily no shell had actually burst in the trench. So I went round to another bit & found that things were a bit more ordered and getting more or less organised. Place, who was asleep at the time, was flung straight off his bed by the shock & rushed out and did awfully well in front, I'm told. When the shelling stopped completely I went back to C Coy and had breakfast. The men who died were buried at about 12 noon and coming from the cemetry the padre met another stretcher going in to the aid-post. I was down at H.Q. for lunch, as all was then quiet. The M.O. (Jimmy) came in a bit late & just said, "Another one for Fritz." And no one spoke for a bit. After lunch I walked home via this 'hot' bit of trench. And I'm blowed if I didn't meet five more stretchers. A sausage had landed smack in the middle of them, and 3 were not dug out for 20 mins & were of course dead. The other two are all right apparently.

21.10.15

I've read over what I wrote last night to see how it reads, and honestly I've not exaggerated a bit. Remember that the men I saw where mostly dazed and a bit 'muzzy'. There were some fine things done in front I've heard since. The crater of this colossal mine is egg shaped (most German craters are) and is about 70 yds long by 40 yds wide!!!! Just try to picture that!

The marvel to me is that everyone near wasn't burnt by the flame, or at least knocked senseless. Owing to the Huns not shelling the casualties were pretty light, I can't say how many owing to [the] censor. I don't think I've ever been in quite such a tight corner before. You had to be a few degrees cooler than an iceberg, think of 10 & do 1 thing at once, give a few orders putting two chapters into 2 words and meanwhile help a couple of poor devils over their last style in your

spare time!! . . . I hope all this doesn't sound too dramatic, or
egotistic(!). You see I can only describe what I saw with any hope of
speaking the truth. I think it's worth recording in more or less detail,
as one isn't priviledged to help, even if it's only an ordinary
policeman's work in peace time, at the biggest explosion on the
Western Front in this War. [85]

Of that Anon –
The same piece of line
24.10.15
SUNDAY

Good People all,
  . . . We're still 'up' but C Coy. has been relieved and is now in the
2nd line about 300 yds behind the firing line. We had about 5 very
quiet days before our move, & now it's quieter still, so we're very cosy
and get 'bags' of sleep . . .
  So far I've always described my dug outs & billets and I'll always do
that so you can remember them by various characteristics. For
instance, first of all we had the one where 'Freddie' lived. Then I went
to the shed where the bed was, & still is. Then I think it was in
reserve at our present Bn H.Q. and then, on the same trip, up to that
place where the mine was, where I had a ripping straw pallet, the
straw being about 10 months old; after that I went to the quiet place
where the roof used to dribble down my neck & shed mice on to me
at various intervals, & now I'm here. This time Pearce and I are really
in a machine gun emplacement, which is not in use. It's a sort of
double affair. Peachy, Rosher (Pearce's servant) & our food are in the
part where the gun fires & Pearce and I are in the shelter for the crew.
Our part is about 6' long, 6' wide and 5' high. Just about room to
change your mind in.
  As you come in the first 7 or 8 times you hit your forehead on the
crosspiece of the doorway and simultaneously catch your foot on a
sandbag which is supposed to keep the rain from running down into
the dugout, a sort of door step. Supposing you only hit the top of
your head on the lintel, that probably won't stop you from pitching
head first down 3 steps on to the table (1' by 2')!! Having entered by
whichever method suits your build best, the actual entrance being 1'6"
across & 2'6" high (Oh Aunt Janet, do be careful) you get off the table
and rearrange the peppermint creams & the hair shampoo; pick up
the cigarettes, dry them as much as possible on Pearce's towel and
put them at the bottom of the box, & slide on to my bed, keeping the

boots (if muddy) well in the air, and then, having gyrated on the − ,
till the legs can be slipped under the table, utter a short thanksgiving
& apply dressings to the parts most affected.

Herewith a ground plan:−

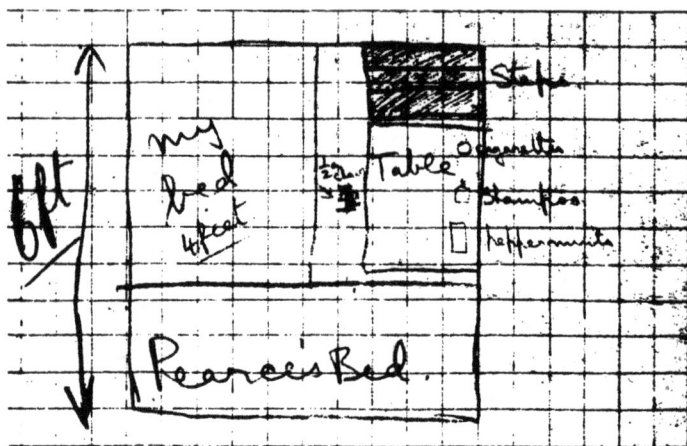

All round the walls are nails and hundreds of things dangle from the
roof, which, remember, is only 5 ft high and strafes it. Peachey's bed
is of rabbit netting on poles. Mine is a strip of corrugated iron resting
on sand bags; it's practically rat-proof, except for the enthusiasts who
miss their footing while navigating the rafters above; in which case
they land with a resounding boom, i.e. if they don't hit you, on the
iron. As you'll see at a glance, 4 feet is not long enough for 6 ft of
expanding humanity. If we roost here long enough I shall grow like a
cockle or a periwinkle. My back & right side are a most curious
pattern, & I expect I look like a coffee blanc-mange, of course it's too
cold to look & make certain!! I'll try to remember to tell you when I get
back to Billets. In spite of this I slept about 8 hrs on end last night and
the night before; you see back here we don't do tours of duty like we
do actually in the fire-trench, but just rove round as the spirit moves
us. N.B. The spirit never moves me between 9 & 6 a.m.!

Our parcels still arrive from Fortnum & Mason's so we dine well,
considering . . .

Jimmy said only yesterday when I went down to Bn. H.Q. for lunch
that I was looking extraordinarily well, & I feel it too. Getting good
sleep is the great thing. Also we have whisky & soda, one glass at
lunch & at supper regularly, & that is a splendid medicin I find. The

water is all right but nothing to send a telegram about (especially as
men say that's a 9d stunt now)! Dear me, how far-reaching the War is.
[88]

> Back in the same
> Billets
> V.s.A.
> 28.10.15

Dear Everyone,
Here we are, ici nous sommes, sur Sommes (almost). I got here
about 1 ack emma this morning, as I 'clicked' a wiring party last night
from 6-10 p.m. putting out barbed wire. Just supervising a party of a
sergeant & 8 men. The moon was rather trying, but we only had one
man hit. I dodged it nicely. You see a machine gun popped a couple
by my left elbow so in case he should put any nearer I rolled away to
my right, & the next one went neatly through the empty sandbag on
which I'd been lying a second before. I'm glad I thought it worth
while to shift a bit; but the fourth one passed my ear and went
through both legs of a poor chap just behind me. I don't think we
were spotted, but one of the men just dropped a crowbar on a tin and
perhaps they heard it and sent a few over on chance. I thought they
were bound to hear this chap groaning, but he was quite plucky, quite
a kid too, about 18. Luckily the huns didn't send over a star shell or
they'd have seen us as this chap was wriggling a bit. We tore his
clothes to shreds pulling him in through some low trip wire, & he was
soon nice and comfy on a stretcher on his way to 'blighty'. That
happened after we'd just started, & we had some bother getting some
of the men out to work again. It took about 3½ hrs to finish, which is
a good spell on a damp night, 'outside'. I believe I've 'clicked' another
wiring party on Friday night, but I hope not, as there's no amusement
to be had sitting on damp grass for 3 hrs. odd.
I suppose we shall be here for about 10 days again, and personally
I've no complaints to make . . . After sleeping moist on 4 foot of
corrugated iron for 5 nights my dear old bed with its dear old douvé
was some experience. I lay in it all this morning, as my wiring party
furnished a good excuse for such awful luxury. [90]

He had not merely 'clicked' one more wiring party, but had been put in
charge of all wiring for the battalion.[2]

Well I didn't much fancy strolling out & getting wet & cold <u>too</u>

often so I went round to the C.O. and found him snoozing in front of
a fire in his bedroom. He was in an excellent mood, so I 'wired' into
him. Now, instead of one party & myself alone, I've got 4 parties and
Rhodes (Lt. in A Coy.), so now I can change the men about & relieve
them. I've got the whole lot to myself to play about with & train for 3
days. Each party is 1 corporal & 8 men, so I've plenty to amuse myself
with in billets. Rhodes is quite a good sort, he's been a cowboy for 9
years & his manner is a wee bit masterful, but he's as cool as an icicle
. . . On these wiring & other expeditions I always have my orderly; I
should love you to see him, his name is Miller, and he's simply
ripping. He's as tough as 'bully' & as strong as ration cheese, a man
(22) of few words, very quick & intelligent withal, & possessed of that
dog-like fidelity & cheery countenance which characterises the
personnel of C Coy. [91]

You might send my orderly Miller a decent parcel will you?
[Billie asked his mother on November 5th]. Send it when you get this
letter. Lots & lots of cheap cigarettes, cake, a pair of khaki mittens, a
little chocolate & some Bull's eyes, etc. . . . send it from "Capt.
Nevill's Mother." Thanks no end. [96]

In due course Mrs. Nevill – elevated to the peerage by Pte. Miller –
received a letter of thanks.

5261 Pte F Miller
C. Coy. 8 Bn. East Surrey Regt.
B.E.F. France

Nov.18.15
Somewhere in the fighting land
Lady Neville
Dear Madam,
    It is with great pleasure I have to acknowledge your lovely parcel.
    It came as a surprize to me and I cannot express my thanks enough
to you for your generosity because what I have done by Capt. Neville
your son any man in C Company would have done the same.
Although he is your son he is a man to be proud of and a man who
every one who knows him is pleased to follow as he is so cool and
collected and his genial manner is a great comfort to every man he
comes in contact with. I have been with him on several occasions
within easy reach of the German trenches and a man for pluck and
courage he cannot be beaten and I might say without any hesitation

that he is respected and admired by every man in his company. Once again thanking you for your generosity and thoughtfulness in sending me such a lovely parcel. Although only an orderly I do my best as I mean to do to the end of la Guerre.
Believe me yours in gratitude
F. Miller

Lady Neville
Tennyson Square
15 Montpelier Road
Twickenham

By now some families of East Surrey officers were making contact with each other in order to exchange news. 'I wonder if you've rung up, or been rung up by the Clares or the Ackerleys,' Billie wrote on September 15th, 'they both seemed to think it would be nice for our parents to keep [in] touch. I fancy they thought their people would get news from you, as I'm a bit more of a writer (for frequency & length only) than they are.'[3] [56]

The arrival of an officer in England, either wounded or on leave, gave families an opportunity to hear about their sons at first hand.

One of our officers hurt himself with a bomb and is now home, probably in Town. If so, go & see him please. He's one of the very nicest chaps going & a great pal of mine. It's Eley, in B. Coy, he's not badly hurt . . . He (young Eley)'ll give you all the news, truly & ungarnished. He was at Cambridge some time ago, & has been in the Merchant Service for the last 8 yrs. & knows the world like I do Twickenham. [74]

I wonder if you've seen Eley yet or heard from him [Billie wrote to Elsie on October 16th]. Say you're my sister & he'll do anything for you & tell you everything. If he asks you it would well repay you to tour down to Colchester to see him. [80]

In fact Eley was in Chelsea, which made Billie suggest an introduction to his schoolfriend, Donald Campbell. 'Campbell would like him awfully I should think.' [90]
Billie kept his family up to date with personal details of those around him. His servant, Peachey, blotted his copybook in various unspecified ways[4] and 'received the boot, and I'm now looked after by a youthful cycle repairer

from Herts. who came out in the last draft. So far he's been quite successful and I think I shall keep him. Peachey used to earn his bread at landscape gardening but since I've started washing twice a week he hasn't had many chances of practising his old calling on me, & what with one thing & another & two more besides that I thought I'd had enough of him.' [99]

24.10.15
Bobby Soames stopped two pieces of shell a few days ago and is somewhere 'behind' for the moment, at Rouen, I think. He's probably got a 'blighty' one. Which as I explained before means he'll get home with it. He lives at Weybridge. He's very nice and quite a pal of mine, & when he does get home, would be a good person to call on. He's very shy and was at Oriel, Oxford for one year, he has two pretty sisters! Joe is very fit, I called on him this morning, his Coy (A) has relieved B coy. in that nasty bit, you wot of. Bertie Clare is still away on a M. gun course, & I doubt if we shall see him back again, his nerves went you know, I think I told you. Don't tell his people.[5] Joe's brother Peter is coming out to fill up the gaps soon. Then Major Clifton our 2nd in Command got pneumonia, Eley hurt himself with a bomb, though he was in the papers as wounded & not accidentally wounded. Cadge (D coy) stopped a whiz-bang, went home with a hole in his neck & is now out again. John Bowen is still with us, but he's laid up with a touch of Dysentry & finally there's young Thorne who was killed.

Roland Heath and Wrightson both joined the Tunneling Company here, & I see them occasionally, so we've several vacancies. Of course you keep these vacancies as long as poss. in the hope that you'll get your own officers back, but sometimes you have to fill them up from the reserve, which means your own officers, when they are well, will probably go somewhere else . . .

Our Coy Sergeant Major [6] has just got a commission & is going away in a day or two. He'll leave a big gap, especially as the sergeant who would have taken his place was shot dead yesterday. He was looking over the parapet in day time at a dangerous place without a periscope, so of course, that's what you expect; but you'd credit a sergeant with more sense. [88]

Leave began for the East Surreys on October 28th, exactly three months after the battalion had landed in France. 'Pearce has promised to call on you, if he can,' Billie told his family. [90] 'I've asked various others to [ring up],' he said in another letter. 'I expect you like it.' [99] The C.O. was among those asked – 'you can ask him for home truths as much as you like (He doesn't know me well enough!!)' [107] – as was the Brigade Roman Catholic chaplain, whom Billie regarded rather more highly – 'he's a topper' – than he did the Church of England padre. Both men did telephone (though there is no record of the questions the Nevills put to the C.O.). So did another officer, Captain Place, despite Billie's doubts – '[he] says he'll ring up but as he's engaged & lives in Ireland he'll have a pretty hectic time as it is.' [90]

'If it's not stopped before my turn, I ought to blow home in about a month, perhaps less. I may stay here for my 8 days, as I'm so nervous about the winter crossing!!!!' [90]

NOTES

1. Captain E. C. Gimson was the most popular man in the battalion, according to Heath. *The 18th Division in the Great War* described him as 'a sort of unofficial second in command of the East Surreys. If a junior officer were worried about matters with which he did not want to trouble the Colonel, he would consult "Jimmy". If the Colonel happened to be not quite satisfied with some particular officer, but did not want to interfere officially, he would tell Gimson to have a word with him.' p.40.

2. Wiring – the erection of barbed wire entanglements in front of the trenches to stop any attack by the enemy – was a much disliked duty which, because it was out in No Man's Land, had always to be carried out at night.

3. It is worth noting that J. R. Ackerley later became a highly regarded writer. However, he was more likely to spend his time in France writing poems than letters.

4. There is no reference to Mrs. Nevill's sending a parcel to Peachey, despite Peachey being her son's servant. (Servant was a personal classification, orderly a military one.)

5. 'Bertie Clare is back again with us, & I think he's better,' Billie wrote later. [90]

6. C.W. Alcock, who returned to the battalion as a second lieutenant in January 1916 [136] and was one of the three officers of Billie's company who went over the top with him on July 1st.

8 TAMBOUR

I'm afraid you've been starved lately for letters [Billie wrote on November 8th], but I seem to have been fairly buzzing about over this wiring business. I'm doing 3 bits to-night and I shall be doing some more to-morrow I expect. Still it's better than trying to imitate an icycle on wire, which is the best one can hope to do at night in bed. [99]

That night's wiring took 3¼ hours, 'and I shouldn't care to walk through it now.' [100] The following night's work, which he expected to take an hour, was cancelled – 'It was too dark to put out wire, so you can imagine it was pretty black. Tonight I hope to get a good deal done, but it's awfully wet.' [101] The following day he was able to record that it had been 'quite success-ful and I'm thankful to say that I've not got that job while I'm up here for the next day or two.' [102]

The battalion was once more in the trenches, having returned to the Tambour du Clos opposite Fricourt. Once regarded as a quiet sector of the line, the Tambour was rapidly becoming what was known, in the jargon of the day, as 'unhealthy'. The front line here jutted out towards the enemy trenches, enclosing a piece of high ground which, though small, was valuable as an observation point. German sappers were attempting to win the area by mining underneath; the British trying to prevent them by doing the same even further underground. In addition to the usual shelling and sniping, therefore, the luckless troops were liable to be blown up at any time, not only by mines going off but also by explosions caused by the car-bon monoxide, given off from previous explosions, which lingered in the pockets of chalk. 'The general uncertainty . . . proved a great strain on the nerves,' recorded the brigade historian with praiseworthy understatement.

For the first part of the tour C company was in reserve, spending

its days & nights doing all the dirty work of the Battalion, such as cleaning & draining the trenches, carrying up meals & stores to the firing line coys. and all sorts of odd jobs.[1] We're still in the same group of trenches, which is awfully nice as you know your way about so well. In a day or two we shall [be] up again in that place where the mine was and that ought to be quite interesting, they've sent off 3 more mines there lately, not so big as that other one, but quite disturbing. It was rather misty yesterday so we were wandering about behind the trenches where you can't go in proper daylight just here, & old Joe found the skeleton of a hun in some old French barbed wire, we identified him by his boots; his identity disc had been taken off his wrist (we have ours on our necks, the hun wears theres like a bracelet) so I expect his people know he's 'missing believed killed'. Talking of Identity discs, we winged a hun busplane soon after it had dropped, one of our buses flew over and dropped a parcel containing all the private papers & discs found on the pilot & observer, & a note saying we'd bury them decently. Another hun then came over, and although we shelled him like blazes, he came on & dropped a flag with a note attached saying 'Thanks'. Somehow I can't work up any animosity against the hun aeroplanes, they are great sportsmen. I don't count Zeps, of course, though that must require a lot of nerve, but it's hardly the game as we play it . . .

I've just had a slight shake (800 yds away) from a small German countermine, no one was hurt apparently & luckily. We're having what you might call 'some slight underground activity'. [99]

The facts of the case [Billie explained to Elsie the next day], are that they were apparently frightened and thought our miners were under them (whereas they weren't) so they countermined and blew in a good strip of their own trenches. We simply split our sides with laughter and the huns are awfully bored about it. [100]

The weather is still perfect [he wrote on November 8th], but, my hat, it's cold at night. We've got those goatskin capes now, but I don't have one as at present my sweater is enough; also they smell – well, perhaps you're having a meal – so I won't say what they smell like. [99]

Two days later he reported that the weather had changed 'to the Cat & Dog variety which is unpleasant.' [101] 'Weather is topping one's boots so they rather counteract each other,' he wrote facetiously to his mother [102], and on the 12th,

It's poured steadily for about 48 hrs, and the trenches keep on collapsing, one now paddles along a sort of elongated grave with sandbags dropping gently on to one. They've issued us with big rubber thigh boots, which keep you dry alright, up to the knees. Last night an aerial torpedo went off in the air about 40 yds away from me, it's the 3rd I've seen, and I don't want another. [103]

Back in Billets
17th

Dear Mother,

Back once more safe & sound, in the same billets. I'm sitting now in front of a ripping fire in a nice warm room and the sun's quite hot to-day. It is ripping. I'm afraid I missed a day or two lately but the conditions the last five days were appalling. As I told you we were in the Tambour and it fell in 15 different places the first night we were up, added to which we had 3 men killed and two wounded and then, when we thought the 'straf' was over they chucked over one aerial torpedo. Luckily she didn't land in the trench & so did no great damage, though one man fainted clean away with the shock. When this all happens in inky blackness and a steady downpour of rain, well – it is a bit trying. It rained without stopping for the first 48 hrs we were in the fire trench, and the 2nd night lots more of the trench collapsed. Oh, it was a picnic. The five days we had in reserve before were not exactly pleasant either, personally I'd been out wiring 4 of the five nights. Well after the rain, everyone being skin soaked, it elected to freeze for 3 nights. Mon chapeau, it was cold. The last 2 days we had snow, about 4 inches at the most. Five days with feet always wet & cold, in an enlarged & collapsing drain made as it were in porridge is pretty rotten. Our Tours 'up' are now to be reduced to 8 days up & 8 down, instead of ten. Ten really is too much I think now. We had about one aerial torpedo per evening this last time. They are gigantic affairs. You can see them by day plainly and by night they leave a trail of sparks which you can also see. I've heard officers in dugouts 200 yds apart both swear it landed on the roof of their own dugouts which shows you how tremendous the concussion is. Out of doors you don't feel them so much as in a dug out, which is rather funny. One real peach went off in the air about 40 yds from me & only blew my cap down over my ears. The pieces of the casing fly into bits the size of grape stones & so do no damage, it's purely concussion & the destructive in a trench or on a dug out, which is enormous. With the aid of Mr. T. Atkins' cooker Pearce and I had soup every evening, then there are huge braziers, blankets, fur coats (for the men) rum, whisky & plenty of food to atone for these discomforts.

The last night I wired a gap between two huge craters where the Germans [are] on one lip & we on the other, with the craters between us. The two fire trenches are about 80 yds apart there, but you can't see each other for the craters except in this gap, so we wired across this gap to keep too inquisitive & bombons huns away. Thorne & some of his gun crew lay out in front of me with two machine guns peeping round the corners of the craters to keep people from disturbing us, it was an interesting bit to do. I enclose a sketch which is too inaccurate to be of any value to a spy (potential) but which shows you the old Tambour. You may wonder why we hold this little bit at all, but it's because of the high ground there. If the huns had that bit they could see right back behind our lines for miles, whereas at present they can't which is very nice for us. [104]

18.11.15

Cheer ho,

All correct, I'm just going to have a hot bath; in fact ½ a beer cask has just come in and now Marker, my altogether excellent new servant, has gone to the cooker, where Cpl. Parr, the cook corporal, a goodly soul, who carries your parcels sometimes you remember, has boiled me a 'dickie'² (dixy, pronounced) of water. Wow.

I found I had not forgotten how to undress, it all came quite naturally & was very interesting. Also I've just had a hair cut & shampoo.

Writing tonight properly, I hope,

    Yrs ever

        Bill   [105]

Billets

This eighteenth night

Dear Mother, Elsie and Doff, eventually Amy, Howard and Tom,

Hail! Hail! Hail! (rain and snow). Silly, wasn't it? Quite. I don't seem to have settled down & had a really long buck with you all for ages & ages, so sit yourselves & give ear. Picture me first if you can; I've just had a glorious hot bath in my room, about 5 o'clock in the afternoon, and now I'm in 'pygies', a sweater, a pair of Jaeger carpet slippers, and my dear fleece lining – the ultra-cosy combine! I've not been out the whole day because for once I've had nothing to do all day; I've not even put my boots on. It sounds almost too good to be

true. I had brekker in pyjamas about 8.30 and have simply lazed in
front of a fire with books and mags the whole blooming day. By Jove,
it is good. To-morrow Pearce goes on leave and I shall be in charge of
the old Company, which will be great sport.[3] We shall be 'up' again
before he comes back, but it's our turn for the 'cushy' bit of line on the
left of our old trenches and after we come down, possibly before
even, I shall be due for leave. Leave, my honies! Now about this
leave. I don't want to see any fodder out of a tin the whole time I'm
home, twiggez-vous? Don't let me see a peppermint or a chocolate &
don't let me stay in a room without a fire, bar my bedroom. I shall
have to live on chocs & peps all the winter I suppose, and your
letters. Toast I should like & coffee, buckets of it, oh my hat, my hat!
A nice fried lemon sole, some haddock! (Don't, it hurts) A chicken!
(help! I shall faint) some fresh, green vegetables! (Stop it, my tummy
aches). And so on, ad lib. I expect you'll find me a wee bit quick
worded, but don't mind that; also don't make unnecessary noises or
bangs, this applies to Tom particularly. I shall visit that youthful
wormlet of course, and perhaps stay a night with Evans as I believe
Lionel will be there, he is now, I know, recuperating. If you see
Donald [Billie's Dover schoolfriend, Donald Campbell] warn him of
my impending approach . . . [106]

Postmarked November 22nd   *New Billets*
Dear Family,
    I'm in a topping place now, an absolute ruin, no civilians live here
at all. I don't think I'd better tell you too much about it as the huns
shell it 'on spec' so to speak, as it is, & we don't want any more round
our ears.
    The officers & H.Q.s of the Coy. are in a topping great house which
hasn't been hit yet. I'm in charge & thoroughly enjoying it all, Pearce
is still on leave . . .
    Twigg & I found a simply ripping dog this morning, a cross
between a collie and an Irish terrier & an Airedale, whatever the
French for that mixture may be. He was hit by a bullet, a stray one
(they often float into the village, as we're quite close) in his front paw
& I'm afraid the bullet's still in. We've bathed & bandaged it and he's
licked the place clean. He simply loves us now & is sleeping by the
brazier in my room now. Officers aren't allowed dogs I believe, but
lots have them. This is quite a valuable one I should think & he's mine
and Twigg's now.
    I'm going to explore the place for souvenirs to bring home, in fact,

loot it. Thousands have already done that, so I don't suppose I'll get much.
    Crowds of love now
      Yrs ever
        Billie [108]

Billets as before
23.11.15

Cheery oh,
    Here we are, sitting in front of a huge log fire with a brazier burning in the middle of the room as well. I think my room was probably the servants' morning room of the house, judging by the pictures & the wall paper. There are quite a lot of rooms with all four walls still standing in this house so we are really jolly comfy. I wish I had a camera as this was once a pretty little village. Now only o<u>ne</u> side of the old church tower is standing leaving the works of the clock exposed in a most pitiable manner. The church bell is now on the ground in our yard, resting from its noisy labours. There's no need for it to find a 'locum' while it's off duty, as there's no one left for it to call to church. I think it knows this as it has a most delightfully peaceful look about it. The great advantage about this village is that you have bags and bags of fuel. You live in one house and send your servant next door to fetch the bathroom ceiling in for your early morning fire. Bathroom ceilings & all ceilings in fact, burn very quickly, the wood's so small and dry. After brekker you start [on] bigger logs from the walls for instance and by night you've got on to enormous rafters which burn toppingly about 5 at a time, and you keep on pushing them towards the fire as they burn up. One cottage lasts a Coy 3 days. There is one bath in the village and she's coming in here tonight and I shall have a boiling soak in front of my two fires & then slip into my flea bag, (wow) which reposes on an enormous 4 poster, which has strayed in here somehow.
    There's a jolly little bamboo dumb waiter by my bed and I sometimes think that the things he now carries will make him open his mouth for all his dumbness! Twigg ornaments the floor in one corner on one of the mattresses of a broken bed elsewhere. All over the ceilings are lines carrying washing & my trench clothes airing. Now & then they descend with a squelching splosh on to the brazier or on to your face. There is a small room leading off this where we wash. My duty consists of walking up to the trenches, where the company is working, once a day. It's been so foggy I've gone up

across the open the last two days. I spent hours yesterday in the fog
searching on an old battlefield, just behind the lines. The ground was
covered with little hastily scraped up trenches, showing where the
French had slowly pushed the Huns back to their present line,
months – almost a year ago now. Equipment, clothes, cartridges,
water bottles & tins were lying all over the place, & we found (we, is
Miller & I) 3 skeletons. Near some old German equipment I found an
old pipe bowl which I thought I'd keep as a memento of a most
extraordinarily interesting prowl. Here and there one found piles of
empty cartridge cases on the ground, showing where a mitrailleuse
[machine gun] (pronounced by T. Atkins mittralose) had been
dragged up. In another place near worm eaten equipment, Miller
found several packets of unused French ammunition showing where
some poor 'poilu' had found his 'blighty one' & had crawled off to the
'aid post'. (Every wounded man is supposed to put his ammunition
where it can be seen by others going on.) I wish you'd been there,
you'd have loved it. Perhaps some day I'll take you all over this
ground & we'll follow it all from my letters & look up everything
again. Of course unless there's a fog, you can't go there at all except at
night, when you can't see. Now & then perhaps an 'over' or a 'stray'
will zip past but the chance of getting hit is one in a million. There's
the old station there too – Fricourt station, in fact, which belongs to
us, but the brethren own nearly all the rest of Fricourt.

LATER

I've just had tea & now my bath has come in and Marker has
discovered 6 holes in one end of it apparently from shrapnel however
they are about ½ way up the side so we're tilting up that end and I
shall be fine, so:–

There's a sweet little oil painting in my room which I shall loot as a
mementoe of one of the jolliest billets I've had. Of course there are no

shops here, but oh! the peace and quiet. Practically every house is
dead level with the ground. I found the village bakery this afternoon.
The ovens were slightly out of order, owing to the intrusion of an 8′4
shell. The house was scattered untidily over the neighbouring fields.
The vicarage & this house, the manor, I should think, are more or less
intact. There are a few others in the same happy condition. The huns
lobbed a shell into the village pond the other day, but as even the
ducks have left it did no damage.

The well is on the dredger pattern – a succession, or endless chain
of small buckets, on a chain, you hold the pail so as to catch each lot
as it tips it out at the top of the well. Each of the buckets makes a loud
'clank' as it turns, needless to say it is just outside my window!! It
works day and night!!!

Those Jersey caramels are ripping, my teeth are aching beautifully,
don't tempt me again, also don't try to get me to see Arthur, or any
other broken reed[5], when I'm on leave, don't mention it! I can get
'Dental treatment' at Amiens, if I want it. I've just bust the glass of my
wrist watch, which is very annoying. On the 26th inst get my blue
suit out & hang it so the creases get out. I shall have to wear it one
day while my uniform is being repaired. Also hunt out my khaki
slacks.[6]

While I'm home I'm going to get a small pocket camera. A fur coat
lining, a proper waterproof coat, not a burberry, you might as well
wear a blooming sieve out here. Also a leather fleecelined long
sleeved waistcoat. A pair of trench boots. I'm also going to have made
a special thing to keep the thighs warm, a mongrel pair of p-nts
(deletion by Censor) made of polar bear skin, or something to keep
the cold out. I shall patent it as 'the only:–

ANTI-RHEUM PANTALOON

or Percy's PATELLA PRESERVERS.

I think I've drivelled long enough now. Let's hope for the 29th or
30th, so far no obstacle has appeared; (touch Timber!) The last two
nights the huns have put up mines that have shaken this house, but
no great damage, one was in front of the Tambour . . .

Crowds of love, dear old things all of you, I'm as well as ever and
as happy as a sky lark, no colds, twinges, headaches, or anything,
don't expect me too well though as I shall come home practically from
the trenches direct.

Yrs ever & love to all

Bill [110]

Although the East Surreys' next tour up started well, torrential rain later caused landslides in all the communication and some of the fire trenches, and also leaked into the dug-outs, making life extremely uncomfortable.[7]

UP
27.11.15

Well, well,

. . . We're having a ripping time up now, lovely weather, awfully cold frosts day & night, but sun as well, and the trenches as dry as a bone, & repair work, drying dugouts for socks, & winter comforts going full steam ahead. No one minds the cold, provided it doesn't rain. As a matter of fact we've got a sprinkling of snow, which makes everything very picturesque. Also a sort of mutual agreement not to shell where smoke is coming out from braziers in dugouts, has grown up between the two sides. Whereas, when we first came out, they used to shell any sign of a fire, & cooking was a tremendous difficulty and only possible at night, now smoke pours out from both lines of trenches during the day & neither side worries [about] it. It's very nice to see their fires, as it gives one something to see, not quite so impersonal as the eternal line of chalk & rusty wire. The poor old huns are as cold as we are, no doubt. I hope they're a lot colder, the blighters; keeping us sitting about here, when I might be working for my degree (I don't suppose.) As a matter of fact I simply love this. Of course now Pearce is away I can watch my own schemes materialising & not merely supervise the growth of Pearce's pet ideas, excellent though they are. [112]

30.11.15

After 4 awful frosts, we had a thaw & rain, of course all the trenches subsided and we've had a pretty hectic time. I took out some wirers to start them on a job and the man behind me was hit through the thigh the second he got over the parapet. So far as I could see it was only a cushy flesh wound, & we patched him up in our telephone dug out, as best we could & he vanished on a stretcher down a crumbling trench on an hrs' journey in the rain, with a cheery "Good night, sir, rather bad luck, wasn't it, sir?" Some man. A chap called Webb & one of the very best. It always is the best who get hit somehow. I had exactly 1 hrs sleep last night and the nights are now 14½ hrs long. [114]

Billie had first mentioned leave as far back as September, in a letter to

Amy. 'Do you realise I've been out over 6 weeks now & after 3 months the
battalion starts getting leave, so I shall soon start reckoning & counting the
days, when my turn will be due. But no, you'll think I'm wanting a change,
but this is delicious really.' [47A] Now leave was beginning to occupy a large
part of his thoughts.

If I get leave, I shall look in at Dover, if I go by F. [Folkestone] on
the way up to town. Jack Schooling [Muffie's elder brother] has had
some more leave, that 7 ft. enthusiast 'wangles' bags of 'blighty'. To
'wangle' is to arrange, or to bring about. You might 'wangle' Muffie
for tea, where as you would 'click' Mr. Schooling if he came! You see
the difference don't you in these words. I like you to keep in touch
with our lingo so you'll understand me on Der Tag.[8] [90]

9.11.15
My leave is now within measurable distance. I think I ought to be
home on or about the 28th of this month for 7 days, or, if not then on
the 2 December for the same time, unless anything unforeseen or
unforeheard about occurs in the interim. It's practically certain to be
one or the other of those times, probably the first, so keep those days
open & free, won't you? I'll fit in a day at Dover to see Tom &
Woodroffe & Evans etc. somehow. Also please & this applies to
Mother, write to Mrs. Schooling & ask Muffie up for a day or two,
saying you're not certain when I'll come but you'll let them know for
certain when. Don't put that off, DO IT NOW!! Negotiation must start
at your end and do work it somehow. Make out a list of theatres
you want to see . . . Don't ask if Tom can come up, I'll go down to
him, and besides it's a bad thing for him to come in term time too
much.
    I don't suppose I shall have much time for sleep when I come as I
shall be at top pressure. It'll take a day to get over the crossing at
least. Then I must buy boots & fur coats etc. I'm designing some fur
underclothes too!!! My old tunic is looking quite a veteran & my cap
might have been on the Aisne or at Mons. Perhaps you'd better warn
Coxes that I'll be drawing all their ready cash at one wild whoop
(probably having my pocket picked at the door on leaving)! Also, all
think of what you want for Xmas. By then I ought still to have about
£80, that's £10 a night while I'm on leave, so I ought to cut a little ice
in the Metropolis. Wouldn't it be sad if I got in the way of a Zep
bombo? Perhaps I'll have frostbite & spend the days in bed! or my
nerves, such as they are, and if they are, may go phut & I shan't dare

cross the street. People back from leave do look fed up with life and they say London's awfully dull. [100]

Mrs. Nevill did as she was instructed; two weeks later Billie was reporting that 'it's simply great about Muffie, she's mad about it.' [108] 'She says she's got a fringe now, it's called Maria locally, she's not certain if she likes it or not. I'm dying to see her with it, don't laugh at it will you, or I shall come back here at once.' [110] There was no mention of a chaperone, perhaps because of Mr. Schooling's reported mellowing towards Billie, though more likely because of Muffie's growing independence. In October Billie had told his family that 'Muff is now parlour and scivy in a Military hospital at Hastings. She starts scrubbing & cleaning at 7 every morning & works all day. I should think it would kill her in about a week, but she says she simply can't hang about at home & do no war work & that's about all she's trained for at present! She's learning V.A.D. work in her spare time; I think it'll do her a lot of good.' [70] By the time Billie returned on leave Muff had left home and was in billets, 'a budding Vic Ack Dom. She works hard from 5.30 to 6 p.m, so I don't know when she'll break down, still it's a good experience for her.'

Billie had hoped for leave towards the end of November, but it was postponed for five days. 'So I shall be at home from the 6-12th practically for certain. I've told Muff, but mind you write as well and say it will be just as convenient & all that sort of thing. Twiggez vous?' [111]

NOTES

1. During a battalion's time up, two companies held the front line, one company was in support and the fourth in reserve. Two battalions of a brigade were up at a time, while the other two remained in billets; in the 55th Brigade's case one battalion at Dernancourt and one (the East Surreys when they were down) at Ville-sur-Ancre.
2. Large iron pot for cooking on an open fire.
3. Billie had originally described Pearce as 'rather a quaint man but tolerable.' [10] More recently, however, he had told Elsie that, 'No one likes him, I don't, as I told you long ago, but I have to get on with him, or what could we do.' [100]
4. Billie occasionally muddled the ' and

" for feet and inches. He must mean 8".
5. His dentist's name was Arthur Reid. Billie had to consult him eventually, when he went home in May 1916.
6. During World War II servicemen reverted to civilian clothes while on leave, but for some reason they tended to remain in uniform during the Great War. Perhaps fear of receiving a white feather, the age-old symbol of cowardice, had something to do with it. As early as August 1914 the *Daily Mail* referred to young women handing out white feathers to any man they considered should be in uniform. Major Irwin, with a D.S.O. to his credit, was given one in the autumn of 1916 while recovering from a wound received on the Somme. Recently

married, he was with his wife at the time. She was not amused.

7. War Diary, 29th November, 1915.
8. German for 'The Day'. Usually taken as meaning 'the day we Germans conquer England', but appropriated by English officers to refer to some highly desired future date, in this case when Billie would go home on leave. He had given definitions of army terms on previous occasions: 'It' is one of these quaint terms . . . for unmentionable things. To be 'for it' is to be going into a hot place under fire, or to do some unpleasant job.' [27] 'A 'cushy' wound, or a 'cushy' job is one which is nice & gets you comfortably home without too much damage & a 'cushy' job is like the artillery or transport people. Anything nice & safe & easy is 'cushy'. 'Blighty,' while I'm instructing you in some of our lingo is Tommy's name for England. A 'blighty' wound is one just bad enough to send you home.' [76]

9 WINTER IN THE TRENCHES

'The great thing on these occasions is the change,' Howard told Elsie, writing in 1918 about leave in England. 'It does not matter if you do yourself to a frazzle as long as you have heaps of things to think of the next few months.'

Billie certainly filled every minute during his leave. He went down to Dover College to see his youngest brother: 'Dear old Tomaso . . . it was topping seeing you down at Dover and I am so glad you love it. Of course I knew you would.' He visited Holmbury St. Mary. 'That is one of the spots I intend to visit <u>when</u> I get leave,' he had written as far back as September 15th. [56] He caught up with various relations: 'It was ripping seeing Maurice & talking to Aunt Janie too; and <u>so</u> jolly meeting the 10 lost tribes at Fullers in that quiet backwater of London.' He went to the theatre, seeing, amongst other shows, a new revue with music by Lionel Monckton called *Bric-à-Brac*. Though he does not mention Muffie's visit, it must surely have been her presence that made him say, 'Bric a Brac & Friday evening generally I need not discuss, I hardly knew one could be so happy!'

It was a successful leave in other ways, too. 'The great point is that I didn't spend very much while I was home, not nearly as much as I'd expected, & yet we didn't exactly skimp, but, Mother, you paid a lot too much. Don't let that occur again please.' [119]

Bad news – or what Billie considered bad news – was waiting for him on his return to the battalion.

> *Tambour*
> 14.12.15

Dear Mother,

I had a topping crossing, slept all the way & had a hot dinner on board. Brekker we got at a Y.M.C.A. hut on the railway coming up. I got a lorry from railhead to V[ille] and after tea there, walked up to the dear old trenches. There I found to my disgust that I had been transferred to D Coy as 2nd Capt and Paul has gone to C. Coy. It is rotten, & I loathe it. Of course I should look on it as a compliment, but it's jolly hard luck when I love C Coy so. I've got Marker transferred with me, my servant, & Miller very much wants to come too, but I don't suppose I'll be able to manage that. Quite a little retinue wanted to transfer with me, which was nice, but impossible to wangle. [115]

'The compliment about my move is this,' he told Doff a few days later, presumably in answer to a question from her, 'C Coy is now without any question the best coy. D is the worst (at present)' [121]. A.E.A. Jacobs, one of C company's subalterns, in Billie's opinion the most efficient, told his parents that he was 'sorry that Nevill has been transferred to D Co (which is not quite as good as the rest & needed a good officer) and we shall miss his merry humour badly.'

During December the battalion had two periods on the Tambour, both of them difficult. 'The Germans are offensive,' Billie recorded, 'though I've not seen one eating! They've given the Tambour over 300 sausages the last 3 days.' [116] He had to reassure Doff a week later. 'No, their 300 odd sausages did practically no damage, about 4 men slightly grazed, that was all.' [121]

It was impossible to be reassuring all the time. Billie reported one particular casualty, wounded just under the German parapet during a night patrol.

Serg. Ruffles, my old wiring sergeant, had his thigh bone smashed in the Tambour craters last night, but managed to crawl back to our lines after people had been searching for him for about 2 hrs. I'm awfully sorry to lose him. He's doing well & probably home by now.[1] [117]

Billie escaped from D company briefly, when he stood in as Adjutant. 'I expect I'll be awful busy, as I'm doing Clare's work while he's on leave,' he warned the family, adding. 'I should say I'm going to try & do Clare's work for him.' [118]

I like doing Adjt. very much really [he wrote on December 20th], but by Jove you want some memory, and by Jove you are busy.

It's all office work and arrangement; and is rather new to me, so I like it. Of course, if you forget anything it's your funeral for a cert. I have a telephone to my bedroom which saves me a lot. Still there are a topping lot of Orderly Room Clerks and they remind me of everything. You find heaps of awfully amusing incidents which help the thing along a bit . . .

I had two topping parcels, pants etc. and most of the things I ordered from shops have come. My leather waistcoat is really ripping.

Yes, I should like another pair of the thick pants. I'm getting a ripping fur lined coat cheap through the Govt. I've got a grand pair of new boots free from the same source also a set of webbing (nice) equipment in exchange for my present leather stuff. So altogether I'm jolly well set up. My Cording's waterproof has not come yet and I hardly expect it as they were making it. I've had to send my new watch back to have the patent spring cover strengthened as I caught it in my coat. The watch goes perfectly . . .

I've got a ripping room now we're back in our old Billet town. I'm in the Adjutant's room of course. It has a fire and a dressing room opening off it . . .

No, I didn't feel in the least flat or mopy when I got back, there's far too much to do to think of worrying about homesickness . . .

No, the aerial torp. department of the hun trench engine Coys. has been replaced locally by a comic kind of catapult, which jerks over about 6 articles, of the size & appearance of a bottle of Whitbreads, at once. These burst with some gusto, but do very little damage. They are quite interesting little souvenirs. One dropped between one of our officers feet on the ground, but did not burst. Some escape!! That was Pegg, a new officer, 'on draught', as they used to say, before the Pub Act.[2] I'll try to keep you posted daily, but I expect it will often only be F.S.P.Cs. (There is a new order that you may write "A Merry Xmas & a H.N.Y" on these cards) till Clare comes back. [119]

'I'm afraid my letters have been awfully scarce,' he told Doff on December 23rd, 'but I don't get a second to myself by day, & it means sitting up at night if I want to write.' [121] 'I'm awfully fit & happy but colossally busy as Adj.,' he said on a postcard on Boxing Day. 'Attending to all the wants, troubles & parents who enquire, Xmas gifts & health, comfort & fighting of 1,000 men is a little wearing. I look forward to the evenings when I can run without appearing undignified!!!' [122] Two days later he added: 'I hope you understand that it's only because I'm so awfully busy, and not because of any seediness, that you have been so starved litterally. (Note the double meaning in litterally.)' [123]

As Adjutant, life in billets was comparatively comfortable.

I'm sitting now in front of a fire in my bedroom. I have the telephone to my bedside and can talk from there to Divisional H.Q.s! I have in fact. We're in an old chateau place & while we were feeding tonight the old, old Madam produced some ripping little glasses & two bottles of wine dated 1878. They are awfully good to us here. My room has some ripping family portraits, one quite like the staircase grandfather, & a dressing room opening out of it. I'm rather too busy to appreciate the real beauty & peace of the place at present.

The Flying Corps officers near these parts were taking several of us to the Divisional Cinema the other night in one of their many cars. We had all herded in & without thinking I said:– "I hope Basil Hallam's in good form tonight." One of them said, "Yes thanks, but I've got a bit of a cold" – & there he was. Basil Hallam Radford.[3] I felt rather an owl. I clean forgot he was about these parts. Rather comic. [121]

Billie's opinion of the Royal Flying Corps had deteriorated since the previous autumn. Commenting on his brother, now with the R.F.C. in Egypt, he said that '[Stanley] <u>does</u> seem to be earning his pay, anyhow, which is more than most of the <u>good</u> old R.F.C. about these parts. Their chief job is lending us cars for the Cinema.' [126]

I'm still enjoying myself out here [he wrote on December 28th, after a week in the trenches]. It's a bit muddy, I know, but then you expect mud. We've got ripping trench boots, and my new coat is really ripping. Also I've got a fur-lined British Warm, it's simply ripping only £3.12.6 off the ordnance. In Town they are £5.5.0. I'm now thoroughly and completely equipped for the winter, I simply can't get wet, or cold ever, now. [123]

The British Warm turned out not to be quite as ripping as he had thought, being too large. He managed to sell it to his C.O. – 'Rather comic,' was Billie's comment – and ordered another for himself, one hopes at the same bargain price. [126]

The East Surreys were back in the trenches in time for Christmas Day. 'All thoughts of fraternising on Christmas Eve was put an end to by Trench Mortars, Sausages, Rifle grenades & whiz-bangs on the part of the Germans,' said the War Diary, adding briefly, 'Our Artillery responded.'[4] Heavy artillery bombardments continued throughout their tour up, as the Germans tried to stop them – unsuccessfully – from occupying the mine craters which lay in front of the British trenches. On December 27th the battalion suffered its first gas attack. Billie was able to be more explicit on this occasion, as his letter home was to be posted in London by an officer on leave. 'The Huns gas & tear shelled us pretty badly at the rate of <u>200 shells</u> in 20 mins. for about <u>5 hrs</u>, some straf. Also they got into the trenches of the next regiment & bagged about 30 men, strafe them. After the gas shelling, no one could see them coming for gas. We have blown a lot of good mines lately & they only one small one.' [127]

Last night up
30.12.15

Dear Elsie,

The real adjutant Clare, has now come back from leave and I shall retire to 2nd Captain D after guiding the battalion with the "mailed fist in velvet glove" through various mines, courts-martial, and what not, as adjutant. Rather a come down but very restful after a pretty hectic 10 days. I expect you'll see our bit mentioned in the papers. It's been quite interesting lately. I enclose a tiny bit of the inside of a 'tear shell' or 'lachrimatory', or 'weeping shell'. I expect you've heard about them. They make your eyes smart and run and your head ache, like billio. I hope this bit will still have its smell, when it reaches you. It can't do you any harm, or blow up, but <u>don't</u> burn it, as I'm not sure it won't make you all cry, and it's an interesting souvenir. I've got a bit of the shell itself, the case, that is to say, which contains this crying gas.

Also we were introduced to the Wipers 'Coal box', about an 8-10 inch shell, which makes more noise even than an aerial torpedo, and a perfectly sweet hole to hide in.

I was well out of it by a good 400 yds as I had to stay at the telephone at HQs as adjutant. I had one or two rather interesting messages, which I've kept as souvenirs. For five hours heavy shelling, we had one man slightly hit in the back, which shows you how awful safe trenches really are. Will you keep all the communiqués which mention 'Westgate' and any odd references to the old Tambour Duclos, to give its full name. Oh, yes, it hasn't been a bit dull the last day or two. Of course I'm awfully well and fit. The other day I had to go down to billets, for a court martial, and to come back here Paull & I both got ponies and one groom to lead them back. My hat, we fairly shifted along, full tilt. How I ever stuck on is a mystery to me now; it was simply great and I'm as stiff as a poker today. [124]

He was mounted again a few days later, when he and Joe Ackerley had to fetch money for the battalion – 'Great fun; you ought to see me on an 'orse!' [126] Two weeks later he was able to report that

My French music & riding are improving daily, as one might say of a young lady at a 'finisher' or home for knock outs. I can ride now much better and have at last got that rising in the stirrups when they trot, which is so hard to get at first . . . To-day John Bowen gave me a riding lesson, we went about 3 miles to a butchers (where I shared the

bed on the landing, with Bertie Clare, about 3 mos. ago) got some
mutton chops, then on to another place (D) [Dernancourt] about
2½ miles – where we called on our R. E. Coy and had tea with
them. Wright, a captain of theirs, is one of the most deelightful birds
I've met, and also Tyler (Beaumont)[5] is in his company too. After
tea, home again 6½ miles trotting all the time – 6½ altogether I
mean. [135]

'I'm beginning to feel quite at home on an horse's back,' he told Elsie on
January 20th, 'which will be a help when I'm a regular. My moustache is
going strong, I hewed him about this morning, and he's looking very chic.'
[136] Thoughts of his future career are evident. When Donald Campbell
sailed from England to join his parents in India, Billie told his family that, 'I
expect I'll meet him there, when I go there with my regiment after the War. I
shall transfer to whichever battalion is going to India, if I can. It's cheaper for
one thing, until I'm senior enough to live on my pay.' [135]
Back in billets at the beginning of January, Billie told his mother that

The good old Division is plugging along at its policy of never
leaving the dear old hun alone for even an after dinner cigarette. Did
you see about the "minor nocturnal enterprise resulting in a few
dozen British prisoners," in the German communique. In our
communique it said – 'A few Germans entered our trench but were
instantly repelled by counter attack.' I'll tell you which was true when
I see you, it happened where I used to live, the 'shed with the bed',
just next to us now. I told you they 'gas shelled' us and 'tear' shelled
us too. A great experience. We're off to the dear old Tambour again
soon, for a short visit. It's getting quite a centre of attraction. I want
you to keep every reference in the papers to our part, Fr — rt, or
south east of 'Mrs. Bull's son'. Did you see the C.O., Thorne, & Sergt.
Conquest were mentioned in dispatches? You'll see a lot about our
part in the papers during the next day or so, I expect. Keep it all,
won't you?
    Leave is starting again soon, & I should be home again in about 2
months or 10 weeks. I'm still as well as ever, & we're having a real
rest this time 'out'. [126]

He decided that he liked his new billet 'quite as much as the old one in
C. Coy. I'm getting to like D Coy. better than I did at first, but I don't as
much as I did C, that is at present; perhaps I shall when I know them better.'
[128]

We have two gramaphones in D Coy Mess <u>with</u> the Bric à Brac
selection. As I write 'Nevill is a devil '[6] is ringing in my ears! Also
there is Mlle Alcinie, who does our washing and mends our sox (?), &
mothers us generally, age 19, & her dear old Mother, a mistress of the
rounded phrase & polished diction of France in its childhood,
between them we learn quite a lot of French, and I hope to be able to
speak quite decently soon. Speak <u>French</u> decently, I mean, of
course!!!!! [126]

He reported the start of a Brigade Magazine. 'I have sent in some oddments, which everyone pretends are very funny, as they are all topical allu-
sions, I won't bore you with them.' [126] This seems to have been false
modesty on Billie's part. 'A sprightly Trench gazette' was how the historian
of the 18th Division described it, while P. G. Heath remembered it as being
'entirely written by [Nevill]; it was somewhat bawdy, full of local "jokes"
and the men loved it.'

He had promised to buy himself a small pocket camera [110] before going
on leave, and did so, taking photographs of the family in the garden at
Twickenham before bringing it back with him to photograph officers and
landscape in France. Security was such, however, that he dared not send
photographs by post (even bought postcards sent home were supposed to
have the name of the place deleted). An officer going on leave took the film
to England to be developed, and another brought back the prints when they
were ready. First Elsie, and later Doff, was in charge at the London end,
though arrangements were complicated by the unreliability of Billie's
messengers.

4.1.16

Did Clare send you all the snaps I took out here of <u>people</u> in the
trenches, he doesn't remember. I have some landscape ones of the
Tambour, & you have <u>their</u> negatives, but I've <u>not</u> got the snaps I took
at home or out here of people, and Clare took 'em to Kodaks, in
Regent Street to be developed. I think you must have them. Anyhow,
<u>if</u> you have them send 1 copy of any that would interest M to
Hastings. And keep a copy of all for yourselves. Send at least <u>8</u> copies
to G. G. Morse, Esq., Thorpe, Norwich. If you haven't as many
copies, send what you have there, & then get the rest done & wait till
I give you another address to send them to. <u>Never</u> send them <u>direct</u> to
me by <u>post</u> . . . [127]

14.1.16

Dear Else,
   This is the next place to send prints to, if you have any to send, (I
want you to keep the 2 & the negatives, which I hope Kodaks send
you occasionally). I order, each time, the negs & 2 enlarged prints for
home, & 6 enlarged prints to be brought out by the officer who takes
them home for me but when I think he won't get them in time he tells
Kodak to send those 6 to you & it's those I want you to send to the
various addresses I give you. Is that clear? [132]

20.1.16

   So Cadge just forestalled you in Regent Street, he left all of them at
his home, like a lunatic, but they're coming out all right. [136]
By May, Billie seems to have been supplying photographs to the whole
battalion.

22.5.16

Dear Doffly,
   Here's a special order from the Colonel for him & the Brigadier.
'Some show', they both loved them & paid for them too, I'm charging
a franc (8d) each.
   I hope you got the other lists from Hetherington.
   Jacobs is posting these.
   Don't forget some for our lot & Nora Soames & The Ackerleys. The
latter are going to ring up, I believe.
   The Soames (there is a Mr. Soames) are moving to Byfleet on
Thursday but letters or parcels will reach them.
   Tell Kodaks to hurry up, as several people have already paid, and
the others won't till they hear they've got them at home.
   I think this will be the last order for a longish time at any rate. [191]

By the end of January Billie was discussing the possibility of leave 'about the
end of Feb. or possibly the beginning of March.'

   Not so very far away now. Only about two more Tambours. We
rather reckon by Tambours. You see it goes like this. One tour up &
no Tamb, billets, then up with Tamb, billets, & up no Tambour, & so
on. Next time up for me, No Tambour . . .
   Sun has been [out] on several occasions lately, in fact buds are
coming spring is almost at hand. Wow Wow!
   By April I shall be in Berlin [here he reached the end of a page] or a
coffin! You didn't expect that when you turned over, did you? Just a
pleasant surprise . . . [136]

Billets
Last Night Down
22.1.16

Dear Everyone,

I know I'm not writing those long rambling letters Doff mentions, like I used to, but somehow I just can't. There doesn't seem to be the need to keep you disalarmed about me now. I mean you know I'm permanently alright & as well as possible always. And now there isn't anything particularly new to tell you about. What is new is mostly censorable & of purely military interest. What!

I found these two daisies to-day, they're the first I've seen & they struck me as being a nice peaceful sort of thing to send from here. Also it's very early for daisies isn't it? anyhow it's a topping sign of spring. Buds are showing on lots of trees too. Tomorrow we go to sausage land on the quiet bit near the Tambour, not in or too near. I say 'quiet' comparatively! I expect you've been seeing all sorts of thrilling things about Westgate lately. Quite exciting ain't it? Don't get alarmed.

Bye bye now heaps of love to all
from *Billie*

Very quiet   *UP*
                                                    All quiet
                                                      23.1.16

Dear Mother,

Here we are again, in the "Empire's furthest flung outpost", i.e. a very snug & cosy dug-out, with a fur coat on & quite happy. I've had a head ache the last 3 days now & a stiff neck today hasn't improved matters. I think I'm only paying the penalty of tinned prawns and tinned pheasant. And I think that with the aid of Savory & Moore's invaluable Camels I've dealt with it. A very engrossing subject forsooth. It has come as a nice change, & has made something to do. 24th. Much better today, thank you. Quite well again in fact . . .

V.B.L. to all
Bill [139]

26.1.16

Dear Anyone,

This morning we did have a little excitement as one of our bus-planes had to come down rather quickly. He or his engine got hit when well over the bosche lines & he volplaned home, just skimmed over our & the Bosche trenches, they all fired at him like sin, of course, and landed about 1000 yards back on a hill. We could see him hop out & then several men ran out from somewhere and they pushed the thing over the crest out of sight. The Huns shelling them all the time. Some of the shells fell mighty close. The other day one volplaned 4 miles and landed with the man wounded, 50 yds only behind our lines! The huns then shelled it & the 35th shell hit it. That was in the papers though & I expect you saw it.

So long and cheer ho. Tomorrow is the Kaiser's birthday so we're looking out for squalls.

V.B.L. to all, *Bill*   [140]

Despite saying that he could no longer write long letters, there were still times when he found himself rambling on, as he had done the previous autumn.

27th 1.16
Second Line Supports
Counter attack Coy

Dear All,

The post's just gone and it's about 5 o'clock. The remains of tea are strewn about the dug out and somehow make it look awfully 'homey'. There's a glorious brazier which reminds me of the tram-line gangs at the end of our road. Those noise merchants who clang 'gas' alarms all night you know. I say 'gas alarms' because nowadays we use lengths of rail and hammers for gas gongs, as well as empty shell cases and mallets. John [Bowen] & Geoffrey Morse & Wightman are in here too. Singing 'The Mountains of Mourne' to a whistling accompaniment, & selections of Bric-à-Brac.

I've got about 8 ft of good earth and steel rails over my head in this dugout, which is a ripping new one, with a wooden floor. I've not felt so secure for weeks. One can lie down knowing that there are only two ways by which you might be killed tonight, namely gas & someone accidentally letting off something. As both of these are practically impossible, I'm pretty safe.

They say the hun is having new prussic acid shells made, a dear thing which kills everything for 20 yds, even grass! Aren't they darlings? I don't suppose this is true for one moment, but if it were, I believe we've a better retaliation.

We celebrated the Kaiser's birthday with a pretty healthy artillery straf. So far the Bosche has hardly retaliated except on some perfectly harmless places, where he's welcome to shell till his head aches. Our trench mortars to-day had some ripping shooting. I saw a lot of barbed wire go up after one fine burst, and after another I saw a body go up, about 30 feet – rather beastly – but better than seeing one of our chaps. Just 6 months ago today we were at Salisbury in the train en route for what we each of us imagined the front was like. Then we all expected it to last about 3 weeks, if we were lucky.

By the way, if you do want to know exactly what the 'Front' is like, read the First Hundred Thousand by Ian Hay, The Junior Sub. It's the best thing I've seen & describes exactly what we've been doing for the last 6 months. Also all the little criticisms of Ian Hay's are exactly my own private opinions.

28th 4.10 p.m.

The Bosche has just blown a huge countermine in the Tambour, it gave me the shake of my life & I was quite 600 yds away. However it did absolutely no damage at all to anyone & they shelled and sausaged as well but nothing even hit the trench! No one hurt.

Cheery oh now

V.B.L. to all *Bill*

29th

Funny, but you remember what I said about being so safe, well I spent 3½ hours in the open 250 yds from the Bosches last night in charge of a party digging a new trench. Their machine guns were beastly busy but somehow – no one quite knows how – none of us stopped anything.

We got back about 4.30 a.m. and I was issuing them rum when we had a gas alarm. You ought to hear the gongs going. It was only that beastly 'tear' gas again, but it's jolly unpleasant, makes your eyes ache & run. We only had a whiff of it as it came over about 3 miles away, but it all blew our way & we knew all about it in no time. It was so misty you couldn't see 40 yds . . .

Things may be said to be fairly humming now.

For 2 or 3 days now we've heard nothing but guns, guns, guns, rumbling and muttering like a heavy sea in a cave – I think that describes it best – about 5 miles away from here. Keep your eyes on the communiqués now, not only the English, as we are about 5 miles from the French left, look up all the places, & you'll see what a beano we're listening to and smelling! Perhaps, or they may not mention it much. Anyhow I'm quite alright so don't you worry.

Crowds of love to all

from *Wilfred* [141]

Billets There
2.2.16

Dear All,
I'm very wicked, arn't I about writing, but somehow I can't do it nowadays . . .
I've sad news for you, namely that we're leaving these ripping billets where we've been all the winter & are moving to a place about a mile away, not so nice. Things are buzzing along round here with some gusto, but I shall be all serene. The fact is we're not going back to the Tambour again. There! I suppose you're glad. I am in a way and in a way I'm not. There's an amazing fascination in the old Tambour, but it can be doocid unpleasant. It was the other [night], just as we were being relieved they lobbed about 180 8.2″ shells into it. Thank goodness I wasn't there. As each of these little pellets weighs 266 lbs & bursts like a torpedo, you can picture the sight. No, you can't, unless you've seen it, you can't picture a 'coal box'. Of course our big 'uns are far better & more accurate, & plentiful. We have the Bosche beat & he knows it. I don't care what happens (don't believe a word in our papers, except the German official, joking apart). We are bound to beat Germany eventually, even half steam ahead as we're going at present. If we settled down to it as a nation like the huns have, we'd be home in 6 months.
Of course you must stand by for enormous casualties, all scratches I expect, in the more or less near future.
Bad luck about Francis [a first cousin]. M. guns are beasts for attention. It's all luck though. Often if you are near one, you get a bullet that throws the earth all over you from about 1 foot away. It might just as well hit you, but it just doesn't, I don't know why. One did catch a chap the other day, I saw him just after. He'd no eyes forehead or nose left. Rather horrid. Read this through carefully, as it's quite long for nowadays. Don't miss any points in it. I got up at 6.30 a.m. & took some men up to the trenches digging all day. Some rest.
V.B.L. to all,
Bill

[The coded message read: The neighbourhood is simply crawling with troops here and guns. We shall be between La Boiselle and Fricourt.]

NOTES

1. Sergeant Ruffles was awarded the Military Medal for continuous gallantry on patrol duty.
2. An act forcing public houses to close during the afternoons to prevent workers spending too much time and money on drink.
3. Although he had played Shakespearean parts, Basil Hallam made his name in light comedy, and was particularly well known for his rendering of the song 'Gilbert, the Filbert, the Nut with the K.' Due to an old injury he wore a steel plate in his leg, for which reason he was turned down by the infantry when he tried to enlist. He joined the Kite Balloon Section of the Royal Flying Corps in August 1915 (after being given a white feather, according to Heath) and at the time Billie was writing was stationed at Buire. He dined several times with the East Surreys – 'an awfully nice chap,' Billie said – and Irwin remembered him leading sing-songs at Madame Godbert's restaurant in Amiens. He did not long survive Billie, being killed on August 20th when his parachute failed to open, an incident described by Raymond Asquith to Lady Diana Cooper. 'The day before yesterday Basil Hallam was killed before my eyes by falling 6000 ft. or so from an escaped balloon. He came to earth in a village ½ a mile

from where I stood . . . shockingly foreshortened, but recognisable by his cigarette case.' Jolliffe, p.288
4. 24th December, 1915. The famous Christmas truce had taken place the previous year, when both sides met and talked in No Man's Land and there was even a game of football. Fraternisation was strictly forbidden in 1915, but did take place – Raymond Asquith defended two Guards officers court-martialled for the offence.
5. Beaumont was the home of an uncle and aunt, Tyler their ex-gardener.
6. One can see why *Bric-à-Brac* was such a success with Billie. *Neville is a Devil* ('an excellent song, sung in the Basil Hallam vein, by Gertie Millar,' said *The Stage*) began:
   Of all the boys in town
       The smartest anywhere
   Was Master Neville Brown
       The chaperone's despair!
   He chased the ladies round
       From Bloomsbury to Balham
   And even cut the ground
       From under Basil Hallam!
   Neville was a devil
   A perfect little devil!
   He trotted after anything with
       curls!
   I tell you on the level,
       At rollick or at revel,
   Young Neville was a devil with
       the girls!

10 CHRISTMAS IN FRANCE

'What a strange Christmas this has been, no doubt for all of us,' Amy wrote on December 27th.

As they would be up on the 25th, the East Surreys celebrated Christmas two days early. Lunch in billets included 2 lbs of plum pudding 'each man . . . to himself,'[1] after which a convoy of lorries took the battalion to the Divisional Cinema at Méricourt.

On the day itself Billie scarcely had time to think of Christmas at home. 'There's far too much to do to think of worrying about homesickness. Besides as I say, & as anyone would tell you, I simply love the life out here honestly and am quite looking forward to the next 2 or 3 months. Then I'll be home on leave again.' [119]

Amy's thoughts, unlike those of her brother, turned frequently to Twickenham during the Christmas season. The pile of parcels, which she and Aunt Annie kept to open on the 25th, summoned up vivid images of home.[2] 'It was nice to see old Tom's writing on the boxes, to say who they were from. I could just imagine the dining room and the getting of them off, and wished I was with you.' On Christmas Day she pictured herself with the family. 'All day I kept thinking about you all & wondering what you were doing, it was a lovely day & I thought very likely you all went for a walk.'

She had had problems with her own shopping. 'I've found it quite impossible [to] get presents here but so want to join in with the others, so am sending £2 home, I'm afraid I'm rather late for the Hoxton do, but I had wanted 10/- of the £2 to go to that, never mind do what you like with it, get something for Adèlé [daughter of the Belgian refugees living with the Nevills at Twickenham] and of course old Nulli [Elsie's fiancé] is included in the family.' [6]

In the base hospitals every effort was made to celebrate Christmas, despite the difficulties involved.

We were awfully busy on Christmas Eve, as we had some <u>very</u> bad cases in. However we had time to make up stockings for some boy officers we had in, which amused them very much so was quite worth while. We were in the ward until 10.30 p.m. then I joined in the Carol singing, & we went round the huts, & to the Americans[3], & then to the men's lines & sang, & I was finally in bed about 2.15 a.m. Our service on Christmas Day was at 6.15 a.m . . . After the service I grabbed my breakfast from the mess, & took it to eat in the Aunt's hut & we opened our stockings together, and wondered what you were all doing . . . We were all on duty all day, I never left the ward except for ½ hr for lunch. Nearly all our officers were too ill to take much interest in anything, we had a frantic phase for ½ hr during the afternoon. At 8 p.m. was our dinner. Being Christmas Day I sat by Aunt Annie. The Home Sisters had made our mess look most awfully pretty, & every table had the dearest little tree, with a tiny present for everyone. I had a bull dog, & Aunt Annie a Father Christmas coming out of a chimney, which made a fan. After dinner some of us went to Aunt Annie's hut, & we sat round, talked, then I went to say thank you to various people & finally to bed about 11.30. [7]

At the beginning of January Amy began two months' night duty. Her particular friend, Cliff, was already on nights, 'so we may as well get it over & be on together for a bit. I hope I shall have more time for writing. The night V.A.Ds seem to.' After only a couple of nights on duty she was able to say that she liked it enormously.

I am in charge of two surgical wards – that is two huts – one only has local men in it, or rather mostly local, & they are all more or less convalescent, but the other, where I sit all night they are quite ill. It is wierd. My first night was awfully wet, & I paddled between the huts in topboots & mack & hood. I was also 'on' with the Sister, such a dear Helen Hurry, daughter of Sir Edward, tonight I am 'carrying on' on my own with one orderley.
Between the two wards I am kept just comfortably going, & really find it a rest. All is peace just now, 2 a.m. & I am not going to disturb them for temps & feeds just yet. At ¼ to 3 the orderly & I will get 5 ready for England, & when they are safely off the morning's work will begin. Breakfast is sent over ready cooked, which is a comfort. I have several mild treatments & a good deal of bedmaking but nothing hard . . . I am also responsible for the night meals, we feed together, which is rather nice. Cliff – my pal – & I see to the meals. She has 3 medical wards, so has more time than I have, she had to get the 11 o'clock meal by herself, but I hope to be able to help clear away after the last

meal, it's such a great opportunity to see her for a few minutes . . .
I must stop now as it's time to get my men ready, washed, dressed
& breakfast over, ready to go. [7]

She was sharing a new hut with Cliff; the extra free time in the day was
spent in domesticity. 'Cliff & I went into P-P [Paris-Plage] to get cretonne for
curtains etc. I enclose a pattern, & am now making a long wall pocket for us
both. I made a curtain for our clothes this morning, & we have covered our
floor with a wide plait straw matting, which looks quite nice. I do wish you
could see it.' One disadvantage of the construction going on around them
was the difficulty it caused in getting to sleep during the day. 'There are so
many new noises to get used to, we have not the matting down the passages
yet, also the store room which is next to us is not yet finished! . . . We have
three banging entrance doors all with steps up or down, which everyone
falls over.' [8]
Being on night duty meant that Amy was unable to see as much of Aunt
Annie as she had in the past.

23.1.16

Night sister has just been round, & as I am very slack let me go over
to see Aunt Annie for ½ hr, leaving my orderly in charge of my
officers. I found her surrounded with letters. She has tried today to
tackle them – over 50 these last few days has she had – & of course
she is more than delighted to get them, but the answering! She is
most awfully tired & nearly in weeps that she had not written to you,
even a line, after your letter about the flat.[4] We were most awfully
interested & I want you to understand that although she hasn't
written, she is always talking about you. Our assistant Matron is away
ill again – for the second time quite lately, so of course it makes her
more busy than ever.

Then the blow fell. Amy poured out the whole story in a letter to Elsie.

I am only to do a month on Night, & then go into the Home –
Never never breathe this, it's just for you family people – Mother Doff
etc., not the Aunts. I love night duty, it's delightful getting the long
morning, & of course I ought to do two mths. the only thing is I see
so very little of Aunt Annie, so to my astonishment she told me she
didn't think it was suiting me! I was to come off after my month –
when Cliff comes off. I then help Home Sister – Sister Foster. I can't
bear to think of it. I like Sister Foster very much indeed but perfectly

hate the idea [of] being in the Home – or rather Mess – & mess it is. I
quite see through it – I see heaps more of Aunt Annie & that's the
only nice part, as I shall get her special meals etc. & wait on her
generally! You know, my dear don't you, Sisters late for meals, no
definite job & never finished – beastly – no one likes it & I have to
pretend I do!
    What a growl, but I feel better now, better tear this up my love, no
doubt when I write again I shall be loving the mess!! [8]

All V.A.Ds had to take their turn helping with staff catering although
many did so, like Amy, with reluctance. Most had volunteered to nurse,
rather than work as cooks or kitchen helps, and in any case came from families with servants and so had little experience in that field. Whether Amy became reconciled to working in the Mess she does not say – 'I find I have no
time for letter writing again, now I'm not on night' – but it is evident from
her next letter, this time to her mother two weeks later, that her annoyance
with Aunt Annie had been short-lived.

    It's been just like a funeral going on today. The Aunt has gone. It's
    too horrible to think about. Everyone is so sad at her departure, & I
    feel like just nothing, it's perfectly beastly. She has gone to be with
    Miss McCarthy, she will tell you where, it's a good deal south of here
    about ½ way between Billie & me . . . Aunt Annie's orders came quite
    suddenly. Miss McCarthy has said she may consider this area her
    own special charge, so she will still be able to come sometimes &
    inspect us. [9]

Miss McCarthy was Matron-in-Chief of the British Expeditionary Force in
France, with her headquarters at Abbeville. Aunt Annie was going as her
second-in-command, taking charge while Miss McCarthy went on leave and
then going on leave herself after Miss McCarthy's return.

    It will be hateful not to have the Aunt to read & share my letters
    with [Amy told her mother], they were always so much nicer to sit &
    talk over with her by her fire these later days, since the wooden huts.
    I can't tell you how absolutely ripping she has been to me, we have
    not had one single jar & it's been no effort to avoid them either. You
    know what I mean, don't you?!
    Today we packed her up, put all her treasures away & stored 4
    [cases] full in the Stores here, & then had her two rooms cleaned &
    the new matron in them by 3.30, not bad as Aunt Annie didn't go

until 2! Of course the new matron Miss Blakely – she knows Elsie – has not got quite absolutely straight yet, but is getting on with it & looked quite comfy when I took her her tea at 4.30.

Aunt Annie had not gone for ever. She planned to call in at Étaples on her way to Abbeville after leave in England. Amy could look forward to receiving news of the family at home then. What Amy could not know was that by Easter she herself would be in Abbeville.

NOTES

1. War Diary.
2. A large temporary building was erected in Regent's Park for sorting the huge amount of Christmas mail for the armed forces. During the week before Christmas 300,000 to 500,000 parcels a day were crossing the Channel, with six special trains and four special boats laid on each day to carry them. The weight limit per parcel was 7 lbs.
3. The United States of America did not enter the war until April 1917 but American doctors and nurses had arrived in France under the aegis of the American Red Cross as early as September 1914.
4. Elsie and Nulli, now officially engaged, were looking for somewhere to live once they were married. This unwritten letter to Elsie seems to have been the last straw, as far as Aunt Annie was concerned. What sort of letters surrounded Aunt Annie, Amy does not say. They may have been to do with family or with work, or they may have been letters of congratulation – Aunt Annie had been mentioned in despatches for the second time the previous autumn. This was not the first time Aunt Annie had worked herself into a state over her correspondence. The previous autumn she had omitted to write a thank you letter to Elsie. On that occasion poor Amy had been left to soothe the ruffled feelings at home. 'I am awfully sorry about the gramophone Elsie my dear,' Amy had told Elsie, 'but Aunt Annie wished to write to you herself about the money she was so awfully pleased about it when I told her & what is more, she told me she had written about it. She would love to have her own Gram. & lend it round, & she was delighted when I told her what the brothers & sisters had done.' [4]

11 FAMILY MEETINGS

'But hark!' Billie wrote home on February 8th, 1916. 'I've got to go [on] a course somewhere, lots of us have been to them and it's my turn now. It lasts a month probably and takes place miles behind somewhere so you needn't worry about my safety for a bit.' [147] He was on trench duty again, but finding it more pleasant than life on the Tambour.

We came up this morning to a new bit, just on the left of where we have been all winter. It's an awfully quiet bit, simply miles from the beerswillers & plug-uglies, quite 350 yds in places! Isn't it ripping, just fancy being as far away as from the tramlines to the little red house on the left there, Mrs. Mons or some quaint name, down the road there by the haunted house (I don't think) no. 25. Our new trenches are simply topping, like a rest billet. We actually run to an officers' mess, & we're in the front line too! I sleep in the mess, & Marker is in a sort of sand martin's nest across the gutter. Baldock, my orderly, who takes Miller's place, shares that with him. John Bowen is round the corner & the telephone & our Mess Cook, a whole hearted enthusiast called Game, are near at hand. Altogether it is quite idyllic. The Complete Warren. There's a coke cellar, lavatory, kitchen, servant's hall & pantry box, & police station all on top of one another & a garage for the trench pumps, 300 rats, a couple of frogs (since deceased) and one mouse, probably a widower, as I can detect the presence of his dead spouse, or is it a gas attack? Forward the sanitary section!!!

The Mess is quite a gin palace, has a table, covers for 6 (i.e. two Daily Mails (B.C.) & a John Bull; an old Louis Quatorze chair from the chateau, just behind; the usual wire entanglement-à-coucher, a shelf or two and a half; a fire place & dummy chimney; with a waste paper sack and a leaky roof. The feature of the whole place is the door. It once fitted on a very nice brougham, or carriage of some kind. The glass window still works & it makes a tophole door. Its fellow is on a dug out in the next sector as part of the roof. The wheels of the carriage are used in a travelling ambulance stretcher and the main body of the carriage is, I believe, a kitchen range. That carriage is doing its bit all right, anyhow. And I should think its owner, the Seigneur of the Chateau, who is scrapping in Champagne somewhere, would be rather amused to go round the lines and see it. The door has his family crest on it, and lends a little tone to the dug out . . .

The weather is lovely now & the trenches as dry as old bones. I say old bones, because since I came out, I've seen a lot of ordinary bones, still in use, which were not dry by any means.

Coming to new trenches is just like going to the seaside, to a new house & hunting ground. It's great fun. No sausages here, or crumps. Only a few whiz-bangs and an odd rifle grenade or two. No more Tambour, still we're near old Fricourt still & get in for any stunts, so we shan't quite lose touch with the War. [147]

A week later he was writing from the 3rd Army Infantry School at Flixé-court, one of many schools of instruction that had sprung up behind the front line throughout the British sector. The majority of courses were organised for N.C.Os and young officers, though there were exceptions – the East Surreys' C.O. was at Flixécourt on a week's course during Billie's time there, and even lent Billie some dry clothes. 'I saw quite a lot of him, which was nice for him wasn't it?' Billie said. [152]

> 3rd Army Infantry School
> B.E.F.
> 14.2.16

Dear Mother,
    This letter must be in answer to several.

I came down from the trenches on the 12th (don't mention it to the Kaiser or he may seize the opportunity for his Spring Push) and after a healthy search found the bed of an officer on leave, seized it, stole a tub, filched some hot water, pinched the washing appurtenances of the lad on leave and had a bath. Possibly you had already guessed that that was the idea. I rode over to Ville (all alone! arn't I a Knib?) had tea with Alcinie & her mama[1], fetched my dirty washing and rode home. Before I left the trenches I went to headquarters for lunch. The chateau is quite close to the firing line and is the most extraordinary mixture you ever saw. The cellars are the bedrooms, they do mess upstairs but a stray bullet often whistles through the window, which is sandbagged up to a safe level. The library is now loopholed and the

books are on the floor, while sandbags are hammered into the
shelves. The whole place is littered with the most lovely books. I took
one half of the New Testament[2], which I thought might be saved and
which was small to carry. I found it under an old smoke helmet
leaning against an ammunition box! I couldn't find the other half
anywhere, which wasn't exactly surprising. The private chapel, of
which the altar is still intact, except the candle sticks (which are
doubtless illuminating some dug out) is now a bomb and general
store. As I came in Jimmy's servant was brushing Jimmy's burberry
on the lectern! [Captain Gimson, the M.O.] The stained glass
windows are more or less alright, you see they're so heavily leaded
and such small pieces. The dining hall is all right too. Upstairs you
never saw such a mess. Every stick of furniture has gone and clothes,
books, ornaments & pictures litter the floor. I must tell you more
about [it] when I see you.

Well, after my bath I had a note asking me to dinner at the Brigade
H.Q. So I rode over & had a great fill up, rode home again and slept
the sleep of the just. The next day I rode over to Buire, Marker & a
Sergeant, who is on the course too, going in the Mess cart, & we all
left Buire in a Motor bus at 10 a.m., having collected various other
parties, for Flixécourt about 14 miles from Amiens, N.W on the way to
Abbeville. There are 100 Captains & Sergeants here & we are having a
course almost identical to the one I had at the Staff College, when I
started. They work us fairly hard but it's a ripping rest. The C.O. said
I was looking a bit seedy, but I didn't feel it, & I think perhaps that's
why he sent me. [149]

Siegfried Sassoon, attending the 4th Army Infantry School at Flixécourt
two months later, also suspected that the course was a holiday for those in
need of a rest. 'It certainly seemed so to me when I awoke on the first morning and became conscious of my clean little room with its tiled floor and
shuttered windows. I knew that the morning was fine; voices passed outside; sparrows chirped and starlings whistled; the bell in the church tower
tolled and a clock struck the quarters . . . on the other side of the street a
blossoming apple-tree leant over an old garden wall, and I could see the
friendly red roof of a dovecot . . . I looked at a chestnut tree in full leaf and
listened to the perfect performance of a nightingale. Such things seemed
miraculous after the desolation of the trenches. Never before had I been so
intensely aware of what it meant to be young and healthy in fine weather at
the outset of summer.'[3]

Flixécourt, or Felixstowe as it's called by the élite, is about the size of Ryde, perhaps not quite so big, more Westgate [Billie told his mother]. It's fairly clean, and we've got ripping billets. I'm awfully lucky, as I live in the same house as our Mess. We mess properly about 12 to a Mess, which again all helps to get trench life & its slackness & mud out of one's mind. Also you meet people here who've been in every scrap & action . . . I share a room (two beds luckily) no sheets, but Stanley's old flea bag is as good as new still, with a man called Whyte in the Sussex pioneers, quite a nice lad. Then we have several canny Scots in the Mess as well. It's a 28 day stunt[4], and will do me a world of good, as we're really comfy & jolly well looked after, everyone is awfully decent & all are gentlemen, so far as I can see, which is saying a lot nowadays . . . [149]

'Let anyone who reads this know that I was four weeks at Flixécourt, and four weeks happy and peaceful – and free, with my books and my work and the heaven of spring surging all round me over the noble country, and lighting the skies with magnificence,' Sassoon wrote in his diary on leaving Flixécourt.[5] Although Billie was less fortunate in the weather – 'The weather has been fiendish lately . . . sleet or rain or hail each day,' [150] followed a week later by five inches of snow – his time there seems to have been equally happy and relaxed.

Sunday [20.2.16]

This morning, there being nothing on for the first time in my life out here, I stayed in bed till 12 & had a real laze. Got up then, had a walk till lunch with several others who'd done the same as me, then lunch & this afternoon we walked out & explored an old mined chateau, something like Corfe Castle and quite as old – there's not nearly so much of it left as there is at Corfe. Very eerie & supposed to be haunted.

The rabbits & lizards keep
The Halls where Monsieur gloried & drank deep
Rotten! poor old Omar. [150]

Weekends were free, with transport into Amiens and Abbeville laid on. 'Last night we all went into Amiens on Motor Buses. Great fun . . . Nottidge, a captain (we're all capts) in our mess gave us all a ripping champagne dinner at the Godbert restaurant.'[6] [150]

During his time at Flixécourt Billie even had time to draw. Lacking the talent of his eldest sister, his drawings give a schoolboyish impression of life on the course. 'In future I will try to illustrate similar features of our

strenuous military life out here & forward them when completed' he wrote, enclosing three of his efforts. 'They may not be true to life, but they are at least animated & self explanatory!! I have labelled anything which may be obscure at first sight.' [152]

There seems to have been a touch of the schoolboy about the officers' behaviour, too.

> On Saturday we were going somewhere on a Motor bus & before we started we loaded it with snow balls on top. All the way, everyone we met was greeted with a volley of snowballs, it was a great rag. Then we had a little dinner party when we got there & bussed home. [154]

One benefit of his attendance at the course was his proximity to Amy. Aunt Annie was still at Abbeville, 'but as I can't get over till next Sat anyhow if then, I'm afraid I shan't see her,' Billie told his mother on February 21st. [152] Three days later he was 'hoping to see Amy this Sunday, for about 6 hrs.' [153]

24 *General Hospital*
B.E.F.
France
1.3.16

My very dearest Mother family & Aunt Annie,

. . . I did have the most perfect thrills last Sunday, at second lunch I had a line from Billie saying he might turn up at about 4, but I had hardly finished reading it when in he walked just about 2 into the Mess. Matron was sweet & said we could do anything we liked, & offered us the use of her sitting room & wanted me to have a supper party there, but as Sister Foster & I are alone in the mess just now I thought it was too much. We went out by the train to as far as you can toward the Villa Tino & then walked & had tea there . . . Billie was looking & seeming very fit indeed, & it was just lovely to have him. We had dinner at Matron's table, & Sister Foster & Cook had in no time made a most delightful little meal. We had 2 knives each & two spoons & the beautiful china plates & the pretty best soup bowls!!

Crowds of love to you all

Amy   [11]

III Army Infantry School
B.E.F.
28.2.16

Dear Mother & Co,

. . . On Sunday I went by devious ways to ETAPLES & saw Amy, it was simply top hole & I thoroughly enjoyed it all, though it was a bit of an ordeal. I was introduced to all A's pals and she seemed to know everyone. If I go next week I know I shan't remember who I've met & who I haven't. In asking the way of some V.A.Ds who happened to know Amy, the magic influence of Aunt A. was at once seen, everyone fairly gushed over her nephew. [154]

I did enjoy that show no end on Sunday [he told Amy], it was simply topping & I shall certainly come again next Sunday, I hope about the same time & for the same time. I got back home about 1.30 a.m. & everything went well. [154A]

Alas, the journey to Étaples the following week turned out to be one of Billie's more eventful trips.

Stranded on the way to
ÉTAPLES
Sunday. 5.3.16

Dear Everyone,

Curious address, isn't it? I'm making a great struggle to reach Amy again and having started at 9 from Felixtowe (compris?) I hoped to get to Eat apples[7] about 12.30 pip emma. However that was perhaps rather too optimistic a view to take of the French railway system and so, here I am at one of the most utterly useless backwood kraals I've ever struck, to wit, LONGPRÉ. I'm only 4 miles on my way so far and it's now 11 o'clock so that's not bad. There's another poor devil who's trying to get to Abbeville, and is with me now. We got here about 10.30, so nice a couple of fresh young officers as you could wish to meet anywhere. We changed here. That is to say, on the advice of a much-braided individual, who confessed to being in the gilded profession of porters & other railways nuisances, we slid gracefully from our cattle truck on to the lines (personally my flight was arrested by one of those long handles which, I believe, work points, or signals) as the train (save the word) skidded through the station.

This place, being one of the most forsaken on earth, of course we discovered in an old carriage our ever ready friend the R.T.O. two of 'em in fact. We explained our troubles and said we wanted the next train for Abbeville. "The 1.20, you mean," he said. "What do you want it for now?" No bally train was going to Abbeville till then; I suggested an express 'peut-être pour Etaples' to the french ticket-seller man and I believe he's injured himself internally, laughing at the idea.

Quelle Vie!

At last we found some lorries and rushed at them & asked if they knew of anything going to Abbeville. "Oh yes," said one, "I believe I might be able to 'elp yer." I can tell you, it sent me 'all-of-a-didder' to hear the magic words. "My mate," went on the merry wight, "do be going to St. Omer tomorrow, I've heard, if his car's ready in time. Yer see," he explained, "We're all waiting to be repaired!"!!!!!! No bon & Na poo[8], ad lib –

Another porter directed us to the "Hotel de France et d'Angleterre" (Wow-Wow) "where all the orficers go, sir." Good work, at last a light in our darkness, and away we tottered, two worn & almost beaten veterans. The Hotel de etc. rather belies its name. You go in, past the dog (if you're lucky) and jump into what appears to be the kitchen and living room of about 20 children & a round dozen of grown &

senior grown-ups, and slam the door on the aforesaid dog (again, if you're lucky). I asked in my polished Parisien if this was really the Hotel de etc. And a buxom wench volunteered the remark 'Yees, een here, eef yew pleese." That sort of thing always annoys me. Well, here we are, "een here" quite a jolly little "dug-out" with a piano and a fire. My brother unfortunate is under the impression that he can play the piano, but as Mark Hambourg himself couldn't manage this toothless harpsichord, you can perhaps dimly conceive the row there is. I have a pair of bones too and occasionally help him through a tricky bar or two. Not the sort of 'bar' you mean! Well, well. We've ordered lunch at 12, omelette, veal & desert (s) N.B. I've put that s in brackets after desert, in case it should be required in the correct spelling of the word, popularly used to denote the fruit & finger-bowl episode of some meals.

I have now been fairly credibly informed that I shall reach ETAPLES about 4 pip emma. A 7 hour journey, but well well worth it. You simply can't realise what speaking to English ladies means. People who in peace times would probably awe, or bore me, act like a strychnine tonic out here, after you've sat glaring at the same two or three faces, in the same everlasting khaki for about 7 months.

It's simply ripping. Any girl French or English has an extraordinary & altogether disproportionate fascination for anyone who litterally hasn't seen anything in skirts for a week or so! You know how desperately shy I am, well it will show you the state you get into, when it comes to me talking to girls in Amiens just to hear a girl's voice for once, after Mr. T. Atkins' backchat or the everlasting 'barks' one gives & hears when drilling. Also it practices one's french enormously. N.B. don't be shocked, I'm not really a fool, though I may look it; and incidentally all this will be eventually communicated to Muff.

Lunch is nearly here now & I can smell the omelette in the nursery next door, so, cheer ho & cheer up, as I believe leave has started again . . . Bye bye & love to all, hope you'll like this letter, it's amused me for an hour.

Billie

Later. Home again. Saw A & had a topping time. Very well & fit & found a letter from Muff awaiting me. time 1.45 a.m. [155]

Postmarked 8.3.16   *24 General Hospital*
                                         B.E.F.
                                         France

My very dearest Mother & Elsie & Doff,

Billie came over again on Sunday it was so lovely to have him. Poor dear, he had taken 9 hrs getting here, wasn't it bad luck. Matron is quite in love with him. She thinks he is such a nice boy & seems quite disappointed there is no chance of seeing him again anyhow just at present. He is hoping to see Aunt Annie next Saturday. Home Sister & Cook were perfectly sweet & got such a jolly little dinner again for us & all the best china out again. Billie presented the cook with two pipes & various kinds of tobacco, & a tin of cigarettes for our 4 orderlies in the mess & the two kitchen boys a tin for each. Cook is a great pal of mine[9], so Billie had to be solemnly presented to him, & the kitchen all stood at attention! Billie was splendid not in the least embarassed & said & did everything right . . . [he] was looking & seemed very fit, he had a tiny cough & wanted Fomamint[10] which unfortunately I could not supply him with.[12]

Billy had mentioned 'his wee bit cough' on February 29th – 'Funny day to write on isn't it?' – and asked for the same thing, though he had called it 'a bottle of Phormamint.' [154] A week later he was able to write, 'A Glorious pharmacy fetched up to-day & was most acceptable. My cough is now cowering in terror at the array of bottles, tins & jars, which face him at every spasm. I'm hoping to see A again next Sunday,' he added, '& Aunt A as well en route, at Abbeville.' [156] At the same time Amy was telling her mother,

All yesterday & today we have been expecting Aunt Annie, & are frightfully disappointed she has not turned up. No doubt I shall hear the reason by this evening's post . . . Hellen Henry has just come back brings us the news, that the Aunt may come tomorrow, Wednesday, so all is joy & peace once more in the Camp . . . I'm just longing to see Aunt Annie & hear all your news, all about the arrangements for the wedding & exactly how you look Mother dear, if anyone or anything is altered in the house, what covers you have on the chairs in the drawing room now . . . oh just hundreds of things. [12]

Aunt Annie must have reached Abbeville by the following weekend, for Billie 'managed to flit over' on the Sunday, but, not surprisingly, failed to reach Étaples as well. 'My Course is over and I'm wandering round France trying to find my Bn.,' he told Amy on March 14th, writing from Madame Godbert's restaurant, where he had stopped for a meal. 'I saw the C.O. to-day & have borrowed a car, off the H.C.C.S. [Highland Casualty Clearing Station at Villers-Bocage, where Billie spent the previous night, more cor-rectly described as a hospital in his letter to his mother] & am on route again for Flixécourt till Thursday. I have been given command of B. Coy now & am very bucked.' [157A] It was another eventful journey.

> *Once more at* FLIXÉCOURT *but*
> *In a New Billet*
> 14.3.16.

Dear Mother & Co.,

Since I last wrote from here, when I thought I was saying goodbye to the place for good, I have travelled most of the way round France, and this letter will be a short (?) history of that wonderful organisation which we've heard so much about. I left 'Flixy' in a bus, with Marker and my valise, not knowing where on earth the Bn. was, or rather where C and D Coys were. A and B are here at F. [Flixécourt] but of course I had to join D [company]. Well we left at 2 p.m. and after 4 hrs in the bus reached HEILLY. There no one knew where we were to go, but after a struggle I found the Bn. i.e. C & D were at RAINEVILLE about 3 hrs back on the road we'd come along! The best I could find was a lorry going back to VILLERS-BOCCAGE at 7 p.m. We crawled off to tea at the officers' buffet, where the Elephant Flapper lives, and ordered tea & omelettes. So far, not so bad. We had just time for the omelette and I wouldn't touch anything till it came for fear of spoiling its taste. In it came & on to my plate. Enter the Elephant Flapper's dog. I stooped to pat the beast's head – crash-splosh, exit & descend omelette & plate. No time for more! Stuffed about 6 cream éclaires in my pocket and 4 in my mouth, paid & fled. I tried to argue that I should not pay for the omelette, as I had neither eaten it nor taken it from the premises, but no, in the hurry I gave in. Reached bus as it was due to go & found it wouldn't go for 20 mins, just not enough time to go back to E.F. & omelette, needless to say.

Started off & at once an enormous storm burst over us. During ride (4 hrs) my head hit the roof fairly regularly as we skipped up milestones & down ditches, with the ease & rapidity of a totally blind slug. At last we got to Villers-B. and I went straight to the hospital there and asked for the Colonel. 'Some' cheek! I found him going to bed & calmly asked for an ambulance to take me to Rainville about 3 miles. He was kindness itself and ordered one at once. So off we went to R. we got there about 11 p.m. Everyone was asleep except one woman, age 90, deaf, blind and nervous. I knocked on her door for about 1 hr and at last discovered that no soldiers had been there for over a week! Na bon! Back to the Hospital. Then I found Marker a billet somewhere & calmly strolled into the Hospital, & found someone, a night sister I think, and laid all before her. She found me a bed in the officers' ward & there I slept in sheets, like a crown prince! In the morning slippered orderlies ministered to my wants & the 'day brother', or whatever he's called, brought me a topping breaker. Then I found the dear old Colonel again, one Douglas, thanked him profusely & asked to use his telephone. After endless talks with everyone in France from D. Haig downwards I found the Bde. HQs. were about 3 miles away. I guessed they'd know where C and D were, so I borrowed the car again, loaded up & off we went. Reached Brigade H.Q. & found a note from the C.O. which had just been telephoned through to Flixécourt, telling me I was to have command of B Coy. & to stay at F in charge of A & B.

I met Mitchell at Bde H.Q. and told him all my woes, borrowed enough to oil my way home again & left for the C.O to report to him on the way back. He saw me & cursed me roundly for being there & off I went again after a chat with John [Bowen]. I hung on to the car, an old taxi, converted, & ordered the man to go to Amiens. We got there about 12.30 & I stopped for lunch. Finally I got back here about 2.30 p.m. having borrowed the car for a few minutes at 10 a.m.! I've got a ripping room here, sheets & electric light! To-night I got 3000 frs & paid my new Coy. & to-morrow I'm going to let 80 of them go in to Amiens for a bust. They'll love it, I know. We leave here on Thursday for CORBIE-sur-Somme. After that I don't think I'd better give you any more names.[11] I will tell you we are going about 4½ miles South of where we have been all the time. Right on the river there. 'Some' spot . . . All marshes & Bosches. No mines, thanks be, & I believe no sausages . . . Don't forget I'm B. Coy. now . . .
Crowds of love
   Yours ever
    Billie   [158]

NOTES

1. This was the nineteen-year-old Alcinie whose billets Billie had been reluctant to leave. He was not the only officer to return to see her. 'Last week we had a visit from Mr. Pegg, Mr. Hetherington, and Mr.

Wigtman [Wightman],' Alcinie wrote, in French, to Billie on February 29th, 'and on Sunday yesterday a visit from Captain John Bowen and Mr. Pegg again. They stayed quite a long time with us.'

2. Now in the Imperial War Museum with Billie's letters.
3. *Memoirs of an Infantry Officer*, p.12.
4. Event. In soldiers' terms a stunt was more usually some action or raid involving danger.
5. p. 63.
6. Amiens, the only big town in the Somme area, had a number of hotels and restaurants, as well as other services, catering for officers and men, but it was Madame Godbert's restaurant that was the favourite of the East Surreys, particularly during the early summer of 1916 when they were at Fourdrinoy and Picquigny. 'One of the finest restaurants in France,' according to P. G. Heath. Siegfried Sassoon talks of 'guzzling at the Godbert'. It was not only that the food was good. Years later Major Irwin remembered the warm welcome given by Madame Godbert, and the way evenings there almost invariably turned into sing-songs.

The East Surreys had several talented pianists and singers, and Basil Hallam was a frequent visitor. Billie had visited Amiens earlier in the year with Captain Flatau of A company, but on that occasion had dined at the impressive sounding Grand Hôtel de L'Univers. 'We had a tophole dinner & saw the Cathedral, all sandbagged & bought stacks of things.' [127]

7. The British soldier anglicised French names in an effort to make them more memorable. Heel Taps was another variation for Étaples.
8. No bon – no good. Na poo – finished, non-existent. From the French, *il n'y en a plus*.
9. Presumably one benefit from working in the Home Mess.
10. Formamint – more usually a cough lozenge.
11. Place names could be used when letters were going to be posted in England. In France security meant that no place near the front line should be named and discretion used with places in the rear. Billie seems to have been inconsistent, even so.

12 COMPANY COMMANDER

'I'm awfully bucked at getting command of B coy.,' Billie wrote home on March 14th. [158] The new command brought him a horse called Betty, but no increase in pay. Indeed he now discovered that, because his name had appeared in the Army list on January 4th as a second lieutenant in the East Yorkshire Regiment, Cox's Bank had been paying him at the second lieutenant's rate since that date – 'and I'm still a temp. Capt. & doing Major's work incidentally.'[1] [165] Despite hoping to work a transfer to the 1st or 2nd East Surreys, while keeping his 'temp. rank of Capt. as long as I'm with the East Surreys, which will be for the duration I hope,' [150] he turned down Elsie's offer of help. 'About the transfer, don't bother about asking that cove, as I've already got several very strong 'wires' being pulled by various people. And in time I hope I'll get it alright.' [150] Meanwhile, he took over charge of B company.

'They're a very decent lot,' he said, 'but now there are only 2 junior subs. to help, Drane & Alcock (the old C Coy. sergeant-major) by name, neither very exciting.' [158] Whether extra officers would have helped with the journey from Flixécourt he does not say; it sounds as though Billie's journeys in charge of a company were as eventful as journeys on his own.

CORBIE

16.3.16

Dear All,

I've had rather a comic day to-day on the whole, but a terribly rushed one. I managed to get the two coys. out of Felixtowe without much trouble, after a few farewell speeches, and we pushed down to Hangest, there we found a train & got on it. Then the fun began. It seems that one is not allowed to scull round France with 380 officers & men, without about 300 red forms – 400 passes, & 700 yellow orders & a few such details. Well I had none at all and it seemed at one period as if we should stay at Hangest for 3 years, or duration. However I found someone who had authority to let the train leave the station, & we coasted off. I told the driver where I should like to go & he knew the way & steered us in about 2 hrs over the rather tricky 20 min. course. On reaching Corbie, we obeyed the invariable rule of dashing past the platform & stopping well outside.

Here we met my coy. clerk. I had procured (?) a bicycle for him the day before and he had ridden on, overnight, to find where our billets were. One does that sort of thing after one's billets have been pinched once, or twice. Our transport lorry, with blankets, cookers, etc. & of course our valises, broke down & has just arrived – 10 p.m. Marker came with it as he missed the train this morning, 'some' youth. We're all quite comfy now & my room has a bed & also a baby's crib, which Madame seemed to think a great asset. She & M'sieur are quite decent. Drane is in the same house.

Our mess is quite a jolly room too, with about 17 girls, from 1 – 30 yrs of age. We played footer with them with the babies (no 5) ball. Beyond saying the prettiest one's name is Madeliene and she has dark hair, I can't stop over 'em.

The coy. is going very well & I'm no end bucked about it. 220 odd men all to myself. Their meals, clothes, pay, & lives too all to my responsibility. They are a topping lot, not unlike C. coy. I rather won their hearts by paying 'em & sending 'em to Amiens to enjoy themselves. To-day I've been cursing the ones who missed the train home! Bobby Soames has joined us again, and now with Drane & Alcock, we're quite a jolly little party. It's ripping having Bobby back again, he stopped a whiz-bang about 4 months ago in the Tambour, you remember. I'll tell you about our new trenches, or rather line, when I've seen it. [159]

'I've been simply humming round getting the company straight & working smoothly,' he told his mother on March 21st, apologising for his neglect of her, and telling her of the battalion's changed surroundings. 'We're not in trenches here, but on outpost in the marshes, very difficult work & trying for everyone but very interesting . . . We have no billets and shall probably be up about 2 months.'[2] [161]

The East Surreys had moved south to the far right of the British line where it met with the French. 'Get the papers for the 27th last & you will see a place called Vaux is mentioned as having been shelled,' Billie told his family on March 30th. 'Vaux is where we are.' [166]

Christian Carver, the R.F.A. officer attached to the East Surreys who spent his days in the observing station in the wood on top of the cliff behind Vaux, described the area in a letter to his father:

Below [the cliff] is a small hamlet from which the wood takes its

name, then comes the river, then a sort of no man's land peninsula
enclosed by a loop in the river, then the German side of the loop. Out
from the village runs a causeway, and at the end, in the peninsula is
our advance post . . . Straight away for a long way runs the river, to
the left is the small village of C. [Curlu], about 2000 yards, to the right
the better known place of Frise, where the recent fighting was. It is
about as interesting a sector as you could wish for. There are
practically no trenches, so you can fairly often catch the huns in the
open, and you can see all his trains and motor transport, etc., in [the]
rear.[3]

Billie described one such occasion in a letter home on March 29th.

The other day we spotted 3 huns dressed in skirts to look like
French civilians, digging a trench across the village green at CURLU, a
hun village opposite, one of our officers took careful aim and fired &
as luck would have it hit him on the 27th of March. He limped away
holding it with one hand & shaking the other fist, helped by the two
others. The[y] reached a house & went in & we whiz-banged it, so
they let out a lot of little French children & of course we had to stop!!!
I'm not romancing! That's true.

He wrote of another incident the following day.

To-day I went up to one of our observation posts with my telescope and
on the far hill I saw three Bosches in the open, one of them had no hat on &
looked very solemnly over here & said nothing apparently, also he seemed
to be wearing khaki, & not the bluish gray of the other two, who were evidently annoyed with this hatless one & gesticulated & waved a map. Altogether I'm positive in my own mind that he was one of the prisoners we lost
the other night when they attacked us & we drove them off again. I noted all
I could about him & if he answers the description of one of our chaps, it will
be interesting to let his people know he's safe.[4] [166]

Life for the East Surreys in this part of the world was very different from
the troglodyte existence they had led in the Tambour. Scouting between
river, marshes and causeway (the only way the enemy could attack in person) had a distinct air of playing pirates about it. 'We hold our bit of the river
and Fritz holds his, and we scout for each other in the park, and chivey each
other among the trees to the north,' Carver said. Although there was no
longer the fear of being blown up by mines at any moment, danger existed
at Vaux quite as much as it had in the north. On March 21st the Germans

attacked Duck's Post, one of the battalion's most advanced posts, in an attempt to blow up the bridges of the causeway.

> 21.3.16
> Last night I went to bed (?) at 2.30 a.m. & was up again at 4.30 a.m. as the Huns attacked a post of the next Company. 150 of 'em against 20 odd and we chucked em out with the bayonet, caught one & killed 4 & wounded several.[5] [161]

Billie continued to send technical details home, presumably for the benefit of Howard and Stanley, who received copies of his letters from Doff.

> *Up. 30.3.16*
> Dear All,
> ... There's a new, (to me) kind of shell the Bosches use here, or rather not a new shell but a new way of using it. It's his 5"-9[6] high explosive, burst with a time fuse in the air like an ordinary shrapnel, instead of bursting on percussion on the ground or a tree. The 5"-9 in the air is usually a great yellow lyddite shell and makes a huge smoke & they are commonly called "woolly bears". The next size in H.E. is 8".2 which is a black smoke shell, and when burst in the air is, of course, a "Coal box". They are the biggest hun shells I've met yet. That was in the old Tambour & I'm quite contented thank you! I've seen bigger English shells, a 9".2 for instance, which is a really huge brute, I've seen it remove 3 houses at a burst in Fricourt honestly; it's "some" sight!
> These 'woolly bears' I was talking about, are very harmless in the air, on the ground they make a hole about 3 to 4 feet deep and about 10 or 11 feet across, that's the 5".9 size, corresponding to our 6 inch! Then they have a light howitzer 4".2, not much good on the whole, & then there are the ordinary whiz bangs, just about 3.1 inch, corresponding to our field guns. A whiz-bang shrapnell is usually called a "pip-squeak". Enough! Today has been perfectly heavenly, bright sun all day and quite warm. We caught some fish, which tasted like mud[7], had a little boating and punting & I shot at some coots and moorhens.
> There has been an enormous lot of anti aircraft shelling to-day by both sides, & this morning I saw a real fight, the machine guns fairly going & I thought every minute they'd run into each other, marvellous steering & fairly high up. At the moment I'm dead cushy, I've got about a week more here & then about a fortnight – elsewhere – & then here again & I hope leave. [166]

2.4.16

Dear Anyone & Everyone,

I hadn't meant to write to-day but I thought it might amuse you to hear that the beloveds shrapnelled us to-day and one of my blankets, which was airing in the sun had nine holes in and another 3. Well, that's not fair; I've gone to great trouble stealing those blankets and they're irreplacable, & now I'll have nine separate draughts.

The major had a whole in his vest & his servant got two in his pants. (Both articles were drying from the river laundry.)

V.B.L.

Billie

5.4.16 (night)

Well, Well. How's everyone?

I was quite sorry to leave the old place but this wood promises to be great fun. It's one crawling mass of blue-bells, cowslips anemones (?) and shell holes.[8] We're all in dug outs & shanties and under odd hurdles or half inside bread sacks, in fact in the usual condition of things. B. Coy is on its own now & so I have everything to myself and it's rather jolly. Since the 19th I've been <u>sort of</u> in charge of two Coys.[9], and had no particular fixed abode, consequently I've lost one or two things, including Mother's scarf, which I'd like replaced at once, several pairs of gloves (most of which I'd already stolen off absent-minded visitors) and one or two oddments.

I've got quite a decent dug-out here & I share it with Bobby Soames, who as you know is a most priceless chap, and who acts as my 2nd Capt. and looks after Coy. pay and one or two odd little worries like that. <u>He's</u> topping. I'm surrounded with orderlies & servants and have a sentry at the door of my dug out all night, so I don't think we shall come to much harm. The sentry is not to preserve my own hide, or Bobby's but to wake us officers up the second there may be any alarm. Talking of servants, I strafed Marker tonight till he moaned with remorse, because the silly blighter had handed in all my blankets when we moved, because he thought they weren't mine!! Blankets, (riddled with shrapnell, cf a letter 2 days ago) on which I'd spent hours of scheming to pinch from attached gunner officers & other quilted bed-bugs. Jacobs & Alcock live down the road about 50 yds away. The bed here (wire netting) looks quite decent. Up till now, I've spent alternate nights on the floor and in a sacking bed, rather rotten really. Rats are noisy but keep mostly on the floor or table, so that's alright. Another great asset is an oil lamp instead of the eternal

candles. Marker will carry this lamp in his hand if necessary for the
rest of the Continental Tour. I'm getting the place in order now,
there's a fire place (no need for a fire tonight) a waste paper sandbag,
four proper chairs, & one imitation, two tables, 3 good shelves and
heaps of nails to hang on, quite topping, not too low either, decent
steps down & a nice door. We have two bowls (?) of flowers & they
will be changed daily. I'm afraid it's a bit far to send for water cress
which we had before. Where we were we used to send the C.O. a
bundle of water-cress & then ask if there might be a rum issue that
night! Simple lessons in strategy!

We're short of butter & milk chiefly, now we're going to start an
account with the A.N.S. or some place, simply for those two things.
We gave up our parcels in C. Coy. because the canteens out here were
so good & cheap. But the bally canteens either sell out, or can't get the
stuff, before the marooned birds like us, with no billets can get at 'em.
I can tell you I'm about ten times fitter than I've been before, which is
saying oceans. Bobby & Jacobs are also very fit, but I'm a bit worried
about Alcock (he's a married man of 34) as he seems a bit seedy & has
a bad foot. You know sometimes I sit down & laugh to myself when I
think what I was before this bally War. Now I've got 200 odd men,
solely under me, to feed, pay, clothe, house, advise on every
conceivable subject, lecture to [10], teach, & order about in emergencies,
organise, act as judge to, in fact every blooming thing, & the funniest
part of it all is that it doesn't worry me a bit or awe me, though the
thought of it in England used to frighten me a bit, but I know I've got
real good officers to back me up & I feel absolutely confident in the
men themselves & that's why I can feel confident in myself, which is
the most important thing. I don't know why I should suddenly
ramble off like that, but it suddenly struck me then again. Don't think
I'm swanking. [171]

Same old Place
4.4.16

Dear All & Sundry,
    Yesterday was great fun. I started off about 12 noon to go to H.Qs
for lunch. When I arrived with one of my new orderlies (Watson, an
ex-page boy at the Tavistock Hotel, Covent Gds & a jolly smart kid
too) I found the C.O. and the Brigadier & a cask of beer. We had a
cheery little lunch out in the open, under some trees, as it was a
scalding hot day again. After lunch the C.O. took me with him to the
Village and we went out to our advanced posts. While I was there

Wightman (scout officer) & an Australian corporal called Ankertel, guided by a French soldier, a native of these parts, who knows every stick & stone in the woods, set off on a daylight patrol.[11] I got leave to join them, took my orderlie's rifle & crept off. We cracked & crashed through the trees for a long way & it was great fun, as we are one end of the wood & the Bosche is the other. We got right through & found a little German breastwork of sandbags. It was pretty exciting hopping over those sandbags as we weren't quite certain if it was occupied or not by day. It is by night we know. It was quite good fun as we were the first people who had ever got into it. Others had seen it. We found little traps all along the path to it, which we carefully replaced in position. In the breastwork we found no Huns but a bomb, a bandolier of ammunition, and two shovels. I got the bandolier as a souvenir, it did have 9 clips of 5 cartridges in it, but I've given 7 away, & now the bandolier with two clips is waiting to come home with me. Alas, I hear that bally leave is stopped again.

The other night the C.O. made me take him out to help remove a booby trap laid on a bridge near here. It was a big shell and if you touched the bridge it was supposed to explode. However Wightman had already crossed the bridge & nothing had happened, so to get rid of it [we] tied wire round each end of it and fastened a long piece of wire to it, went away about 30', lay down & heaved it off the girder (which is all that's left of the bridge, after it was blown up months ago) and it fell harmlessly into the water & did not explode after all. Still it's interesting work fingering these booby traps. [169]

Billie seems to have given up reassuring his family of the lack of danger, presumably because he knew it was pointless. In any case, tragedy came close to home with the death of Muffie's younger brother, Peter Schooling, on March 30th, after he'd been up only one day. 'You'll write to Mrs. and Muff won't you? If you haven't already heard & written.' [170]

'It was bad luck about Peter wasn't it?' he wrote on April 5th. 'I'm so sorry for poor old Muff, & the others, mais c'est la guerre, as everyone says & it's very true.' [171] 'Peter Schooling was hit clean through the head & died in 10 mins without becoming conscious again,' [182] he said later, but as this was the standard reassurance to the bereaved it is impossible to say whether this was true or not. Billie had a letter from Muff, 'she's staying with the Stoops at Byfleet[12]. She didn't want to leave Mrs. S. herself, but Mrs. S said, quite rightly, that she'd better go & try to forget about Peter and enjoy herself as much as possible.' [180]

I go to Vaux Village tomorrow [Billie wrote on April 7th, enclosing a map which was to be posted, with the letter, in England]. Now I'm in Vaux Wood. I've just come from Royal Dragon's Wood. The French are in Eclusier. We are in the Moulin de Fargny & the Bosche is in Curlu . . . Keep this map. You'll find Fricourt up north. I've put a X on the Tambour. Also I've marked in my Billet at Ville, when with D. Coy. And Heilly where the Elephant Flapper lives. I've filled in the line roughly from Hamel to Fargny Mill, where the trench line ends. We hold as outposts the whole front from the Mill to Eclusier. I've marked Duck's Post, one of our most advanced posts. The wood just beyond is Lodge Wood where we patrol & Bosche hunt. I don't think I've said anything that the Bosche doesn't know already, so it's alright . . .

 Cheery Oh & Love to all
  Buckets of love
   Yours ever *Bill*   [174]

Living in Vaux – 'a sweet little riverside resort, really charming, duck shooting & fishing good, shelling fair to middling, accommodation fair, but would stand improvement. Sun provided. Good well water. Cuisine distant but good' [175] – B company occupied 'a huge great cellar, used by my predecessors as a Zoo for bats & mice, so far as one can judge! As you can't see more'n about 2 feet, you can't judge far!' [175] The cellar housed

Soames, Jacobs, a telephone, 7 bats & about eighteen grown up rats & of course self . . . The trouble about this cellar is that all the different quarters (ours, servants, orderlies, telephonists, etc.) are only separated by hanging blankets & we hear one or two things which perhaps weren't meant for our ears. Jacobs has a tin whistle & what with my bones[13], we make a bonny din. The clock in the signal office has a tick like a kettle drum & promises to keep us all awake easily . . . I heard a chap say the other day that he thought the next generation would be born with their boots on & sleep with their eyes open. I wonder! [175A]

Unfortunately they took to 'gypsying in the woods' [178] just as the weather changed. 'We were really more comfy in the Village than in this wood where we are now, but both are heaven compared to the Tambour or any trenches in fact.'

I pity the poor brutes in trenches this weather. We do stroll about in the open like kings, still an occasional whiz bang makes you feel you'd like a trench handy before the next one comes. A blighted sniper nearly bagged me the other day, though; I didn't think he could see me, but I was talking to one of my orderlies in Lodge wood, and it hit the tree just between & behind us. You see the careless hun bird had seen two & knew we'd bolt after the first shot, so aimed sort of at both of us, & sort of hit both us, only just missed both. Needless to say we ran to cover, & he squirted one after us for luck, which went well over. I don't mind huns firing into the dark over a parapet in a promiscuous sort of way, when one's wiring, because you know it's a fluke if you stop, or hinder one, but a well-trained sniplet with a telescopic-sighted accurate rifle firing at 600' in bright daylight should be avoided with speed. That's the first time I've had occasion to run for about 2 months, and a hundred yards about did me down, such a state of stagnation does one get into. I do (with the men as well) half an hour's physical drill every morning, one [hasn't] spare time for more, or one gladly would . . .

Last night the Bosches elected to let off every gun, howitzer, cannon, musket fouling piece & blunderbus, which he could lay hands from 2 – 2.30. I sprang out had a good look round but it was just on our left. A lot of our guns fired and the brethren heaved a lot of 'express trains' over us on to roads & things behind. There was quite a lot of ill feeling on the whole & an immense quantity of old iron in the air. It was a fearfully impressive sight to stand & watch. A faint wiff of tear gas (very pleasant in small quantities as I told you) added a little extra charm to the scene. We were all happily asleep again by 3 a.m., except Jacobs who I sent round with some rum, to buck people up a bit. [179]

A week later they returned to the cellar.

We've just taken over that wood where I found the Bandolier, and consequently it's meant a lot of readjustment of sentry posts & a lot of careful surveying by day & night. I've spent the last two days tramping through the wood, which is only about 4 yds deep in quagmire. It's all settled up now, & the C.O. came down this afternoon to look round & was quite pleased. It's quite nice to sit down & write to you all, feeling really happy & contented. The C.O. took Soames back to H.Q. to tea with him & as Jacobs is at Duck Post and Alcock is wiring in the Wood till after dark, I'm all on my lonesome in our celler, with the orderlies & telephones etc. It's beautifully peaceful, & quiet. I suppose we must be at war still, the paper says so. But you never know what to believe nowadays. [182]

Easter in 1916 fell on April 23rd, St. George's Day and the anniversary of
Shakespeare's birth.

A Happy Easter to you All [Billie wrote on Easter Saturday], I'm
afraid this will be late for Easter, but I thought of it alright too early
and when the right day came I'd no time; besides all that, it's so
curious to write a cheery Easter letter on Maundy Thursday or Good
Friday, especially when you're wet through & it's still raining! [183]

Both Billie and Amy found regular worship difficult during their time in
France. 'Church or any help of that sort is not to be had here,' Amy com-
mented, when asking for a helpful book for Lent. 'Church of a sort is, but
not much of it & it's only too easy to get slack.' [12] The previous autumn she
and Aunt Annie had always attended the 6.30 communion service on Thursday mornings. [5] Night duty put a stop to that.

One thing against night work is it's almost impossible to get to
church, there is a service at 8, but of course you are not really due off
until then – however that's no excuse, as you can hand over your
report to the Staff nurse, or whoever happens to be the early one on,
but these last two Sundays, I just felt it was quite impossible to keep
awake, we have not been sleeping well in our new huts up to the
present. [8]

While not as scathing as Robert Graves, Billie does back up Graves's con-
tention that Church of England padres tended to remain at the rear; though
he charitably blamed both circumstances and Headquarters – 'The padres
themselves are quite willing but they don't seem to take opportunities with
small parties, they like to get whole battalions together right back in billets.'
[177] He was quite prepared to take action himself to remedy the situation if
necessary – 'It's Sunday to-morrow and I am taking the whole Battalion at
Church Parade in the morning,' he wrote on one occasion. [58] Communion
was particularly difficult.

This morning I was able to go to an early service in an old
schoolroom [he told his mother on October 10th]. It's the first time for
3 months I think, and the fact that I was the only one of "this
congregation here present" made it none the less impressive &
helpful! At Church Parade later on, it was very noticeable that the

men were far more attentive and sang much louder than at home, although there were so few left to come. That man Geeves is still our Brigade Chaplain, though I'm afraid he's very badly treated by the authorities and no one helps him much. And a Brigade in action (half always in the trenches) is a pretty scattered parish. [74]

'It's about mid-Lent now, isn't it?' he asked on March 29th. 'I've given up billiards, washing & theatres to mark the season properly. [165] 'Leave is another thing I've given up during Lent,' he added on April 4th. [169] But Lent was not a matter for jokes.

Same cellar

9.4.16

Dear Mother,

. . . As today is the Vth Sunday in Lent & no parson has taken a service for us for at least 6 weeks, I think longer, I'm taking a little short service myself tonight after tea for those of B Coy who are not actually on posts. Just the Confession, Gospel, Lord's Prayer, Creed, a tiny address on Easter & Lent, & a couple of hymns. Hetherington is going to come down from the Wood & help us with the hymns. He sings beautifully. It's not much, but it's just something & as I've told you before I think it's disgraceful how few services we get out here.[14] I may not be a pukka padre but I'll bring something home to 'em. I was going to hold it in the Church here, but I'm afraid it might not be liked by the R.Cs here in the Coy., or a French soldier who lives here as a guide, so we're having it in the open. [177]

Billie even had difficulty organising the services for Easter Day. 'Would you believe it I had to go down & worry away at H.Qs and then write a long letter begging for them. The padré was alright about 'em, but H.Qs are awfully slack in that way, I'm afraid. However it's alright now.' [183]

A very, very, happy Easter to you all [he wrote home on the day itself]. To-day is perfectly lovely, absolute summer weather. We had morning service in anti-shellfire formation in the Wood, and H. Communion in the new H.Q. dugout afterwards.[15] This afternoon we've been boating & fishing. [184]

'One little scene comes to my mind,' J.C. Drane, one of Billie's subalterns, told Mrs. Nevill in a letter of condolence the following August. 'On Easter Sunday morning, at his invitation, the Chaplain came up to the trenches, and there, in a front line dug-out, we, Billie & I partook of the Holy Communion. I shall never forget it.'

NOTES

1. 'My pay at Cox's has been adjusted now to that of a Capt. alright,' he reported two weeks later. [182]
2. 'When I do get leave I shan't have had my clothes off since March 18th anyhow,' he wrote on March 30th. He did not go on leave until the beginning of May.
3. 30th March, 1916.
4. Unfortunately he never mentioned the incident again so it is impossible to say whether he was romancing on this occasion.
5. In fact the German casualties occurred during a counter-attack organised by Pearce before dawn that same night. Only 2 dead were found. The prisoner was the first German taken by the 55th Brigade.
6. Billie must mean '5.9 inch', and similarly throughout the letter.
7. 'Jimmy, the Surreys' M.O. pulled out a 6 lb pike on a trout cast after 15 minutes of the best, last night.' (Carver, 21 April 1916)
8. He sent some of the bluebells home – 'I hope they won't be dead when you get them.' [172] Bluebells being notoriously short-lived, Mrs. Nevill must surely have been tactful rather than truthful when acknowledging their arrival, for a week later Billie was writing that he was 'so awfully glad the flowers arrived fresh.' [180]
9. The second was D, his old company, while John Bowen was away.
10. While still at Flixécourt he had asked for 'the biggest War Map of the whole of Europe, fairly soon, & also a map of the world as well, for lecture purposes. Not too big, like you have in schools.' [150]
11. The story of Scholari, the guide, typifies the tragedy of many Frenchmen during the war. Before 1914 he had run phosphate mines in this area. After serving with his regiment in Lorraine he returned to his own neighbourhood during the winter of 1916, to act as a guide for the British. His mother and fiancée

still lived in Curlu but as Curlu was in German hands, Scholari had had no contact with them since 1914. However, from the observation post above Vaux he was able to watch them through the telescope as they picked vegetables in their garden. Scholari was very popular with the British, 'a most excellent and brave soldier', according to the regimental history, '[who] resented any patrol being sent out which did not include him'. 'He simply lives to kill Huns,' Carver said. Two weeks after Billie's letter he was killed while out on patrol. Lt.-Col. Powell, the East Surreys' C.O., recommended that some English military honour should be conferred on him and given to his relatives. There does not seem to be any record of this being done and in any case it is difficult to see what award he could have been given. The French were more generous to foreigners. Aunt Annie was one of those to benefit, being awarded the Legion of Honour.
12. The Stoops were old friends of the Schooling family. Their daughter and Muffie had shared a governess until Muffie went away to school at the age of 12.
13. 'Will you send me out a pair of 'bones' like niggers rattle you know,' Billie had asked on February 2nd, adding, 'This is important.' [143] 'Bones' were the nineteenth-century negro's equivalent of Spanish castanets, two pieces of rib bone, usually that of an ox, which were held between the fingers & rhythmically clacked. 'The bones you sent are good,' Billie wrote on February 28th, 'but I should like a set of larger ones please.'
14. Contrary to Billie's belief, the War Diary records church parades on numerous occasions. Heath thought that part of the problem stemmed from the unimpressive personality of the Church of England chaplain. The

Roman Catholic Capt. Aveling, in contrast, was an erudite, charismatic man, a Jesuit who was not above proselytizing on occasion (Heath suspected this was as much to irritate his Anglican colleague as for any religious reason), as a result of which attendance at the duller C. of E. church parades dwindled while that at Catholic ones flourished.

15. The Divisional History records that on Easter Sunday 'a truly impressive Church of England service [was] held in the quarry near Dragon's Wood hard by the East Surreys H.Q. The Boche was so near that there could be no singing and the prayers had to be said in low voices.' (p.34)

13 SPRING LEAVE

Despite the still wintry weather, signs of spring were beginning to show in the countryside around the camp at Étaples.

Postmarked 8.3.16   *24 General Hospital*
                                                    B.E.F.
                                                    France

My very dearest Mother & Elsie & Doff,
    . . . The woods round here are just perfect. Gordon & I went on Saturday & got heaps of wild daffs, enough to make the eight tables in the mess look very jolly, the undergrowth was all periwinkle and just the anemonies beginning then the daffs & a few oxlips, & presently it will be a mass of hyacinths, really they are a sight. I did so wish you all could have been there to see them, & yesterday some of the sisters came back with heaps of little sweet violets, from somewhere, quite possible to manage from your 2 – 5 off time. The weather has been unspeakable lately, snow, frost, cold winds, & now sleet rain, perfectly beastly, the trenches must be worse I suppose, but the men don't wear cotton frocks in them! [12]

But the strain of the past winter was beginning to tell. For Amy there had also been the additional strain of having to serve two masters for so long. In much the same way that Billie tried to reassure his family but chose words that were only likely to increase their anxiety, Amy wrote home on April 9th,

Don't worry over my wheeze & cough, they are going strong. Everyone is so awfully kind & sensible about it. I am up & about but not on duty, of course I do little things such as the flowers etc. The thing is I'm not to catch another cold, & am to get rid of this cough before going to the new work. I am to go to Hardelot, where Aunt Annie went for her little rest, it's a charming spot, right up in the sand hills & pines ½ [hour] from the sea, & I know Lady Gifford &

Miss Inglis & one of my favourite sisters are there, so I shall have a lovely week. Breakfast in bed every day!! & just laze about & do nothing. Get all my letters written up I hope. So I shall just get my leave feeling very extra fit, & also my hands will have a little chance of getting healed up. It really is good of them to look after me. It's quite an unheard of thing to be up & about, a lady at large & still in the camp. I'm not to get tired or do tiring things, & am having extra milk. I really & truly feel quite well, only you know how alarming my cough & wheeze would sound to those unused to it. [13]

Well [she wrote a week later], here I am. I have wheezed & coughed to some purpose at last. This is absolutely delightful. There are no rules, or I should say just one, & that is you must have breakfast in bed! Well I'm in a real comfortable bedroom, with proper furniture & a spring matress, and a fire in my room when I go to bed at night, & every comfort. Lady Gifford & Miss Inglis are absolute dears, also there is one of my favourite sisters from 24 having a week's rest as well, so we walk & talk together. The country is ideal, beautiful pine woods all round, with sand hills, you just get to the top of a sand hill & then you see the sea, which is only 2 mls off. I've not been down yet, but certainly shall one day. A bus from here goes into B [Boulogne] every day. Sister Davies & I went in it yesterday with some of the others & Lady Gifford & Miss Inglis. I had to get a pair of house slippers, I couldn't be here without any, & of course you never have a chance to wear any in our hut life. The joy of a bathroom under the same roof, & almost next door to you, your shoes cleaned, & hot water bottle filled for you, warm rooms to come to, & no parafine smell or lamp to fill anywhere. Breakfast is brought to you at nine, Lady G. brought me mine this morning, & you get up when you like, it's pelting today & I'm very glad I'm not running like a rabbit backwards & forwards in it, from the mess to the kitchen, it doesn't help a cough, but is healthy if you haven't one. Each morning of course I have from habit awakened at 6, & then with a sigh of content, rolled over & gone to sleep until my breakfast has arrived . . . There are about 20 sisters convalesing here, but sprinkled about in the various rooms, you don't come across them much. Also Sister Davies & I are out as much as possible & they all prefer the fire. I am very spoilt & have a room to myself, absolutely topping. I feel such a lady, & can wear my coat & skirt, & no cap, so I have to do my hair properly, it was such a nuisance yesterday, it refused to be done, it's getting quite long & thick!! from the long rest of no back combing! [14]

Amy made little of her illness. 'You know I always sound so much worse than I really am, which is a pity, because it agitates everyone so much that doesn't know my wheezy habits' [14], and insisted that she was 'clearing up beautifully, as I always do, with the lazy treatment – hot milk at night & mid-day.' However, she did appreciate the break from hospital routine.

> *Still at Lady Gifford's*
> Ap.17th

My dearest of dear Mothers, Elsie & Doff & Tom,
  Isn't it terrific luck to get this lovely rest before my leave. I didn't know I was tired until I had this lovely chance to rest . . . I still wake up each morning about 6.0 & then quietly roll over & sleep another good three hrs, & wonder already, if the other life in the huts & the "rabiting" round as we call it is only a dream. I didn't really feel tired getting up at 6.30 last week, & yet I don't feel the least inclination to do it now . . . I can't tell you how absolutely lovely & beautiful it is here. Tiny bits remind me of Holmbury, only the pines are all on such beautiful sand hills, & at the top of each you get most perfect views of the sea, which is only 2 mls off. I walked there with one of the sisters one day. It's a pity Tom can't spend some of his holidays here. Perfectly charming little golf links, a lovely castle, & wild boars in the forest to add to the excitements of the walks. I expect to go to 2 Stationary Hospital on Monday. [15]

It was the first mention of a move. No. 2 Stationary Hospital was at Abbeville.[1] So, since her transfer to the Matron-in-Chief's Headquarters, was Aunt Annie. It is impossible not to see the latter's hand behind the move.[2] Certainly Amy was reluctant to leave Étaples. 'I'm very sorry to be leaving 24 for nearly everything except Aunt Annie. I feel I'm leaving such a lot of friends behind.' [15]
  But Amy was not one to dwell on regrets, and in any case was pre-occupied with thoughts of her coming leave. 'Only about a fortnight now & I shall be home, I can hardly believe it. This week is gently breaking me in, for the comforts of life again.' [14]
  This was to be a particularly important leave, for Elsie and Nulli were getting married. After hesitating for a long time because of the difference in age – Nulli was twelve years younger than she – Elsie had agreed the previous Christmas to become engaged. 'I can't tell you how pleased I am Elsie has the ring,' Amy had written then, 'not that it really makes a scrap of difference, but I should love to see them both, old Nulli purring like a sleek tabby cat.'[3][6]

The wedding was planned for May, though it does sound from the letters as if there were one or two unexplained hitches. Stanley was still in Egypt but it was hoped that the other members of the family would be able to attend. Arranging leave was difficult enough, however, without trying for a particular date. The wedding and hopes of leave take up space in the letters of both Billie and Amy but it was the latter who was anxious to learn all the details.

I am just longing to see Aunt Annie to hear all your news [Amy wrote on March 8th, while waiting for her aunt to call in on her way to Abbeville after leave in England], all about the arrangements for the wedding.

What about Nulli, I do hope he was refused on account of his eyes, it would be back luck if he had to go now.[4]

I tremble to think of my leave due next month!! think of it, but as all leave has been stopped this month I'm thinking how behind I am, many dozens due before me, they do speak hopefully & say you can sometimes do an exchange. Elsie can't get married without me. Tom will I suppose have to give her away! He can if he has been confirmed. Has he said anything about his classes? [12]

How are the dresses getting on, & all the other preparations [she asked on April 14th]. I'll soon be home to give a hand. I shall be quite at home laying places for so many on the day. How simple it would be, if we could just make everyone do with one plate, spoon, knife and fork.

I can't conceive why the Aunt ever thought it possible for me to have 14 days [she said, two days later]. It seems to me ½ the sisters are arranging their leaves for sister's or brother's weddings . . . oh it's too horrible to think about but yesterday we heard all leave was to be stopped from the 18th & I shall live in agonies in case it's not open again by the 28th, so many poor dears are dreadfully disappointed. [15]

Billie, too, was facing disappointment. 'Leave has just been stopped again this morning!!!' he announced on April 12th, at the end of a letter in which he complained that he had not had a 'sniff of leave for 4 months and more,' – unlike the C.O. who, as Billie had pointed out the previous week, was 'going on leave, for his third time, today, I believe.' [172]

Most of the battalion have had two goes now, but of course it [is] just the fortunes of war and lately I've been too interested in the company, and the sector to want to go. But now I've been to each bit of this sector and it's raining – well – I could do with a night in pyjamas, or even an hour or two in bedroom-slippers, some nice fried sole, and a good revue and a good rag & binge, somewhere. [179]

Leave is still stopped [he wrote on the 15th], but it may come on again soon. It would be great if I could get back with Amy and both of us be [home] for the Wedding. But perhaps now Nulli has broken free at last, those arrangements will all be altered. Poor old Elsie, but still somehow you couldn't picture Elsie being married quietly and calmly. She's sure to be late, or forget the day, or marry the wrong man, or something exciting will happen I know. [180]

'How nice to have Tom home to look after the presents,' Amy said. 'I'm glad they are rolling in.' [15] Whatever had happened, or was happening be-tween Elsie and Nulli (the mystery is never explained), the wedding was presumably going ahead. Billie's present was sent through his mother.

Here is a cheque for ten guineas. I want you to buy £10 worth of 5% Exchequer bonds repayable in 1920, for Elsie and Nulli as a wedding present from me.
Elsie has asked me not to give her any more than the five pounds towards the headache cure, so I won't now. This will be jolly nice for them in 1920 as it will have grown a good bit, to about twelve pounds. They can of course get at it any time they like at the Market price at the moment. She seems to like one Bond, so I thought I'd get her a couple more to go with IT. If, for some reason or other they don't get married now, then buy the two five pound bonds for me, will you, please?
I'm telling Cox to buy me £25 worth for myself, and of course they would go with [the] rest of my belongings according to my will, which Uncle Leonard has. But I shall have 'em myself in 1920, by which time they will have grown to just over £30.
I'm hoping to save enough now to keep myself in the Army after-wards without calling on my capital at all . . .
With VBL from
    Wilfred
The odd 10/- is for Easter eggs to everyone I know at Twick. The Prossers, The Boddys, the servants, everyone. [181]

By Easter Saturday Billie was hopeful that he would be able to wangle leave by hook or crook, round about the 26th-30th of this month! Don't count on it, you're too old soldiers to do that, I know, but unless leave stops again, which is highly improbable (mind you, it's not on again yet but will be, I'm sure), or unless I collect any unnecessary old iron, which is equally improbable now for a bit, I should be home over the 6th. What a rag, Amy How [Howard] & I all clicking each other like that, 'some' stunt. [183]

Because there still seemed some doubt however, Billie eventually applied for special leave,

and the C.O. is going to try & work it. When I say special leave, I mean leave at that special time, as leave has started again. I may arrive the day after, as the C.O. wants me to stay with the Bn. during our 3 day march back to our rest billets at Picquigny, beyond Amiens. I've got to see the C.O. this afternoon & I'll probably hear something more definite, anyhow I'll post this now to raise your hopes, and very likely I'll send a card later to-night if I've time. I spent an awfully interesting morning going all round the French lines in the Bois de la Vache, where the Bosche got [to] when he took Frise, 3 months ago. Lor! the shell holes. [185]

A postcard   25.4.16
My Dears,
    The C.O. has promised to get me home somehow, on the Staff boat if necessary, by the 6th. I should sail on the night of the 5th, give me full particulars of the times of every movement on the 6th & I hope I'll pick you up about midday. I shall be home for about 9 days, as leave has been lengthened from 8 to 10 days! [186]

                                                              As Usual
                                                              26.4.16
Blighty oh Blighty, in about a week. Programme. 4th. the 6.15 from Amiens to Boulogne, ordinary french train, not a leave train, and then if I can get over that night I shall, but I'll probably have to wait till the 5th & sail then. 6th. Folkestone, London, where I'll ring up home for instructions, it's too late for you to write to me, now, so leave instructions won't you?
    You must write and ask Muff up of course, so as not to clash with Howard, if possible.
    Warn Cox's to have a lot of money in about then!
    Don't let too many relations know!

I shall try to work a night at Dover with Evans [a master at Dover College], but they'll all be on leave too. Then you may have to put up Woodroffe [an old schoolfriend].

Hang out my blue suit & brush my bowler.

Destroy all tinned fruit, & lay in vegetables, potatoes particularly, as we've had none for 4 weeks now. Sheets, sheets, sheets!!! I don't want to see a candle flame either. And as little bacon, tea, and ordinary white cheddar cheese, as possible! I think I'll go & see Arthur Reid, as I've had toothache for the first time in my life lately.[5] The weather is glorious, I hope it'll hold, but the gnats are – deletion by censor! I shall leave during our march back to billets so with that & six weeks & more up, don't expect me too spruce & correct. I may not be able to wangle Boulogne, which will mean staying the night there & going to Havre next day, and on in the ordinary way. Boulogne is only for Staff, Colonels & Nurses.

Cheery oh, isn't it great,
    VBL to all
    Bill [187]
P.S. I've still a good week to get hit in. WPN

A postcard   27.4.16
Only 8 more days now! I shall have a lovely ride in to Amiens for a start off, and a perfect morning. Don't forget to ask Muff up, or I shan't come you know! Everything points to leave continuing smoothly. A regiment near here, did a stunt & laid out about 50 huns. VBL WPN

                                                               29.4.16
Dearests,
    I've just sent off a parcel of old clothes, be careful with them. The shirt has fought its last fight, and the pants & vests are "to be in England now that April's here! Shelley [in fact Browning]". There are a few other oddments which you'd better treasure up till the "Hero's Homecoming", in 3 reels twice nightly; or "Why girls leave home", in three parts!!

    I believe I shall have to do 3 days' marching just before I come home, after 6½ weeks practically sitting still in one spot, so don't mind if I want to have brekker in bed just one morning.

    I had a hot shower in Suzanne this morning, and I've hardly

scratched since, it's ripping. The weather is still heavenly, and I'm dying for my leave, it's sure to be stopped, I know.

Crowds of Vic Beer L.

Yrs

Bill

Billie's letters give the impression that the wedding was taking place on May 6th. Whatever the planned date, Elsie and Nulli were married on May 2nd by Nulli's father, in the parish church at Teddington. Tom gave Elsie away. Amy was a witness. Neither Billie nor Howard managed to 'click' the exact date. Howard arrived home while Billie was still on leave but the day after Amy had returned to France.

NOTES

1. Stationary hospitals were comparatively small hospitals on the line of communication between casualty stations behind the front line and base hospitals along the coast line, the latter having to be near ports from which the wounded could be evacuated to England when necessary.

   Mrs. Nevill got the address wrong again and had to be corrected. 'I expect to go to '2 Stationary Hospital on Monday, Mother dear, it's not 2 General as you wrote in your letter. 2 General is miles away and I might never get your letters.'

2. The following year Aunt Annie did move Amy, from No. 2 Stationary to No. 8 Michelham in Dieppe, a convalescent home for officers, where the lightness of the work made it almost a convalescent home for nurses, too. Though Aunt Annie may have organised the move out of consideration for Amy's health, Amy objected strongly at the time. However, she did later ask her mother to 'tell Aunt Annie I love it all, & thank her just heaps for

sending me here. I know I was a little pig about it, but she understands I don't mean all I say.' [22]

3. Nulli's real name was Arthur Bond. He had met Howard when they were both working at the Bank of England. There are differing opinions as to the origin of his nickname. An airship, launched at about the time Arthur joined the Bank, had been called Nulli Secundus; Tom Nevill suggested that Nulli was named after that because his friends thought him a bit of a 'gasbag'. Arthur's nephew, however, thought that the name came from Nulli's recurrent use of the phrase 'second to none'. Whatever the reason, he was so called for the rest of his life.

4. 'I can't tell you how glad I am about Nulli's commission,' Billie wrote on April 23rd, so Amy's hopes were not fulfilled. In any case conscription had not yet been brought in so Nulli must have volunteered. He served in the R.N.V.R., as paymaster like Howard.

5. Not true. See p.105 and p.129.

14 PREPARING FOR BATTLE

'Wasn't it just the worst luck possible, missing Howard by a day, I really nearly wept,' Amy wrote from No. 2 Stationary Hospital on May 17th, after a difficult return journey to France. The boat had been late leaving Folkestone, she had spent a 'hateful' noisy night at the Louvre Hotel in Boulogne, and when she arrived at Abbeville it was 'too hot for words, we nearly melt all day, not an atom of shade.' She had enjoyed 'every minute' of her leave, but the old homesickness returned as soon as she crossed the Channel. No. 2 Stationary was much smaller and cosier than the base hospital complex at Étaples, however, and she was soon well settled.

This is such a jolly little camp, everyone is so friendly & nice. Miss Nunn is Matron, her brother is in the Bank of England & knows the boys. We have a dear little Badminton court, & play most mad games 6 a side, reminds me of the boys at home . . . There is no talk of my going back to 24. I don't much think I want to now, I'm settled here, our little hut looks quite nice, & we have really a very happy time. [17]

Billie did not refer to his leave on his return to France, but there was no doubt that, despite the excitement of the wedding, it had been less enjoyable than his Christmas leave.

The visit to the dentist was one reason; Arthur Reid's treatment had been radical.

'I should so love to see Billie with his teeth,' Amy wrote from France, 'did he have a very bad time, & are they an enormous improvement, but they are sure to be.' [17]

Alas for the fond sister, it seems that they were not. According to Joe Ackerley, Billie's new teeth were to be the East Surreys' new weapon in the coming attack. It would seem that there had not been sufficient time for a proper fitting. The resulting bad fit enabled Billie to produce a death's head grimace when he smiled which the Surreys expected to finish off any 'gibbering imbecile' of a Boche encountered in the enemy lines.[1]

There were problems with Muff. Billie continued to receive parcels from

Hastings after his return to France, but in a letter to his family written in
June he said, 'By the way, in case there's any doubt in your minds (& this is
confidential) Muffie & I are <u>not</u> in any way engaged and never shall be. If
Stanley gave you or Uncle Leonard a letter of mine with reference to my will,
I <u>don't</u> want the part of it referring to Muff acted on. It was only a note to
you personally Mother, & not a legal document.' [197]

However Billie enjoyed sharing his leave with Howard[2], and together the
brothers went out to buy footballs for Billie to take back to France for his men
in the 'Big Push' that everyone knew was coming.

The Allies had originally planned to attack simultaneously on three fronts in
1916, with the British and French attacking side by side on the Somme. German strength would be diluted, being also occupied on the Russian and
Italian fronts. On the Western front, the battle-hardened French army
would compensate for Kitchener's men's lack of experience.

Then, in February, came the German assault on Verdun. France suffered
such huge losses during the following months that she demanded, more
and more urgently, that the British should bring forward the attack on the
Somme in order to divert German troops from Verdun, giving July 1st as the
latest they could stave off defeat. Reluctantly, Sir Douglas Haig, the British
Commander-in-Chief in France, agreed and set June 25th as the date,
although this barely gave Kitchener's New Armies time to complete their
training.

The 18th Division had been withdrawn from the Albert area at the beginning of May, supposedly for six weeks' rest but, as it turned out, to undergo
intensive training for the coming offensive. The East Surreys were in billets
at Picquigny, north of Amiens, when Billie joined them on his return from
leave, after a journey that, as usual, had not been entirely trouble-free.
'Arrived safely. Good journey. Kit <u>not</u> found yet,' he reported home on May
18th.

Rehearsals of the attack before a battle had first proved useful at Neuve
Chapelle in 1915 and, as a result, were routinely included in preliminary
training for an offensive. During brigade training at Picquigny, therefore,
trenches were dug in an exact replica of the German front-line system as
seen from the air, and numerous practices of what the East Surreys' War
Diary insisted on calling the 'Abnormal Attack' were carried out. There were
a number of failures, largely due to heavy rainstorms at the time. One full
dress rehearsal with contact aeroplanes and flares took place in the presence
of Sir Douglas Haig himself. The East Surreys were also inspected by Sir
Henry Rawlinson, who was responsible for the coming battle. On May 28th
brigade sports, at which Maxse presented the prizes, gave a day's respite

from hard work, but there was little time during this period for leisure activities such as letter-writing.

> The weather is horribly hot, we are all training horribly hard, and altogether everything is going on quite smoothly [Billie told his mother on May 27th]. I expect to be here about 1+ m south of Picquigny, for another week or so, and then the dear old trenches again, where I don't seem to have been for years now. The Company is going on A1 and doing awfully well. I've had about a letter & a half since I got back, but never mind.

However Billie did have time to organise a visit to Abbeville with Thorne. It is a curious incident. Thorne was 24, a Cambridge Blue who had not only won the Military Cross for bringing his brother in from No Man's Land the previous autumn, but had also been mentioned in despatches since. There is no explanation as to why someone of his age and character should be looking for the sort of wife that he apparently wanted. Billie was casual when telling Doff about it:

> Picuinguy
> 22.5.16

> Dear Doffly,
>   . . . Oh! by the way, had you heard Thorne has promised (to me) to marry Amy. He wants an elderly, really nice, not pretty wife, so I've written Amy about it, and I'm taking him over to see her soon, then he's going to Flixécourt for a month. [191]

One would have thought, considering the purpose of the visit, that Billie might have taken more care over the journey. Perhaps, given the intensity of training, the two men had difficulty getting away at a reasonable hour. 'I took Thorne over to see Amy the other [day],' Billie wrote on the 27th, 'we arrived about 9.30 p.m. & stayed till 11, she was in bed when we arrived!!' [192] Two days later he was telling Doff that Amy, whose thirty-seventh birthday was the following week, 'has decided not to marry Thorne as he's too young.' [193] It was an amicable refusal, however, for Thorne continued to visit Amy on his own while attending the course at Flixécourt.

On June 10th the East Surreys returned to the front not far from Carnoy, to face the German trenches in front of Montauban, the brigade history describing every member of the battalian as 'full of fight and knowing exactly what his role was to be in the great battle'[3]. 'A wee bit wet & muddy but otherwise quite nice to be in a trench again,' Billie reported. 'This is a nice quiet spot, on the whole, but a wee bit noisy.' [194] The line was in fact being heavily shelled, and on the night of June 13/14th there was an intense bombardment, during which there were fears of an imminent German attack. Regrettably not all the casualties were caused by the enemy. Some of the British field guns returning fire were firing short into the East Surrey trenches, A and C companies being the worst affected, though Billie's B company also suffered.

> *8th East Surreys, B.E.F.*
> *14.6.16*

Dear All,

Quite well and happy, though we had some beanfeast about midnight & this morning early, as the Huns opened one of these hurricane bombardments on our trenches. I was just going off to bed when it started, so my beauty sleep was a bit disturbed. All alarm arrangements went like clock work, and the company were simply splendid. Far from crumpling us up our fire & our artillery behind was so good they never left their own trenches at all and after about 1½ hrs of solid flashes and bangs and crashes all was quiet. I simply cannot very well describe one of these night bombardments. Picture, say 20 electric railways flashes at once continuously for 1½ hrs. & throw incessant over head thunderclaps and if you think that out you'll get some idea of what it looks like. Of course there are nasty sides to it, especially afterwards, but I think the Bosch got more than he gave. When I have seen these shows from a mile away, say, I've always thought how awful they are but now and at the time I don't and didn't mind a scrap. It's so continuous it's like being in a tube, with all the windows rattling. Read this carefully and you'll get a bit of an idea of some of these "2 lines in the Communiques" bombardments.[4]

Love to all [196]

Later, during a couple of days out of the line, Billie described the incident to Thorne.

> *Bray*
> *22.6.16*

Dear Corny,

Cheer up. We had one of those hurricane & very intense bombardments, you know the sort, for about ¾ of an hour, starting about midnight on the 13th but owing to the perfectly magnificent

way the men manned the parapet and the steady & deliberate fire
they kept up & also owing to the tremendous response by our
artillery, no Bosche ever reached our trench or tried to. We gave 'em
hell, and I don't think there's a shadow of doubt that they meant to
cut us out but damned soon found it was we who were opposite &
not some dud exponents of the gentle art of keeping cool. The men
were great & it has put their tails up no end. In half an hour we had
the following men hit, about my sister's age & yours added together!!
Santler was killed.
   Give my love to Amy
      Yrs
         W.P.N.

                                                          18.6.16
Dear All,
   I don't doubt for a moment that you are occasionally writing to me,
but as you persist in putting D instead of B̲ Coy, that is probably why
I've not heard for several days from anyone, but Howard[5]. However
I'm very fit & happy. We're not actually in the line now, but only 400
yds back. We had 5 days up and as it rained all the first 4 days, and as
we were very heavily shelled the 5th it was pretty rotten. We were
congratulated by the next division for the way we stood it, in fact
everything went quite smoothly and I never felt any anxiety about
them getting into our trenches, though the shells were dropping like
hail & how anyone lived I don't know. I had about 50 in my face I
should think and so did everyone, but somehow the bits get past you,
though some of us stopped some, I'm afraid. It was really awfully
topping to walk round and see the men, all quite happy, & yelling
out, "Come on Fritz, we're here" & such like expressions as "Come
right in & don't bother to knock first," etc. etc . . .
   The weather has at last cleared up and it's quite sunny.
      VBL to all
Pencils, ordinary lead ones, about 6 and don't look for more than
F.S.P.C.s for a bit.
      Bill [197]

It was at this time that he told the family about Muffie, and mentioned
his will. 'I want you to do as you think best about it, supposing there's any
need for you to think about it at all. There'll be about £100 I think at present.
But I daresay you won't even have to think about it. I seem pretty bullet
proof.'

On June 20th the battalion left the trenches 'after a fairly healthy going,' as Billie put it, for three days' respite at Bray.

> I got on Betty [his horse] for the first time since we left Fourdrinoy about a fortnight ago & we skipped [like] young lambs especially when a crump went off about pretty close. I think in a week's time the papers will be quite amusing for you to read at this rate, they're jolly good now arn't they?
>
> I'm going to look for Ruthven [a cousin] after tea today, but I don't suppose I'll find him, anyhow it will be a decent ride & I want some exercise, although I'm tired out with work, which sounds funny.
>
> So long now
> love to all
> Bill   [198]

The date of the attack, set for June 25th, had been postponed to June 29th. The East Surreys returned to the front in time for the opening of the British bombardment on June 24th. 'Quite all right so far,' Billie wrote on the 24th. 'We're 'up' now & there's 'some' noise.' The bombardment was intended to destroy both men and artillery in the enemy trenches and cut the barbed wire in front, thus enabling the British to stroll across No Man's Land and take the German line without loss of life. It was so powerful that the sound of guns could be heard on the other side of the English Channel, and the vibrations felt as far away as London. Unfortunately, it failed to achieve its purpose. The British artillery was not heavy enough to destroy the German dugouts or the machine-gun emplacements which were too deep and too solidly built[6], and the ammunition used was not effective against barbed wire. In any case much of it was faulty, up to a third failing to explode. Knowing none of this, and remembering the shortage of ammunition from which they had suffered the previous autumn, the East Surreys were impressed by the bombardment.

UP. UP. UP.
26.6.16

Dear All,

Still alive. Why? Ask me another. We're having the time of our lives now. I'm longing to tell you all about it. All I will tell is, what the Bosch already knows. Namely, that he's been shelled hard for 48 hours now, day & night. It's a wonderful sight. Watch the papers & keep them.

Love to all W.P.N.
Bill

Our Front Line
Some spot
27.VI.16

Dear Else,

I'm afraid my letters simply <u>aren't</u>, just now. Let's hope things will improve, that is as far as spare time goes.

For twenty-two days on end we've been working hard, all hours day & night, my personal sleep time being from 2 am – 3.30 & from 4 am – 8 usually but that's when I'm lucky.

Most things out here now are of course a deadly secret, but I can [tell] you what the Germans and everyone near for miles knows already, namely that for 172 hrs the Bosche has had shells & shells & shells deluging on to him in his trenches, his dugouts, his roads, his billets, his everything, day and night. Lord what a ghastly thing war is nowadays. It's things not men that count. Every trick which science & chemistry can perform comes in. Villages vanish in an afternoon!! A wood becomes a desert of hills and hollows, all while you look on. The old Bosche doesn't take it all sitting either, he picks out some object and fairly soaks it in shells. Sometimes on a bright sunny afternoon the whole landscape is hidden in smoke from shells.

The other day I saw a 12″ shell land in a brick field, and the cloud of brick dust hung over the whole view for half an hour.

I've seen complete trees fly 70 or 80 feet in to the air and houses (you know these mud & timber walled French villages) go down flat like cards.

The other afternoon our heavy guns shelled the ground near the cable of an observation Balloon, a huge German one which could overlook everything we did, and while no one could wind the cable and lower the balloon because of the shelling, two of our aeroplanes raced over and in a cloud of anti-aircraft shells dropped incendiary bombs on the balloon

I never saw such a sight, it flared up like nothing on earth, (which it was) and dropped like an enormous thunderbolt in one flaming mass to the ground.

Picture the end of those two Bosche observers.

Now and then Bosches jump out in broad daylight and rush over to our trenches and surrender, saying they can't stand it any more.

An officer surrendered at Fricourt & we had two on our right this morning in Broad daylight. Well, we've been chosen to stay up for this bombardment & stay I suppose we shall. At first I had a headache, but now well I just don't care a hang, one is sort of hammered by the sound.

Amy is the person to write to for my news, as she is getting our home parcels through her hands. I can't give you news probably but A might.

Cheerho & cheer up. I must stop now, yrs ever old thing, I had long letter from CP, Monica, and Nancy Ackerley[7]! V.B.L. to all
        Bill [202]

The show was preceded by seven days' bombardment, seven days of inconceivable unique Hades [Christian Carver told his parents on July 7th] . . . Standing on top of the mess, you could see a great wall of smoke running out of sight to the South – the French. Meantime the East Surreys were getting a bad doing; they were holding the Brigade front and were also to be the right assaulting battalion. It is difficult to realise how much is put back.

Also our heavies are bound to have accidents and trench mortars have a habit of dropping in the wrong front trench.[8] In fact, as Gimson (M.O. E.S.R.) said, 'There can't absolutely be any worse hell than this.' So on the third day yours truly set forth with his umbrella and carpet bag to try & comfort the poor old Surreys a bit. There I spent the remaining five days, not very cheerful ones, for waiting while death stalks broadcast is apt to try everyone.

On June 28th Colonel Powell handed over command of the battalion to Major Irwin before leaving for Corps Headquarters, where he had been ordered to report as reserve Brigadier.[9] Later the same day Maxse visited the East Surrey headquarters to announce that bad weather had caused the attack to be postponed once more, this time to July 1st.

At No. 2 Stationary Hospital in Abbeville, preparations for the coming battle meant there was no longer time for games of badminton. On the same day, June 28th, Amy wrote home. 'We get more busy every day, but have had our staff increased thank goodness . . . It was 9 p.m. when I got off last night, no time off for lunch, a cup of soup in the bunk, & ¼ hr tea & off at 8.30!' [19]

Cornelius Thorne, still formal despite the proposal of marriage, wrote to her from the Army Infantry School in Flixécourt[10],

                                        Thursday 29th June 1916
My dear Miss Nevill,
    They now inform us they are going to continue to keep us on here "till required", so it may mean yet another week of it, and I expect I

shall turn up yet again to see you this week end. I now look especially
to you for news because I think you will probably be getting it more
direct and first hand than I shall, and I am eager for the least fragment
of information you can give me about my own people. Lord, how I
hate being here just now! I don't think that at the moment of writing
Billy has shifted from where he was, but he will very likely do so to-
morrow (Friday). I hear that up in front we have been bombarding the
Hun with some effect these five days past, & several of them have
come over, here & there, and surrendered. One Boche said that where
he was our artillery had so effectively put a barrage on their
communications that they had been able to get no rations up to the
front trenches for three days & that all he had had was a single mug
of coffee during all that time.[11] It sounds almost like cruelty to
animals; but it's a game of "either kill or be killed", and the Hun on
his side has no mercy. Thank God that now-a-days I think we are top
dog.

    Cheer-oh & so forth!

      Yours sincerely

        Cornie Thorne

If I come on Saturday or Sunday I shall expect to find you busy & will
only look in for a moment in the hope of being able to gather some
news. C.T.

On June 27th Billie sent his family a Field Service Post Card, with a line
through every sentence but the first, which read, 'I am quite well.' The following day he wrote his last letter home.

Dear Else,

    Thanks for a chit of some length and liveliness. I think you can put
a good deal of faith in what Mrs. Pollard says about the end of the
war.

    As I write the shells are fairly hairing over; you know one gets just
sort of bemused after a few million, still it'll be a great experience to
tell one's children about.

    So long, old thing don't worry if you don't hear for a bit. I'm as
happy as ever, yrs ever *Bill* [203]

NOTES

1. Ackerley, page 50.
2. 'No leave will ever seem the

same without dear old Billie,'
Howard wrote after his next

visit home, 'and I missed him most awfully and could not help thinking of last year's leave when he and I were home together.' (27th February, 1917)

3. p. 10.
4. The message reads, 'In half an hour twelve killed & forty wounded,' which does not agree with Billie's letter to Thorne, as the latter's age plus Amy's (24 + 37) makes 61. The regimental history records three officers and nine men killed and forty two wounded.
5. Howard had just taken part in the battle of Jutland, but Billie makes no mention of this, nor does he refer in his letters to Kitchener's death by drowning on June 6th, when the cruiser taking the Secretary of State for War to Russia struck a mine and sank.
6. The British were aware of the depth of enemy emplacements, having captured one in the Somme area earlier in the year. The previous autumn, Maxse had circulated a paper for a divisional commanders' conference after the battle of Loos, with a diagram of a concealed German machine-gun emplacement. 'Coming as a surprise to the attacking force they [the emplacements] can inflict considerable damage before they are captured and

destroyed and may even hold up an attack.' (Dated 16.11.1915, IWM 69/53/6) However those planning the coming attack did not make use of this information.

7. Aged sixteen – perhaps the reason for the exclamation mark.
8. The battalion suffered badly from both German and British fire between June 24th and 26th, A company being persistently shelled throughout one night by a British battery, which was identified and stopped only the following night.
9. According to Heath, Col. Powell had 'gone round the bend'. However, Heath and the C.O. did not get on, so perhaps the former's words in this instance should be regarded with some suspicion.
10. Amy, too, remained formal. 'Thorne sent me on a splendid letter of Billie's,' she said, sending it on herself to her mother. [19] She made no reference to Thorne's proposal in any of her letters home.
11. Haig took comment of this sort from German prisoners as proof that the bombardment was succeeding in its purpose, without realising that German artillery was largely unaffected.

15 THE BATTLE OF ALBERT

One of the most controversial aspects of the battle on July 1st[1] was the way in which the British were ordered to attack: at a walking pace uphill (for the Germans held the high ground) towards the German front line and its heavy artillery. Rawlinson took it for granted that German artillery would have been wiped out by the British bombardment, and the German wire cut. The attack would therefore be a walkover. Haig, the cavalryman, would have preferred rushing tactics but deferred to Rawlinson's greater experience as an infantryman.[2] One reason for Rawlinson's insistence on the slow pace was his fear that the inexperienced battalions of Kitchener's New Armies would disintegrate in a rush attack.

Some of Kitchener's officers themselves wondered how both they and their men would react in a battle situation. The East Surreys had discussed it in the mess as far back as April. It was Billie (who, so the divisional history said, 'held as vastly important the study of his men's mental and temperamental characteristics,') who suggested that the men should be given footballs to dribble before them as they attacked over No Man's Land.[3] Football had been important to the battalion ever since the Codford days. During the previous winter, Association Football had even been considered part of brigade training during the battalion's time in billets, with every platoon expected to put a team forward for matches. Believing that so familiar an occupation would calm the men, Billie sought permission from Major Irwin, who sanctioned it, 'on condition,' Irwin remembered years later, 'that he and his officers really kept command of their units and didn't allow it to develop into a rush after the ball . . . if a man came across the ball he could kick it forward but he mustn't chase after it and I think myself that it did help them enormously. It took their minds off it.'[4]

Having received Irwin's permission, Billie took Howard with him to buy the footballs while they were home on leave. Family tradition is adamant that three footballs were bought, not four, and that only two were taken to France. Certainly no more than two were used, despite newspaper stories afterwards that told of four.

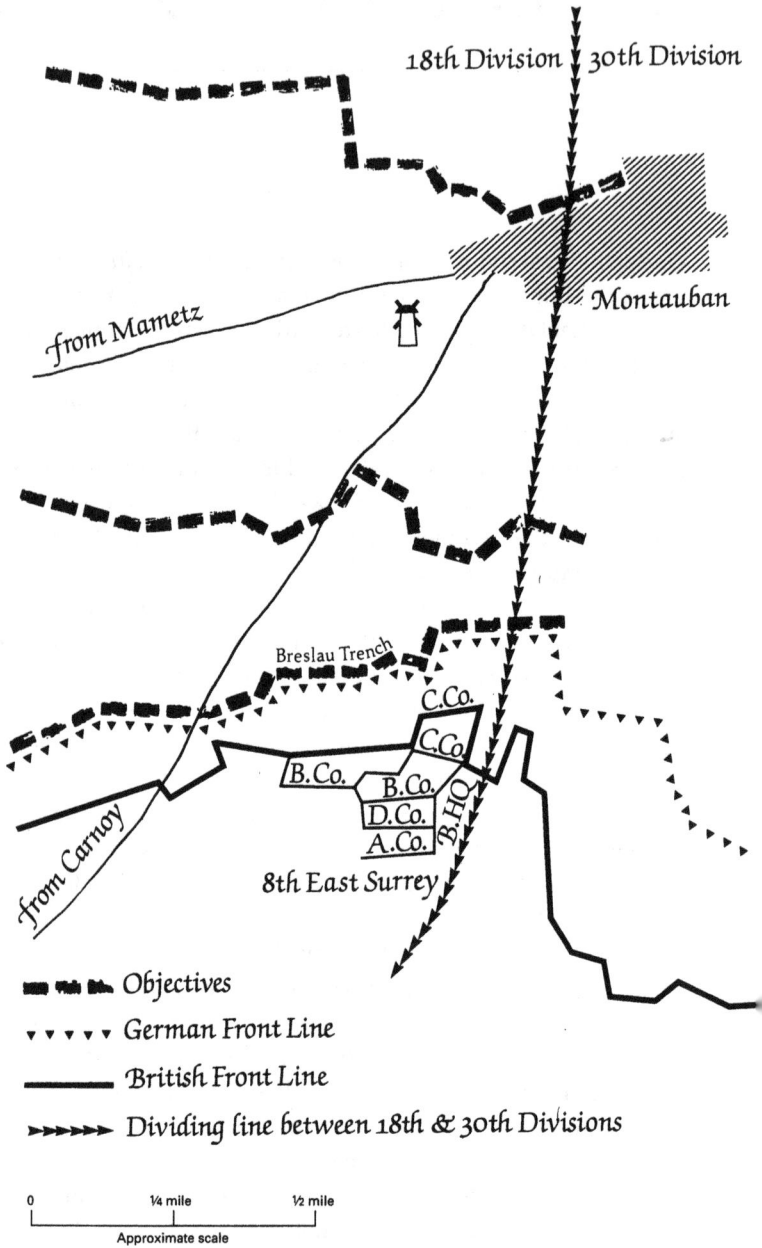

18th Division 30th Division

from Mametz

Montauban

Breslau Trench

C.Co.
C.Co.
B.Co. B.Co.
D.Co.
A.Co. B.HQ

8th East Surrey

from Carnoy

Objectives

▼ ▼ ▼ ▼ German Front Line

British Front Line

►►►►► Dividing line between 18th & 30th Divisions

| 0 | ¼ mile | ½ mile |

Approximate scale

Position of the 8th East Surrey Regiment, 7.30 am, 1 July, 1916

I am afraid the newspapers didn't give quite the right story of the
footballs [Alcock told Doff on July 27th]. There were two footballs, &
on one was printed:– 'The Great European Cup-Tie Final. East Surreys
v Bavarians. Kick off at zero.' On the other in large letters was this:–
"NO REFEREE", which was W.'s way of telling the men they needn't
treat the Hun too gently.[5]

The 18th Division was given the task of securing the western end of the forti-
fied village of Montauban and Montauban Ridge, running west towards
Mametz, and then advancing and occupying the high ground south of
Caterpillar Wood. The first objective of the East Surreys, lying on the right
of the division, was Breslau Trench; their final objective was the last houses
of Montauban and 300 yards of the road west along the ridge. B and C companies under Billie and Pearce were to lead the attack, followed by A and D
companies led by Flatau and John Bowen. C company's section of the front
line jutted out into No Man's Land, giving it a shorter distance to the German front line. B company would therefore emerge first and as it came up to
C company's trench, C would move out and the two would continue together in an extended line. General Staff instructions current at the time
stated that no attack should start more than 200 yards from the enemy. The
distance C had to cross was 120 yards. B company had 400.

The East Surreys spent June 28th and 29th behind the lines in Billon Valley. Exhausted by their time in the front line, where the noise of the artillery
bombardment taking place overhead had aggravated the strain of trench
warfare, they did little more than lie about on the grass and sleep.

Friday the 30th was hot and sunny. In the afternoon the battalion moved
off by companies to take up their battle positions. 'We were very young,'
Irwin remembered. '. . . I took it for granted that the wire would be cut, that
we would massacre the Bosches in their front line, get to our objective and
then be told to do something else, but my whole feeling was that now we
were starting to move forward . . . we were all very optimistic.'

There had been summer storms during the previous three days; the
trenches were consequently several inches deep in water. To make matters
worse the enemy kept up a desultory shelling through the night, making
rest impossible and killing three before the attack had even begun.

Captain Flatau of A Company spent the night writing letters to his family,
post-dating them 2 July, a pointless exercise as it turned out for he was killed
the following morning. Ackerley read Conrad's *Lord Jim* for the fifth time.
Bobbie Soames, Ackerley's best friend, told him, 'I'm going to be killed
tomorrow. I don't know how I know it but I do.'[6]

During the night B and C companies removed the barbed wire in front of their trenches. Ammunition, grenades, sandbags, flares and tools were issued. Each man carried sufficient food to last him forty-eight hours.[7] Breakfast came up at 4.30 a.m. and with it the rum ration.

Writing years later, Ackerley complained bitterly of the visible differences between officers and men – revolvers instead of rifles, rank marked on their cuffs – that had marked officers out as targets for the German sniper. The divisional history, on the other hand, records that for this very reason officers changed into men's uniforms for the attack. Like so much that happened on the Somme it is difficult to differentiate between truth and hearsay.

Irwin, Clare the adjutant, and Christian Carver, who was liaising between the battalion and the artillery, installed themselves in the battalion headquarters' dug-out. Irwin was sorely tempted to lead the East Surreys into battle himself, but had always understood that battalion commanders should lead from behind, only going forward when the attack had lost its impetus.[8] Billie and Pearce visited the dug-out just before dawn, according to Carver 'both absolutely radiant and declaring everything for the best'.

By 5.30 all companies were in their battle positions. At 6.30 the Germans opened a barrage on the East Surrey trenches which caused a number of casualties and completely flattened B company's trench in a number of places.

The morning had been misty, but at 6.30 the mist lifted and from then on the weather was, as described by Siegfried Sassoon, 'of the kind commonly called heavenly'.

At 7.15 Clare left the headquarter's dug-out and went up to the parapet to observe the attack. Finally, at 7.27 a.m. on Saturday July 1st, 1916, Billie and Bobby Soames, his second in command, led B company over the parapet into No Man's Land.

'Zero hour at last. One just heard a wild cheer above the continuous roar to tell one that the 8th East Surreys were on their way to get their own back at last.'[9]

'I saw an infantryman climb on to the parapet into No Man's Land, beckoning others to follow. As he did so he kicked off a football; a good kick, the ball rose and travelled well towards the German line. That seemed to be the signal to advance.'[10]

Only four officers of the Company were allowed to go over the parapet (W.P.N., Bobby Soames, Evans & I) [Alcock wrote on July 15th[11]], and we were for it in the first line, up with Pearce's Coy. Five minutes before 'zero' time (7.30 a.m.) your brother strolled up in his usual calm way, & we shared a last joke before going over. The

Company went over the top very well, with Soames & your brother
kicking off with the Company footballs. We had to face a very heavy
rifle & machine gun fire, & nearing the front German trench, the lines
slackened pace slightly. Seeing this Wilfred dashed in front with a
bomb in his hand, & was immediately shot through the head, almost
side by side with Soames & Sgt. Major Wells.

   Poor Nevill willingly and intentionally gave his life at the
beginning, fearlessly urging on some men who were badly held up by
fire and wire [Alan Jacobs told his parents]. My God, how I wish I
could have led my platoon myself[12]; Nevill would not have needed to
run up to the front wave then. All our best men and NCOs are gone
and when one sees the remains of a fine battalion (still enough
perhaps to inspire the new men we expect with our traditions and
reputation) one realizes the disgusting sordidness of modern war,
when any yokel can fire a gun that may or may not – chance entirely –
kill a man worth fifty of the firer. But we must bear these losses
silently, for it is the way that lies before us and the only way to
Victory.

   At 7.50 a.m. the adjutant reported that the battalion was in the first line of
German trenches. According to the regimental history, Billie and Bobby
Soames were killed just outside the German wire in which both footballs
were found the following day[13]; Pearce was killed in No Man's Land and
Flatau on the parapet of Breslau trench (though Ackerley, whose company
commander Flatau was, said that the latter was shot through the heart
before taking a step). By mid-afternoon B and C companies, the two that
had led the assault, were reduced to one officer and roughly twenty other
ranks apiece. Seven of the battalion's officers were killed in all, and one,
Pegg, mortally wounded. Joe Ackerley, Alcock, Morse and Hetherington
were among the wounded, as was Billie's servant, Marker. 'I shall never forget the smell of it,' Ackerley said of the battlefield. 140 other ranks were
killed, 272 wounded and twenty missing. Such losses were not exceptional –
Middlebrook lists thirty-two battalions that lost more than five hundred
men each in the one day – and the 18th Division as a whole comes low down
in the table of casualties.

   The dead officers were buried together in Carnoy valley the following
Monday afternoon, with Irwin, Gimson and six representatives from each
company present. Though all the East Surreys wanted to attend, it was
thought inadvisable. The Germans were still shelling the valley intermittently and the men were kept dispersed.

   The 7th, 18th and 30th Divisions all gained their objectives on July 1st, the only divisions to do so. Montauban was the first village to fall, Mametz the second. The 18th Division advanced 3,000 yards from its original trenches on a front of 2,500 yards to secure the line between the two villages. Unfortunately, Rawlinson had expected little from this section of the line, did not believe the reports of victory, which were in such contrast to reports of disaster and confusion elsewhere, and failed to exploit their success. Land that was there for the taking on July 1st had to be bitterly fought for in the days and weeks to come.

Amy was the first of the family to learn of the attack, in a letter from Thorne at Flixécourt.

Saturday, 1st July 1916

My dear Miss Nevill,

As you will have heard they went over at 7.30 a.m. this morning. I don't suppose I shall be over to see you to-morrow as we are more or less standing by here. The latest news received here gives the position some three or four hours after the attack started. We had then got forward at intervals all along the line from Gommecourt to the Somme. Casualties comparatively light. Operations in our own area were particularly successful as Montauban & Mametz had already been taken, & our division's objective was on the line between the two, so we must have got there very rapidly without much opposition. I expect they will have paused there for a bit to make good, and to let other people on the flanks come up who had met with more difficulty. The French on our right meanwhile were doing well also. They had broken through in front of Hardecourt & had taken Curlu . . . 10.30 p.m. News as follows of position of this afternoon-evening. All operations between the Ancre & the Somme (Authuille to Maricourt) entirely successful, all the first day's pre-arranged objectives having been reached. North of the Ancre we were this morning held up at Beaumont-Hamel but had captured Serre: the communications in this quarter having broken down no further news is available. Prisoners: The French have already sent back 3000 during the day, the British 2000. But with us I think a statement of the number of prisoners we did not take would be the more interesting!

To sum up we have now got the Boche first & intermediate systems on almost the whole front attacked. The next "jump" will be his second line. If we can do that the third line should be pretty easy, & then we get into open country. The only thing I want now is news of the regiment, and to be allowed to join up myself.

Yours v. sincerely   C.T.

(I do not sign name because if one mentions places one should never mention at the same time names of any units or one's own name.)

'Even if you get a War Office telegram,' Billie had written to Elsie the previous February while at Flixécourt, 'you must never take that as final. Our Mess President here, for instance, was reported killed in the paper & his people got a wire confirming it, but he was only slightly wounded.' [150]

But no news came of Billie, false or otherwise. With nearly 60,000 casualties on July 1st, many of them lying helpless in No Man's Land for days afterwards, it was scarcely surprising that the War Office took so long to inform the next of kin. It was Amy who had to break the news of Billie's probable death to the family, having learned it from wounded East Surreys at No. 2 Stationary Hospital.

A week after the attack the Nevills were still hoping that she might be mistaken.

> 15 Montpelier Road
> Twickenham

On a bus   July 6th 16

Dearest A,

We have not heard a word from the War Office, & Cuthbert Smith has been up & they (W.O.) have heard nothing, & say they are sure to have heard by now. So we are hoping it is not true. Poor girl. What a lot you must have suffered – it was sweet of you to write so much but how terribly trying it being so uncertain. Poor Mother is being so brave. Elsie brought your letter over this morning while I was at school & I am now on my way over to her as it is the last of her 'At Home' days, & she is coming home with me this evening. She has decided to carry on this afternoon as if nothing has happened. Poor girl it will be hard for her.

By the time you will get this something definite will be known. I can't believe it's true as the War Office knows nothing . . . It must be awful for you now.

Ever so much love
   from *Doff*

Of course I have been awfully anxious about old Bill [Howard wrote on July 8th] he must be having a pretty strenuous time now & I am longing to hear what his next letter will have to say. Be sure and let me know if you do get a line from him tho' I very much doubt if he will get any chance of sending even a F.S.P.C.

Letters began to arrive from France. The first came from Major Irwin.

3.7.16

Dear Mrs. Nevill,

I hardly know how to begin to write this letter at all. It seems almost an impertinence to try to sympathise with you in such a dreadful loss, but I feel it my duty to tell you how your son Capt. Nevill met his death. He was in command of one of our leading Companies in the attack on Montauban on the 1st of this month, and led his company most gallantly and with the utmost coolness up to the German front line trench, where he was shot. Death must have been absolutely instantaneous. He was one of the bravest men I have ever met, and was loved and trusted by his men to such a degree that they would have followed him anywhere, and did follow him that morning through an inferno of shell, rifle and machine gun fire. We feel his loss most deeply as a brother officer, who was not only the life and soul of the mess, but also a most capable and fearless soldier. He started his company in the assault by kicking off a football which his men dribbled right up to the German trench. I have been able to get that ball since, and will of course send it to you if you should want it as a memento of him, but I and all the other officers of the Battalion would be very grateful to you if you would allow us to keep it as a regimental trophy, and in memory of your son's gallantry. We have recovered his body and have buried him in Carnoy cemetery with our six other officers who were killed.

We have put a heavy wooden cross on the grave with their names on it, and at the end of the war will put a permanent memorial there.

Yours sincerely,

A. P. B. Irwin

(Major Cmdg 8th Batt. E Surrey Reg.)[14]

Captain Nevill was always simply worshipped by his men & his charming personality & delightful humour had soon made him the most popular of our officers [Jacobs told Mrs. Nevill]. With his brilliance as a soldier he was always my ideal hero as an officer & a gentleman, while as a personal friend it is now that I fully realize that I loved him as boys rarely love one another. It is only by the willing & noble sacrifice of our very best that our country can gradually restore peace & justice to the world. I only wish for your sake & for his country's that I could have taken his place.

Christian Carver's mother wrote to Mrs. Nevill, enclosing her son's letter describing the attack on July 1st (Pearce's mother was sent a copy). 'Perhaps when quite done with you would let me have this letter back – It reads like a Heroic Poem, these two with their Radiant faces at Dawn – and then the call home . . .'[15]

On September 20th Howard acknowledged two letters Mrs. Nevill had sent on to him from Stanley.

I thought they were splendid and expressed my own feelings very much better than I could have done. I, too, cried for most of the first afternoon that I heard the news, as I have not since I was a child. There are not many families, Mother, that are such real friends together as we are, and we pay for that great privilege all the more when one of us is taken, but we have the great joy of the final meeting, where there is no more parting, to look forward to.

The British public became aware of the failure of the 'Big Push' only with the publication of the seemingly endless casualty lists. As the scale of the disaster became apparent, newspapers seized on the football story as a piece of good news. 'How the local men fought in the great advance,' trumpeted the *Thames Valley Times* on July 12th, 'Playing football under fire.' On the same day the *Daily Mail* published a poem written by Touchstone in the style of Henry Newbolt, called 'The Game'. The *Illustrated London News* commissioned R. Caton Woodville, their most famous artist, to illustrate the incident, sending him to visit Hetherington in hospital to verify the details.[16]

The Germans, too, seized on the story and used it for propaganda purposes, in their case to demonstrate the stupidity of the British, circulating the Caton Woodville drawing with captions in ten languages, the English version of which described the incident as 'an English absurdity: Football play during storm attack. All English newspapers laud the "heroic deed" of an English major . . .'

Both footballs were recovered from near the German trenches the day after the attack and brought to England.[17] A special parade was held at Kingston Barracks, the East Surreys' regimental depot, to celebrate their arrival. One ball was inflated and displayed to the drawn up ranks, the band of the depot played regimental marches, three cheers were given for both the East Surreys and the King, and the National Anthem played. The speech of Colonel Treeby, the depot C.O., was no doubt typical of many made by army officers in England, with little imagination and no knowledge of the new kind of warfare being waged overseas. He compared the winning of Waterloo on the playing fields of Eton to 'this war . . . being won by our football heroes to-day. Our men have played and are playing the game. We

are still in the scrum, it is true, but the ball is being carried forward, and we
doubt not that in God's good providence the goal for which we are fighting –
the goal of freedom, justice, and lasting peace – will soon be won.'

The battle of the Somme continued until November 14th, 1916, in a series of
attacks on a smaller scale to the one on the first day but all as ferocious,
fought in mud that was as bad as the notorious mud round Ypres, and indeed thought by those who fought in both areas to be worse. It took the
British army 137 days to advance six miles, in which time they suffered over
400,000 casualties, 58,000 of them on July 1st. Alan Jacobs was killed at the
beginning of August near Armentières; and on September 30th, a year
almost to the day after he had won the M.C. bringing in the body of his dead
brother, Cornelius Thorne was killed on the south face of the Schwaben Redoubt. Later that day Bryan Paull, who had been involved in the mix-up
over Billie's captaincy papers, was killed during the Surreys' successful
assault on the Redoubt. By the end of 1916 there were few officers left of the
battalion that had sailed from England in such high spirits less than eighteen
months before.

Half a million men took part in the attack on July 1st, every one of them a
volunteer. In all, Kitchener's armies raised a total of three million men, but
even this number was not enough and conscription was brought in later in
1916. 'Idealism perished on the Somme,' said the historian, A. J. P. Taylor.
After July 1st there can have been very few officers who looked radiant
before going over the top. Now there was only a dogged determination to
carry on and win the war.

The following summer Sir William Orpen, the war artist, came to the
battlefield. 'No words could express the beauty of it. The dreary, dismal
mud was baked white and pure – dazzling white. White daisies, red poppies
and a blue flower, great masses of them, stretched for miles and miles. The
sky a pure dark blue, and the whole air, up to a height of about forty feet,
thick with white butterflies: your clothes were covered with butterflies. It
was like an enchanted land; but in the place of fairies there were thousands
of little white crosses, marked 'Unknown British Soldier,' for the most part
. . . Through the masses of white butterflies, blue dragon-flies darted about,
high up the larks sang; higher still the aeroplanes droned. Everything shim-
mered in the heat. Clothes, guns, all that had been left in confusion when
the war passed on, had now been baked by the sun into one wonderful combination of colour – white, pale grey and pale gold.'[18]

In March 1918 the area became a battlefield once more. The Germans
broke through the Allied lines, recapturing in one day all the ground the
Allies had struggled over for four months, and went so far beyond as to

threaten Amiens. Albert was occupied, the hanging Virgin finally toppled by the British to prevent the enemy using the tower as an observation post, as they had themselves done. Ville-sur-Ancre, the village where D company had been so happily billeted with Mlle. Alcinie and her mother, was reduced to rubble and, as Amy wrote to Elsie, 'in all probability Billie's quiet little corner all trampled on.' [64]

It was, however, the beginning of the end. Germany was suffering from terrible shortages as a result of the British blockade, and the German army, exhausted by its advance and the casualties it suffered, was in addition demoralised by finding such a huge quantity of supplies lying about in the overrun British lines. Moreover, American troops were now arriving in France. With the Allies' new offensive that July and Haig's surprise attack near Amiens on August 8th, Germany was doomed. At 11 a.m. on November 11th, 1918, the Great War came to an end.

NOTES

1. The battle on July 1st was originally and more appropriately named after Albert, the town through which so many of the men had to march on their way to the front, and is so named in regimental histories. The River Somme meandered through the French sector only.

2. The French, who did use rushing tactics, were entirely successful on July 1st and suffered fewer casualties than the British. However, their artillery had been more concentrated and thus more effective which helped their assault. It also helped the British 30th Division attacking on the French left.

3. It had been done before, by the 1st battalion of the London Irish Rifles at the battle of Loos the previous year, though it is not known whether Billie had heard of the incident or not.

4. Interview with Imperial War Museum.

5. 'They did kill Germans,' Colonel Powell said of the 8th East Surreys. 'General Maxse told them to.' (Maxse papers.) It was Maxse who was credited with the phrase, 'The

only good Boche is a dead Boche.' 2nd Lieut. Janion, the first East Surrey to reach the enemy trenches and the only unwounded officer in C company, was reputed to have killed 15 Germans on the way. He was awarded the D.S.O.

6. Parker, p.23. *The Everlasting Terror*, a poem by Ackerley, dated June 30th and dedicated 'To Bobby', was published in *The English Review* the following November.

7. Maxse had noted the previous autumn that the 24th Division had had no rations with them and nothing to eat or drink for forty-eight hours during the battle of Loos. 18th Division instructions dated 24.6.16 warned against eating any food found in enemy lines, or drinking water from wells or ponds there. (Maxse papers.)

8. Which was what happened. Irwin went over the top himself at 9.45 a.m. in order to gather the remnants together, reorganise the attack and carry it forward. Thirty-one battalion commanders or acting commanders were either killed or subsequently died of wounds on July 1st.

9. Carver
10. Pte. L. S. Price, Middlebrook, p.124.
11. The letter is addressed to 'Miss Nevill', presumably Doff.
12. This was the first time that ten per cent of the officers and N.C.Os had been kept back in a major attack, in order to have experienced men to train the replacements of those lost and to provide a nucleus for the reformed battalion. 'We are rapidly 'licking' our new battalion into shape, & our task is made so much easier because of the inspiration given by those who are gone,' Alcock told 'Miss Nevill' (see above). He was writing on July 27th, 'the anniversary of our landing in France, & we all hope that we shall keep at hand grips with the Bosche & get the war finished soon.' Alas, it was less than halfway through.
13. There is some doubt as to whether Billie fell immediately or near the German wire. In support of the latter, the War Diary says that the first part of B company's advance was made with very few casualties. Private Sorrell, writing to Mrs. Nevill, said, 'our Gallant Capt. fell at the German front line, and I passed him when I was crawling back, shot in the head and Death must have been instant. We had lost three out of four of our officers and they all lay within twenty yards of each other.'
14. All letters of condolence quoted are with the Nevill papers at the Imperial War Museum.
15. Carver had distinguished himself in the early stages of the attack on July 1st. Receiving an F.O.O. report that the Germans were falling back on Montauban Mill from where they would be in a position to inflict heavy casualties, Carver, as liaison officer, directed a 4.5 battery on to the mill so quickly and with such accuracy that the Germans were forced to run, abandoning their machine-guns. Carver's action went against the orders laid down by Rawlinson; he should have first referred back to Corps Headquarters some five miles behind the line. Had he done so authority would have come too late for any action to be effective. Middlebrook points out (p. 279) that those divisions which followed the C-in-C's advice most closely on July 1st were those which suffered most and achieved least. With an independent commander like Maxse at its head the 18th Division was not one of them. Carver was to die of wounds a year later, two weeks after his twentieth birthday.
16. A probably more accurate drawing is in the Regimental Museum of the Queen's Royal Surrey Regiment at Clandon Park, Surrey, but it was the Caton Woodville drawing that appealed to the public at the time, and is still the better known. Touchstone's verses were reprinted in the East Surreys' Christmas card that year, one of which was sent to Mrs. Nevill by Sgt. Cutting, with an inscription, 'My Officer & – My friend' and the wish, 'May the Season be made brighter by the knowledge that the memory of your son will live forever.'
17. Both footballs are on display today, one in the Regimental Museum at Clandon Park, the other in the Queen's Regiment Museum in Dover Castle.
18. Orpen, p.36.

EPILOGUE

At 12.15 p.m. on the 11th of November, 1918, Howard Nevill wrote to his mother

We have just had the news that the armistice has been signed and hostilities have ceased. I must just write a line to you but I really don't know what to say. Everything is so strange for the moment, & one can't quite take it all in. One thing I must say and that is how much I and all of us have admired the plucky way in which you have carried on this last four years, we are really proud of you and what you have done. It is you who have made the sacrifices very much more than we and I know that if dear Billie were here he would say just the same.

It was 1920 before the surviving members of the family were reunited. There had of course been leaves during the war but none had coincided as they had in the spring of 1916. Howard was in south Russia when the war ended but did not return until 1920 when he went back to the Bank of England. From 1944 until he retired in 1949 he was Secretary of the Bank, the first to be appointed from within. In 1952 he became Secretary to the George VI National Memorial Fund and was appointed C.V.O. in 1953.

Stanley remained with the Royal Flying Corps in Egypt where he was C.O. of a large engine repair depot. He was mentioned in despatches in 1917, awarded an O.B.E. (Military) in the 1919 New Year's Honours List and returned to England and his own engineering business in 1920.

None of Amy's letters survive from the year following Billie's death. She remained at Abbeville during the rest of the battle of the Somme. 'For goodness sake pray they may not be like the corresponding six months of last year,' she wrote in September 1917, when telling her family that she had signed on for another six months. By this time she was nursing at a summer convalescent home for officers at Dieppe where the work was much lighter than at Abbeville – 'it's just been a most glorious holiday' [23]; when that closed at the beginning of the autumn she was sent to No. 7 Stationary Hospital at Boulogne.

In November 1917 the matron of No. 7 asked Amy whether she would be prepared to travel further afield. Initially Amy said no – 'I had awfull feelings I must see you & consult you' – but regretted her decision almost immediately. When she heard that two more nurses, 'serious & red stripers' were wanted [red stripes were awarded for efficiency to V.A.Ds nursing in military hospitals] . . . I just felt it was the only thing to do, obviously we are much wanted & it was an opportunity not to miss . . . Do write & tell me you all think it was the right thing to have done.' [31] At 10.30 p.m. on November 14th, she and her friend Lord were told to be ready to leave at 5.30 the following morning. Their first stop was Abbeville, where Miss McCarthy Matron-in-Chief, 'was very charming & wondered what you thought of my going, also Aunt Annie.' [32] Here they joined a group of nurses for a journey expected to last nine days. Their transport was an ambulance train which at least meant a smooth ride. Amy was unperturbed by the discomforts of travel. 'I slept on the top shelf of three layers, thirty of us in the coach, it really was a "scream",' she said of the first night. 'Our supper last night enamel basins of tea, bread & butter & cheese & jam, one knife for the thirty!' Their destination – 'No one knows where we are going, except hope the engine driver!' – turned out to be No. 11 General Hospital in Genoa where the group arrived late in the evening of the 19th, 'none of us having had more than the merest lick in cold water for 5 days!'[35]

Amy remained in Genoa until February 1919, with one leave in England during the summer of 1918. In January 1918, she learned she had been awarded the A.R.R.C, a decoration instituted by Queen Victoria for 'special exertions in providing for the nursing of sick and wounded soldiers'. Her reaction was typically modest. 'I really can't believe it,' she told her mother '. . . I feel so absolutely & utterly unworthy of it, & so awfully sorry for those who have not got it & I feel have earned it so much more than I have. It was splendid to get your congratulations . . . – but – really I do feel a fool, & beg of you never to put R.R.C. on my letters.' [47] It was, as always, the family that mattered. Ten days after she had first heard, when she still had 'not yet recovered from the shock,' she told Elsie, 'my great joy is, that you are all so pleased.' [50]

For some time Amy seriously considered taking up nursing as a career. Discovering that the time V.A.Ds spent nursing abroad would be allowed to count as part training towards a hospital certificate after the war, she handed in her name as one interested, along with other V.A.Ds in the hospital, 'not to bind ourselves in any way, – but just for the authorities to know if there were sufficient V.A.Ds willing to finish their training, to make it worth while to make any special arrangement. I can't help thinking, as I'm confirmed 'old maid' that it would be a very good thing, & need not take m

away from home more than you wish & I shall be a much more useful member of society where ever I go.' [27] Six months later she was still considering
the possibility. 'The more I think about it, the more I'm convinced I must
have something at my back . . . & so be a really useful member of society, &
able to earn an honest penny.' [64] Howard thought the idea 'jolly sound',
but in the end nothing came of it. The decision was Amy's. 'I have entirely
made up my mind not to do a general training, it would take me too completely away from Mother.' [21st September, 1918]. She was the only un-
married daughter left in the family, with a mother already in her sixties
(Mrs. Nevill lived to be 92). No doubt Amy knew where her duty lay.

Aunt Annie, like her sister, lived into her nineties. She went out to Malta
as Principal Matron in 1916 ('I do hope Amy gets out to Malta, a change will
probably do her a lot of good,' Howard said, but on this occasion any plan
for Amy to join Aunt Annie did not succeed). The following year Aunt
Annie was recalled to France to take Miss McCarthy's place as Matron-in-
Chief in France when the latter became ill. In the autumn of that year she became Principal Matron at the War Office in London. In 1919 she was
appointed Matron-in-Chief of Queen Alexandra's Imperial Military Nursing
Service, a post she held until 1924 when she was appointed Matron-in-Chief
of the Territorial Army Nursing Service. She was made a Dame in 1925, and
was much loved and highly respected by all with whom she worked. Age
did not change her: the next generation of Nevills remember her as auto-
cratic even in a wheelchair.

No one knows why Billie should have written about Muffie Schooling as
he did in his last letters. She was seventeen at the time of their last meeting,
Billie nearly twenty-two, with the responsibility of two hundred and fifty
men on his shoulders, and knowing that the biggest battle of the war was
imminent. They may have quarrelled during that last leave – only too easy
in the emotionally charged atmosphere of the time and with such a gulf between them – and lacked the opportunity to make it up. Certainly Muffie's
own family, including her son, assumed that she would have married Billie
had he survived.

Later in the war Muffie met a patient in 'hospital blues', who asked her to
marry him. She turned down his proposal and continued to do so. Eventually she gave way, her son thought because she found life empty after the
war and could see no other future. They married in the spring of 1919. She
was twenty, he thirty-four. There were two sons of the marriage, one of
whom went down with the *Neptune* in December 1941, at the age of 19. Life
was hard for women of Muffie's generation.

General Maxse's training abilities were recognised in 1918 when he was
appointed Inspector-General of Training to the British Armies in France. He

ended his Army career as G.O.C.-in-C., Northern Command, after which he embarked on a second career at the age of sixty, that of commercial fruit grower. During his time in France he had marked how the French grew fruit trees on cordons and espaliers; now he planted out his Sussex estate in similar fashion and during his later years (he too lived into his nineties) made a significant contribution to the art and science of fruit growing.

Major Irwin finished the war as Lieutenant-Colonel commanding the 8th East Surrey Regiment, having gained two bars to his D.S.O. and been mentioned four times in despatches. With the disbandment of the 8th battalion he returned to a Regular unit, serving with the 1st East Surreys for the remainder of his army career, which included fighting the Bolsheviks in North Russia. In 1922 he was appointed Assistant Secretary to St. Thomas's Hospital in London, became Clerk to the Governors in 1928 and House Governor in 1940. The Second World War brought additional responsibilities and it was largely due to his organisational skills that a replacement hospital in the country was set up so quickly and so efficiently after St. Thomas's was badly damaged in the air raids.

Joe Ackerley went on to become a writer and was Literary Editor of the *The Listener* for twenty-five years, during which period he came to be regarded as one of the great literary editors of his time. His autobiography, published posthumously in 1968, was dismissive of Billie, referring to him as 'the battalion buffoon', though letters in the Nevill collection, and indeed Ackerley's own letter of condolence, give the impression of friendship. Certainly there are more photographs of Ackerley in Billie's collection than of any other officer. Ackerley's memory may have played him false after so many years, or perhaps he had been influenced by changing attitudes, for in later, more cynical years, the football incident that had caught the public imagination in 1916 came to be regarded as no more than an act of stupid bravado. One recent commentator has even described it as preposterous, ignoring both the reasoning behind the idea and the difficulty of persuading men over the top for the first time. There were other means of persuasion. Alcohol was one – though not always successful. Middlebrook quotes an incident on July 1st when too much was distributed, with men incapable as a result. Compulsion was another. Some officers, Vera Brittain's brother among them in an action which gained him the Military Cross, forced their men over at gunpoint. Irwin's verdict – 'I think myself that it did help them [the men] enormously. It took their minds off it' – suggests that the footballs provided a more satisfactory alternative.

Argument and controversy persist to this day over World War I, but for the majority of those who answered Kitchener's call to arms the issue was straightforward. Billie saw himself as defending France (twice overrun by Germany in less than fifty years) and opposing what he described as 'hunnism'. J. M. Mitchell, the ex-professor, older than Billie and probably a family man, was looking to Germany's ambition beyond France when he wrote of Kitchener's armies as 'this extraordinary volunteer movement of men in defence of their wives, their children and their homes'.

Whatever disagreement exists, there is none over Rawlinson's orders for the morning of July 1st. All authorities agree that his tactics doomed the attack from the start. As a result the British Army suffered the worst day in its history, its casualties for the one day exceeding its casualties in the Crimean, Boer and Korean Wars combined.

Similar tactics had been tried before, in a battle also begun, coincidentally, on July 1st, with the same devastating effect. At Gettysburg, Confederate troops had attacked the enemy across open fields, marching shoulder to shoulder on to Union gun batteries wrongly presumed to have been obliterated by a previous artillery bombardment. In less than an hour sixty per cent of the Confederates became casualties. Pickett's Charge lost the South the battle of Gettysburg and ultimately the Civil War. Present-day visitors to that battlefield can listen to an account of an action that is eerily like that of the Somme. But Gettysburg had been fought fifty-three years before the Somme. Presumably the British military did not consider battles of the American Civil War worthy of study.

After the war the French Government considered turning the devastated battle area into a national park. The area had been fought over four times; not a village survived. Gradually, however, the former inhabitants crept back, rebuilt their homes and began tilling the ground once more. In 1929 another Golden Virgin was placed on the newly constructed basilica in Albert. Shattered woods regrew; crops flourished over the old battlefields. Today, weekend huts and caravans proliferate along the banks of the Somme; fishing and duck-shooting are popular in the marshes below Vaux. It is difficult, looking over the fertile rolling countryside now, to picture the devastation that once covered the landscape.

But signs of those times are never far away. The cratered ground of the Tambour du Clos remains fenced off and uncultivated, zig-zig indentations in the rough grass indicating the line of the trenches in which the East Surreys lived and died. Heilly Château, Headquarters of the 18th Division during the winter of 1915/1916 and site of the Elephant Flapper's buffet, was never rebuilt. And the many cemeteries are a continuing reminder of war.

Billie Nevill lies in Carnoy Cemetery with other East Surreys who were killed in the battles of 1916. Ironically, when he had hoped to transfer to a

Regular East Surrey battalion, the badge on his headstone is that of the East Yorkshire Regiment to which he had been gazetted.

Carnoy is but one of dozens of cemeteries that mark the site of the British front line in 1916, some large, some small, some close together in places where the fighting was heaviest. In each, the names of the dead it contains are listed in the cemetery register, while Lutyens's memorial arch at Thiepval lists the names of the dead whose bodies never were found. Today few are left who knew the men who died and no-one will ever know what they might have become or achieved had they lived.

In his letters Billie Nevill has put flesh on to the bones of just a few of those names, and in his writing has given the reader a glimpse of the talents that were destroyed on the battlefields of the First World War.

MILITARY INFORMATION

Regiment – an administrative and tactical army unit acting as the parent body of several battalions. The loyalty of individual soldiers went to the regiment rather than to the British army as a whole.

Battalion – the 'family' unit of the army, at full strength made up of thirty-six officers and a thousand men, commanded by a lieutenant-colonel (usually referred to as colonel), with a major as second in command. An adjutant dealt with the administration, the quartermaster saw to supplies. Four companies (A, B, C and D) of approximately 250 men made up the fighting force, each commanded either by a major or more usually a captain, with a second captain to assist. The companies themselves were subdivided into four platoons of sixty men apiece, led by a subaltern (lieutenant or second lieutenant).

Division – the largest fighting unit in the British Army, totalling approximately twenty thousand men under the command of a major-general. It was made up of three brigades of four battalions each, plus a pioneer battalion of fighting infantry trained in field engineering, for the labour and construction work necessary in trench warfare. Each division had its own artillery, manned by the Royal Field Artillery. Normally two R.F.A. officers were attached to each battalion in the trenches to act as Forward Observation Officer and Liaison Officer.

The 18th (Eastern) Division was made up of the 53rd, 54th and 55th Infantry brigades. The 8th battalion of the East Surrey Regiment belonged to the 55th Brigade, together with the 7th battalion of the Royal West Surrey Regiment (the Queens), the 7th East Kents (the Buffs), and the 7th Royal West Kents.

WEAPONS

Coal Box – German 150 mm howitzer ('five-nine' or 5.9"). The shell exploded with a dense cloud of black smoke, hence its name.

Heavy – A large-calibre cannon or howitzer. It had a high trajectory which meant that the shell descended almost vertically onto its target.

Jack Johnson – Another name for the coal box. Called after the black American world heavyweight boxer. Also known as *Crump*.

Minenwerfer – A trench mortar or small field gun for throwing high explosive shells from the German front trench into British lines.

Whizz-bang – A light shell fired from German 77 mm field guns. It had a short range and low trajectory; consequently, the shell arrived almost simultaneously with the sound of it being fired.

ABBREVIATIONS

Gen.	General
Maj.-Gen	Major-General
Lt.-Col.	Lieutenant-Colonel
Maj.	Major
Capt.	Captain
Lt.	Lieutenant
2nd Lt.	2nd Lieutenant
Sgt.	Sergeant
Pte.	Private
C.S.M.	Company Sergeant Major
A.O.C.	Army Ordnance Corps
B.E.F.	British Expeditionary Force
C.-i.-C.	Commander-in-Chief
C.O.	Commanding Officer
F.O.O.	Forward Observation Officer
G.O. C.-i.-C.	General Officer Commanding-in-Chief
O.T.C.	Officers' Training Corps
R.E.	Royal Engineers
R.F.A.	Royal Field Artillery
R.F.C.	Royal Flying Corps
V.A.D.	Voluntary Aid Detachment

DECORATIONS

D.C.M.   Distinguished Conduct Medal. For distinguished conduct
in the field. Introduced in 1854. Awarded to warrant
officers, non-commissioned officers and men.

D.S.O.   Distinguished Service Order. 1886. Given in recognition
of especial services in action of commissioned officers.

M.C.   Military Cross. 1914. In recognition of distinguished and
meritorious services in time of war. Awarded to captains,
lieutenants and warrant officers.

M.M.   Military Medal. 1916. For bravery in the field. Awarded to
warrant and non-commissioned officers and men.

R.R.C.   The Royal Red Cross. 1883. For special exertions in
providing for the nursing of sick and wounded soldiers
and sailors (airmen were added later). 1st class recipients
were known as Members; 2nd class as Associates.

V.C.   Victoria Cross. 1856. The highest award for gallantry.
Awarded to all ranks of all services.

SOURCES & BIBLIOGRAPHY

Imperial War Museum

The greater part of the unpublished material quoted in the text comes from the Nevill collection in the Department of Documents at the Imperial War Museum – the letters of Amy, W. P. (Billie), Howard and Stanley Nevill, together with letters received by the family after Billie's death.

The papers of General Sir Ivor Maxse (69/53/5, 6 & 7)

'Fifty Years After', the memoirs of P. G. Heath (DS/MISC/60)

Interview with Lt.-Colonel A. P. B. Irwin, recorded in 1973 (Department of Sound Records (000211/04))

Public Record Office

The War Diary of the 8th East Surrey Regiment (WO 95/2050)

Select Bibliography

AUTHOR UNKNOWN *History of the 55th Brigade* (privately printed)
J. R. ACKERLEY *My Father and Myself* (The Bodley Head, 1968)
HILARY BAILEY *Vera Brittain* (Penguin Books, 1987)
ALEXANDER BARRIE *War Underground* (Muller, 1962)
VERA BRITTAIN *Testament of Youth* (Gollancz, 1933); *Chronicle of Youth* (Gollancz, 1968)
J. BROPHY & E. PARTRIDGE *The Long Trail: What the British Soldier Said and Sang in the Great War* (Deutsch, 1965)
MALCOLM BROWN *Tommy Goes to War* (J. M. Dent, 1978)
CHARLES CARRINGTON *Soldier from the Wars Returning* (Hutchinson, 1965)
CHRISTIAN CARVER *Christian Cresswell Carver* (privately printed)
ROBERT GRAVES *Good-bye To All That* (Cassell, 1929)
GARETH M. JENKINS *Zeppelins over Bury* (Moyse's Hall Museum, 1981)
JOHN JOLLIFFE *Raymond Asquith: Life and Letters* (Collins, 1980)
MICHAEL LANGLEY *The East Surrey Regiment* (Leo Cooper, 1972)

LYN MACDONALD *The Roses of No Man's Land* (Michael Joseph, 1980)

MAJ.-GEN. SIR W. G. MACPHERSON *Official History of the Great War – Medical Services General History*, 4 volumes (H.M.S.O., 1921-24)

BERNARD MARTIN *Poor Bloody Infantry* (John Murray, 1987)

MARTIN MIDDLEBROOK *The First Day on the Somme* (Allen Lane, 1971)

CAPT. G. F. H. NICHOLS (Quex) *The 18th Division in the Great War* (Blackwood, 1922)

AN OFFICER *The New Army in the Making* (Kegan Paul, Trench, Trübner, 1915)

SIR WILLIAM ORPEN *An Onlooker in France 1917-1919* (Williams & Norgate, 1924)

PETER PARKER *Ackerley* (Constable, 1989); *The Old Lie: The Great War and the Public School Ethos* (Constable, 1987)

COL. H. W. PEARSE & BRIG. GEN. H. S. SLOMAN *History of the East Surrey Regiment* (The Medici Society, 1923)

JULIET PIGGOTT *Queen Alexandra's Royal Army Nursing Corps* (Leo Cooper, 1975)

SIDNEY ROGERSON *Twelve Days* (Arthur Barker, 1933)

SIEGFRIED SASSOON *Diaries 1915-1918* (Faber & Faber, Ltd, 1983); *Memoirs of an Infantry Officer* (Faber & Faber, Ltd, 1930)

PETER SIMKINS *Kitchener's Army* (Manchester University Press, 1988)

JOHN TERRAINE *The Smoke & the Fire* (Sidgwick & Jackson, 1980)

DENIS WINTER *Death's Men* (Allen Lane, 1978)

INDEX